Sir George Cornewall Lewis

An Essay on the Origin and Formation of the Romance Languages

Sir George Cornewall Lewis

An Essay on the Origin and Formation of the Romance Languages

ISBN/EAN: 9783741178962

Manufactured in Europe, USA, Canada, Australia, Japa

Cover: Foto ©Andreas Hilbeck / pixelio.de

Manufactured and distributed by brebook publishing software (www.brebook.com)

Sir George Cornewall Lewis

An Essay on the Origin and Formation of the Romance Languages

AN ESSAY

ON THE

ORIGIN AND FORMATION OF THE

ROMANCE LANGUAGES:

CONTAINING

AN EXAMINATION OF M. RAYNOUARD'S THEORY ON THE RELATION OF THE ITALIAN, SPANISH, PROVENÇAL, AND FRENCH TO THE LATIN.

BY
THE RIGHT HONOURABLE
SIR GEORGE CORNEWALL LEWIS.

SECOND EDITION.

LONDON:
PARKER, SON, AND BOURN, WEST STRAND.
1862.

PREFACE TO THE FIRST EDITION.

THE following Essay was originally written with the view of being published in the *Cambridge Philological Museum*[1], as a criticism of M. Raynouard's researches into the history and formation of the Romance Languages. The discontinuance of that journal having left me no alternative, but to suppress altogether what I had written, or to print it as a separate work, I resolved after some hesitation to adopt the latter course. I am fully conscious that much still remains to be done for the systematic exhaustion of the subject discussed in it: but as M. Raynouard's writings have now become scarce even in France; as they are rarely met with, and are little known in this country: as moreover a reference to many other books is re-

---

[1] *The Cambridge Philological Museum* was published during the years 1832 and 1833. The Author contributed to it some papers on classical subjects. It was edited by Archdeacon Hare and the present Bishop of St. David's, Dr. Thirlwall.

quired which can only be procured in foreign libraries; and as there is no extant work of authority which contains a general view of the history and grammatical structure of the Romance languages, I have thought that the results of my researches would be acceptable to some persons who might be desirous to obtain a connected view of the entire question, without consulting a variety of books and scattered essays, of very different degrees of accuracy and value, in which alone the desired information can now be found.

The problem, of which a tolerably complete solution is offered in the following pages, is one which cannot fail to interest all who have considered the intimate connexion of the development of languages, as well with the political history of the communities by which they are spoken, as with those refined processes of thought, of which language is at once the exponent and the evidence. In this point of view the origin and progress of the modern dialects of the Latin are marked by peculiarities, which give them a predominant title to attention. Having arisen within a purely historical period, they are free from the elements of uncertainty which embarrass all enquiries into the origin of most other languages; while their descent from the language of the great Roman nation, and their actual diffusion over all the west of continental Europe, invests them with a deep interest in the eyes of all who take a connected view of the ancient and modern condition of these important communities.

On the other hand, the subject presents to the linguist and metaphysician a clear and full exemplification of the progress of a language in discarding its synthetic, and introducing analytic forms; of the progress by which, at the same time that its dictionary is enriched, its grammar is impoverished; that while its substance is improved, its form is deteriorated: a fact affording plentiful and interesting materials for reflexion, inasmuch as it offers the only certain instance in which the general course of civilisation does not tend to refine and improve all the instruments and appliances of the human intellect.

1835.

PREFACE TO THE SECOND EDITION.

This Essay was composed in 1833, and was published at Oxford, by Mr. Talboys, in 1835. Since its publication the elaborate work of Diez, on the Grammar of the Romance Languages, (*Grammatik der Romanischen Sprachen*, 3 vols. Bonn. First edition 1836—1844. Second edition 1856—60,) has appeared, followed by his Etymological Dictionary of the Romance Languages (*Etymologisches Wörterbuch der Romanischen Sprachen*, 8vo. Bonn. First edition, 1 vol. 1853. Second edition, 2 vols. 1861—2). The *langue d'oil*, or the French language, has likewise been subsequently illustrated by the copious grammar of Burguy, *Grammaire de la Langue d'Oil; ou, Grammaire des Dialectes Français aux Douzième et Treizième Siècles*, suivie d'un Glossaire. Berlin, 3 vols. 8vo, 1853, 1854, 1856.

These works have, to a great extent, superseded my Essay, and might seem to have rendered

[1] The references in the following Essay are made to the second edition of this book.

its republication superfluous. Having, however, been informed that its re-issue in a new edition would be acceptable to English students interested in the science of language, I consented to reprint it, for the following reasons:—My Essay had a special object; namely, the refutation of M. Raynouard's theory on the derivation of the Romance languages from the *langue d'oc*, or language of the Troubadours;—and this object is consistently pursued throughout the entire enquiry. Now, the grammars of Diez, or Burguy, though they do not adopt this theory, nevertheless contain no detailed investigation of it, and they assume the truth of the opinions which my Essay endeavours to establish by proof. The grammars in question, moreover, although they afford more copious illustrations of the Romance languages, and particularly of their syntax, than my Essay, consistently with its limited scope, pretends to furnish; yet do not present the theory of their derivation from the Latin in so compact a form. I may add that my Essay still remains the only English work in which this problem is treated at length, and in such a manner as to enable a student to form an independent judgment respecting its solution.

PREFACE TO THE SECOND EDITION.

In revising this Essay for republication, at an interval of nearly thirty years since its composition, I have not attempted to make any material alterations either in its substance or in its form. With the exception of a few unimportant corrections, I have limited myself to the addition of such references to the works of Diez and others, published since the first edition, as seemed to me to be likely to be useful to a reader. These insertions in the notes are included within brackets.

The importance and interest of the philological problem, which is treated in the following pages, are much increased by the fact that it lies entirely within the historical period; and that not only the original and the derivative languages, but also the circumstances attending the transition, are known by authentic evidence, and by an unbroken tradition. It is therefore a problem which admits of solution by demonstrative arguments, and without a recourse to a series of hypotheses and conjectures, weakening as the chain lengthens.

LONDON,
October, 1862.

CONTENTS.

CHAP. | PAGE
I. THE ORIGIN OF THE ROMANCE LANGUAGES . . 1
  § 1. STATEMENT OF M. RAYNOUARD'S THEORY RESPECTING THE ORIGIN OF THE ROMANCE LANGUAGES. 1
  § 2. EXAMINATION OF THIS THEORY IN THE PRESENT WORK PROPOSED. 5
  § 3. PRELIMINARY EXAMINATION OF THE HYPOTHESIS THAT THE ITALIAN LANGUAGE WAS FORMED FROM A PLEBEIAN FORM OF THE LATIN LANGUAGE 10
  § 4. NATURE OF THE CHANGES IN THE LATIN LANGUAGE PRODUCED BY THE TEUTONIC INVASIONS 16
  § 5. VARIETY OF THESE CHANGES . . . 28
  § 6. GENERAL OBJECTIONS TO M. RAYNOUARD'S PROOFS OF THE DERIVATION OF ALL THE ROMANCE LANGUAGES FROM THE PROVENÇAL . 34
  § 7. USE OF THE WORD ROMANCE . . . 50

II. THE FORMATION OF THE ROMANCE ARTICLES AND NOUNS FROM THE LATIN 54
  § 1. ARTICLES . . . . ib.
  § 2. FORMS AND INFLEXIONS OF NOUNS . . 57
  § 3. GENDERS OF NOUNS 112
  § 4. FORMATION OF NEW NOUNS BY AFFIXES . 119

III. DEGREES OF COMPARISON, PRONOUNS, AND NUMERALS IN THE ROMANCE LANGUAGES . . 147
  § 1. DEGREES OF COMPARISON . . . . ib.
  § 2. PRONOUNS 150
  § 3. NUMERALS 162

CONTENTS.

CHAP.		PAGE
IV.	FORMATION, CONJUGATION, AND SYNTAX OF VERBS IN THE ROMANCE LANGUAGES	166
	§ 1. Formation and Conjugation of Verbs	ib.
	§ 2. Syntax of Verbs	191
V.	PREPOSITIONS, ADVERBS, AND CONJUNCTIONS, IN THE ROMANCE LANGUAGES	197
	§ 1. Prepositions	ib.
	§ 2. Adverbs	209
	§ 3. Conjunctions	224
	§ 4. Concluding Remarks on M. Raynouard's Hypothesis	243
APPENDIX		251

CHAPTER I.

THE ORIGIN OF THE ROMANCE LANGUAGES.

§ 1. It is now nearly twenty years since M. Raynouard published at Paris two grammatical treatises on the Romance language, one containing an account of the rules of that language before the year 1000: the other, a complete grammar of the language of the Troubadours as preserved in their extant poems. These two grammars, accompanied with an introduction on the antiquity of the Romance language, and researches on its origin and formation, composed the first volume of the series which he has since continued under the name of *Selections from the Poetry of the Troubadours*. The poems, which form the four next volumes of his collection, were published by him from various manuscripts belonging to different public libraries of France and Italy, but especially from a manuscript in the king's library at Paris. Before the publication of this work, there was no printed collection of the poetry of the Troubadours in existence; and the few single poems contained in the treatise of the Abbé Millot and some other works of French and Italian writers, had for the most part been derived from inaccurate copies, and had been

CHAPTER I.

imperfectly explained by the editors[1]. As forming part of the same series, though not so closely connected as the preceding volumes, M. Raynouard afterwards put forth a comparative grammar of the modern Latin languages, considered in their relation to the language of the Troubadours. His entire undertaking will have been completed, when the dictionary of the Romance language, which he announced some years ago as being in a state of forwardness, shall have been laid before the public[c]. To those who are acquainted with M. Raynouard's labours, it is unnecessary to speak in praise of publications of which the merits have been so generally and so justly admitted: to those who may not have met with them, it may be proper to say, that by his industry and original researches he has made known an European language and literature almost wholly forgotten since the extinction of the independence of Provence: and has thrown a greater light on the origin of the modern Latin lan-

[1] See an account of these works in Diez, *Poesie der Troubadours* (Zwickau, 1827), p. v.—ix.

[c] M. Raynouard died on the 27th of October, 1836, at the age of seventy-five, in the year following the original publication of this essay. His *Lexique Roman; ou, Dictionnaire de la Langue des Troubadours*, was published after his death, under the editorship of M. Paquet, in six vols. 8vo, the first of which bears the date of 1838, the second of 1836, the third of 1840, the fourth of 1842, the fifth of 1843, and the sixth of 1844. The first volume contains, 'Recherches Philologiques sur la Langue Romane,' p. ix.—xlii.; 'Résumé de la Grammaire Romane,' p. xliii.—lxxxviii.;' and 'Nouveau Choix des Poésies originales des Troubadours,' 1—580. Vols. ii. to v. inclusive, contain the *Lexique Roman*, or Dictionary of the ancient Provençal language; the sixth volume contains a short *Appendice* to the *Lexique*, and a *Vocabulaire Alphabétique des Mots disposés par Familles dans le Lexique Roman*.

In the Introduction to vol. ii., consisting of pp. l.—xcii., M. Raynouard declares that he expounds the numerous affinities between the

guages, their mutual relations, and their early structure and syntax, than perhaps all the other writers on these subjects collectively. In addition to the works here mentioned, his criticisms in the *Journal des Savans* form a complete history of the various publications of ancient French poems, and other writings connected with the philology of the Romance languages, called forth by that taste for the early native literature which his example and investigations have greatly contributed to create of late years in France. It is not indeed without reason that M. Raynouard's fame has spread itself through the learned public in Europe; that Schlegel has said that he has done more for the history of the French language than all the academicians of his country[1]; that by his means the study of the Troubadour poetry has taken root both in Germany and Italy, and that parts of his labours have been reproduced by writers of both those countries. In England, however, as far as I am aware, M. Raynouard's works have not attracted even among scholars and philologists the attention which they unquestionably deserve: and therefore I propose in the

six neolatin languages, namely,—1, the language of the Troubadours; 2, the Catalonian; 3, the Spanish; 4, the Portuguese; 5, the Italian; 6, the French. He proceeds thus :—

'J'entreprends, pour la lexicographie des ces idiômes, ce que j'ai tâché d'exécuter pour la comparaison de leurs formes grammaticales.

'J'ose espérer que le résultat de mes investigations démontrera évidemment l'origine commune des diverses langues de l'Europe latine, et ne laissera plus aucun doute sur l'existence ancienne d'un type primitif, c'est-à-dire d'une langue intermédiaire, idiôme encore grossier sans doute, mais qui pourtant était dirigé par des principes rationnels, notamment quand il s'appropriait, sous des formes nouvelles, plusieurs des mots de la langue latine,' p. i. [Note added in 1802.]

[1] *Kritische Schriften*, vol. i., page 356.

present work to lay before the reader such an account of the principal parts of them as may enable him to form a judgment of the nature and value of their contents; though at the same time I shall sometimes take the liberty of departing from the order in which M. Raynouard has arranged his materials, and shall investigate some collateral questions relating to the origin of the Romance languages, on which he has not fully expressed his opinion.

In order to effect this purpose, I shall proceed to give an abstract of the principal contents of M. Raynouard's Grammar of the Troubadour language, inserting in their proper places the corresponding forms and idioms in the Italian, Spanish, and French languages, which are adduced in his *Comparative Grammar*[1]: so as to present in the most important points a tolerably complete parallelism of the Romance tongues. In this manner it will be made evident what relation the Provençal language, or the language of the Troubadours, bears to its cognate dialects of the Latin: and the reader will be enabled to judge of the truth of M. Raynouard's theory with respect to their origin, which I will now state as nearly as possible in his own words. He conceives that the Romance language, formed from the corruption of the Latin, was common to all the countries of Europe in which the Latin had been spoken, and is preserved in a pure form in the poetry of the Troubadours (*Gr. R.* p. 5,

---

[1] In this Grammar M. Raynouard constantly compares the forms of the Portuguese as well as of the Spanish language. For the sake of brevity and clearness I have omitted the Portuguese; as, although it deviates in many respects from the Spanish, nevertheless there is such a fundamental resemblance between them, that the same general arguments apply to both.

6.)[1]. It was a regular fixed language, having constant rules (*Gr. Comp.* p. ii.) and was universally understood over Roman Europe (*Gr. Comp.* p. xxix.) And this was the common source from which all the modern Latin languages were derived (*Gr. Comp.* p. ii.); so that all the characteristic marks and idioms of each of these languages are traceable in the mother tongue (ib. p. iv.), and the resemblance of the forms of certain words in these languages is sufficient to prove, not only a community of origin, but also the existence of a common intermediate type, which has modified both the Latin and other languages by operations of which the characteristic marks and the perfect unity may still be recognised (*Gr. Comp.* p. 30).

§ 2. Such is M. Raynouard's theory with respect to the origin of the Italian, Spanish, and French, and their dialects. He does not place them on the same line with the ancient Provençal or Langue d'oc, deriving them all, as sister languages, directly from the Latin: but he considers the Romance as an universal language, which arose from the corruption of the Latin in the middle ages, which was severally modified into the Italian, Spanish, Portuguese, modern Provençal, and French, and of which we have a faithful transcript in the poems of the Troubadours. In establishing this theory, M. Raynouard in some degree resembled the prophet mentioned in the Bible, who was required not only to interpret the dream, but also to divine what the

---

[1] In the following pages, the references are made to the separate edition of the *Grammaire de la Langue Romane;* but the miscellaneous treatises which belong to it are quoted as they are collected in the first vol. of the *Choix des Poésies des Troubadours.*

dream was: for before he could trace the relations of the modern Latin languages with the Romance, he had first to discover the Romance itself, to explain its structure, and to ascertain its grammatical rules[1]. When we consider the novelty of M. Raynouard's investigations, the multiplicity of unperceived relations which he brought to light, the extent of his erudition, his unwearied industry, and his scrupulous accuracy of citation, it is no wonder that his theory should have obtained general assent, as his works deserved general admiration, among persons occupied about the history of the Romance languages. Even before the publication of his *Comparative Grammar*, and when his theory had merely been put forward as an hypothesis, Perticari, in a treatise which has been much admired in Italy, adopted his views on the origin of the Italian: considering (to use his own words) 'that the Latin was the grandmother, while the Romance was the mother of the new

[1] The same theory had indeed been previously advanced by others as a conjecture, but only as a conjecture. M. Raynouard's merit consists in assigning definite reasons for that which was before a mere guess. Smollett, the novelist, in his *Travels in France and Italy*, gives an account of the origin of the Romance and its relation to the other dialects of the Latin, which exactly agrees with M. Raynouard's views, though I am not aware whence he borrowed it. ' The Patois, or native tongue of Nice (he says), is no other than the ancient Provençal, from which the Italian, Spanish, and French languages have been formed. This is the language that rose upon the ruins of the Latin tongue, after the irruption of the Goths, Vandals, Huns, and Burgundians, by whom the Roman empire was destroyed. It was spoke all over Italy, Spain, and the southern part of France until the thirteenth century, whence the Italians began to polish it into the language which they now call their own. The Spaniards and French too improved it into their respective tongues. From its great affinity to the Latin, it was called *Romance*, a name which the Spaniards still give to their own language.' Letter xxi. vol. i.

languages now spoken over a large part of Europe[1]:' which Romance (he says in another place) was the common language of Europe for more than five hundred years[2]. The same theory has been adopted by Champollion-Figéac, by Sismondi in the later editions of his work on the Literature of Southern Europe, by Niccolini[3], Lampredi, and Ugo Foscolo: and it is received by Balbi as the established opinion in his Ethnographic Atlas[4]. A few writers, such as Daunou, in the *Journal des Savans*[5], Galvani, who has published an Italian work on the Troubadour poetry[6], and a contributor to the *Florence Antologia*, have faintly expressed a dissenting opinion, or rejected some of the arguments by which the doctrine has been supported: Schlegel alone has expressed his entire dissent from this theory; and has stated succinctly in a short work published at Paris many years ago[7], what appears to me to be the true explanation

p. 334. The mention of the Huns is probably an oversight, as they did not establish themselves in a part of Europe where, according to Smollett's view, the Romance language was ever spoken.

[1] 'Quindi possiamo dire che la latina veramente fu avola, ma la romana fu madre delle nuove favelle che ora si parlano in tanta parte d'Europa.' *Scrittori del Trecento*, lib. i. cap. 7; and see *Difesa di Dante*, cap. vii. ad fin. et 10.

[2] 'Quel comun sermone romano che per 600 e più anni tutta occupò l'Europa latina.' *Difesa di Dante*, c. 44.

[3] Discorso in cui si ricerca qual parte aver possa il popolo nella formazione d'una lingua, (Florence, 1810,) p. 8.

[4] See Balbi, *Introduction à l'Atlas Ethnographique du Globe*, p. 106 —75. Bernhardy likewise, in his *Grundlinien zur Encyclopädie der Philologie*, p. 188, appears to consider the Provençal as intermediate between the Latin and the other Romance languages.

[5] *Journal des Savans*, 1823, p. 68—90.

[6] *Osservazioni sulle Poesie dei Trovatori*, p. 515, note.

[7] *Observations sur la Langue et la Littérature Provençales*, par A. W. de Schlegel. Paris, 1818. [The theory of M. Raynouard, as to the derivation of the Romance languages from a common type, in-

of the origin of the modern Latin languages, and some of the chief objections to which M. Raynouard's system is liable: but no one has undertaken to refute, or even to examine in detail, M. Raynouard's demonstrations, although it might have been expected that among a nation so jealous of the honour of their language and literature as the Italian, some critic would have arisen to question the truth of a theory which takes from that language the reputation which it has hitherto enjoyed of being the first-born of the ancient Latin. The objections which I shall propose to M. Raynouard's system do not, however, arise from any national feeling, or literary jealousy: the difficulties which I find in his argument presented themselves unsought; and it is only because no one better versed than myself in the literature of the middle ages has undertaken the task of examining his theory, that I shall in this work lay before the reader my grounds for venturing to reject an explanation supported with so much erudition and ingenuity.

There is perhaps no problem connected with language which admits of a completer solution than that which respects the modern European languages formed from the Latin[1]. Unlike the origin of most languages, it lies within a purely historical period: the language of the

termediate between them and the Latin, is examined and rejected by Ampère, *Histoire de la Littérature Française au Moyen Age* (Paris, 1841), p. 20—93.]

[1] 'La langue Romane (says M. Raynouard) est peut-être *la seule* à la formation de laquelle il soit permis de remonter ainsi, pour découvrir et expliquer le secret de son industrieux mécanisme: j'ai mis à cette recherche autant de patience que de franchise, et dans le cours de mes investigations grammaticales, j'ai eu souvent occasion de reconnaître la vérité de l'axiôme, "non quia difficilia sunt, non audemus, sed quia non audemus, difficilia sunt,"' vol. i. p. 104. Among the other

native population, the changes which took place in their political condition, the race and languages of the invaders and of the other foreign nations with which they came in contact, all are certainly known: and although the early stages of these Latin dialects, when they were merely barbarous and unfixed jargons, formed by the intercourse of natives and strangers, spoken chiefly among illiterate persons, and used neither as the language of the government, of legal instruments, nor of books, are not only (with the exception of a few words) wholly unknown, but lost without hope of recovery; yet the events which accompanied and occasioned their origin are matter of historical record; and if we cannot always say, with certainty to what precise cause the changes which the Latin underwent were owing, our information enables us at least to obtain negative results, and to exclude undoubtingly many hypotheses which might be tenable if we had merely the languages without a contemporary history of the times when they arose. The same is the case with the English language: without looking to its structure or examining the etymology of its words, we should be justified in rejecting an hypothesis which should derive it from an union of the Anglo-Saxon and the Greek, or the Anglo-Saxon and the Celtic; as we know that the invaders, who formed a new tongue by their intercourse with the native Anglo-Saxon population, spoke not Celtic, or Greek, but Norman-French. When on the other hand we look at the Latin, we find by analyzing its forms and words, that it contains a Hellenic and a barbarous element, and is therefore probably a

European languages, however, the English, as well as the modern Greek, has been formed since the time of memory.

mixed language formed by the union of different races in one community[1]: but what were the component parts of the nation (though the historical traditions afford materials for conjecture) is a matter of extreme uncertainty, and we may as well infer such a mixture of populations from the form of the language, as account for the form of the language by the mixture of the populations. It is therefore peculiarly important to explain, so far as the present state of our knowledge permits, the formation of the Romance languages: as they may furnish a sure point of comparison for other mixed languages whose origin lies before the dawn of history, and which can only be illustrated by means of their analogy with those of a more recent date.

§ 3. Before I proceed to examine M. Raynouard's account of the Provençal language, it will be proper to say something on a theory of the origin of the Italian, proposed by some native writers; since, if it could be established, it would apply with equal force to the other languages of the same family. The hypothesis to which

[1] Lassen, in Welcker's *Rheinisches Museum*, vol. i. p. 301—4, objects to dividing the Latin into a Grecian and non-Grecian part, and says that it might as well be divided into an Indian and non-Indian, or a Teutonic and non-Teutonic part. It is however to be observed, that though all these languages are derived from a common source, yet there is a closer affinity between the Latin and the Greek, than between the Latin and the Sanscrit or the Gothic. Moreover, when Lassen says that the Latin bears no marks of being a mixed language, like the English and Persian, he forgets Otfried Müller's remark with respect to the Latin passive voice, and the progress which it has made towards analytic forms. The want of a power of forming compound words in Latin, which its cognate tongues possess in so remarkable a degree, (see Livy, xxvii. 11, 'Faciliore ad duplicanda verba Græco sermone,') seems likewise to prove that the mixture of a heterogeneous element had enfeebled the capacities of the original language.

I allude is that in ancient Rome, and in Italy, after the
extension of the Roman dominion, there were two dialects or forms of the Latin language: one spoken by the
upper classes, and educated persons, and used as the language of government, of the tribunals, of the laws, and
of literature; while the other, universally spoken by the
lower classes, and differing essentially in structure from
the high Latin, was never written until the middle ages,
when it became the general language of Italy, or (as it
is now called) the Italian. This theory, first proposed by
some writers of little note[1], is illustrated at length by
Maffei, in his history of Verona: the same view, in its
unmitigated shape, is likewise followed by Lanzi, in his
work on the Etruscan language[2]; by Bonamy, in the
Memoirs of the Academy of Inscriptions[3]; and has been
more recently maintained by Ciampi, a Florentine writer,
in a separate dissertation[4]. A nearly similar account of
the existence of a low Latin dialect is given by Muratori
and Perticari, although both these writers admit the
influence of the Teutonic invaders on the native language
of Italy, which Maffei and Lanzi altogether exclude;

[1] See their names mentioned in Perticari, *Scrittori del Trecento*, c. 5.
[2] 'Non furono straniere lingue che in Italia lo (il latino) estinsero: fu un linguaggio di volgo, che fin da antichissimi tempi annidato in queste contrade, anzi in Roma stessa, e restatosi occulto nei miglior secoli, si riprodusse nei peggiori; e dilatandosi a poco e prendendo forza, degenerò in quella che anco per questa sua origine possiam chiamare volgar lingua d'Italia.' Lanzi, *Saggio della Lingua Etrusca*, vol. i. p. 331.
[3] Vol. xxiv. p. 597—666. Bonamy's explanation embraces the Italian, Spanish, and French.
[4] Ciampi, *De Usu Linguæ Italicæ*. Pisis, 1817, 4to. An excellent review of this book (which cannot now be procured even in Tuscany), and a refutation of the arguments on which it is founded, by M. Raynouard, may be seen in the *Journal des Savans*, 1818, p. 323—31.

CHAPTER I.

Muratori in particular has laid great stress on the changes introduced by the conquerors of Italy, and has pointed out the German origin of a whole series of Italian words. It is not indeed very easy to ascertain the precise opinions of Muratori[1] and Perticari[2] on this subject; for, as they rest on a confusion of things which ought to be distinguished, the statements of their arguments naturally partake of the ambiguity on which the

---

[1] Thus he says, *Dissert. It. Med. Ævi*, vol. ii. p. 1013, E., 14 A. 'Incompertum sane est, ne dicam falsum, eo præcipue tempore, quo Gothi et Langobardi in Italia dominati sunt, *natam*, atque ad culmen suum perductam fuisse vulgarem Italicam linguam, quam ad exprimendas cogitationes nostras nunc usurpamus.' But he adds, p. 1016 E. 'Itaque non immerito opinemur, præcipue sub Langobardorum regno Latinum sermonem, antea in barbariem multam prolapsum, gravius corruptum atque immutatum fuisse, ita ut faciem novæ linguæ lingua Italici populi tunc præferre cœperit. *Nam quod nonnulli sensisse videntur, eam ipsam Italicam linguam, qua nunc utimur, a Latina seu Romana adeo diversam, vel florente romani imperii fortuna, viguisse, somnium est nulla confutatione dignum.*' And again, Diss. 33, p. 1101 C. 'Quum tamen longe plures semper abundarint in Italicis urbibus et agris incolæ Latini, propterea primas retinuit ubique Latinorum lingua, sed simul impedire nequiit quin ex tanta colluvione septentrionalium populorum potentius in dies corrumperetur et antiquas voces adulteraret, aut iis voces gentis dominatricis immisceret; præsertim quod officia fere omnia, et publica munera tum sacra tum profana Langobardis dominantibus conferrentur.'

[2] See *Scrittori del Trecento*, c. 5—7. In c. 6, speaking of the effects of the invasion of the barbarians, he says: 'Segnendo adunque la partizione dantesca, diremo essere presto mancato il latino illustre, ma il rustico essere in quei tempi rinnaso.' In c. 7, he says that he 'has traced the history of the *lingua rustica*, discovered its ancient origin, showed how it prevailed for a long period of time, and afterwards under the name of Romance was polished in a better age.' In another place he says, ' non dalla barbarie Vandala nè dalla Gota, ma da questo volgar romano propriamente l'Italico fu prodotto.' *Difesa di Dante*, c. 7. Nevertheless he distinctly admits the influence of the Teutons, ib. c. 8: thus he says: 'non fu nò perduto nè rinnovato in quel devastamento Italico *tutto* il vecchio parlare.'

arguments themselves are founded. The confusion in question has (as M. Raynouard has remarked[1]) arisen from overlooking the distinction between *style* and *structure*, from inferring that because the lower classes of ancient Italy used ungrammatical and vulgar forms of expression, therefore they spoke a language which differed in its inflexions and syntax from that written in books and current among educated persons. Doubtless illiterate people in ancient Italy, as in all other countries, frequently committed grammatical errors[2], and used low words in their conversation: doubtless the countrymen employed words which had been disused in the towns, and had become provincialisms: doubtless professions, as soldiers, lawyers, farmers, etc., had certain peculiar terms not generally current through the community. On the other hand there was a style of writing and speaking adopted by the upper classes, correct in grammar, admitting no mean and vulgar expressions, free from provincialisms, and the cant phrases of the camp, the country, or the forum; the standard of composition as established by critics and grammarians on the models of classical writers; the *lingua aulica* or *cortigiana*, as it was called by Dante, after the political institutions of his day, in opposition to the *lingua plebea*, the unpolished idiom of clowns. It was this pure and correct style which the grammarians of Rome taught to their scholars,

[1] *Gr. Comp.* p. xlvii.—viii. See also the criticism cited above in p. 11, [4].
[2] Thus Quintilian, I. 6, 45, says: 'Quemadmodum vulgo *imperiti* loquuntur, tota saepe theatra et omnem circi turbam exclamasse barbare scimus.' Hence in c. 6, § 27, he says: 'Non invenuste dici videtur aliud esse Latine aliud grammatice loqui,' that is, it is one thing to *speak* a language, another to speak it *correctly*.

and of which they treated in their works; like the Greek rhetoricians and elocutionists who taught their pupils to use a more elevated and grammatical diction, but not to speak in a different language from the vulgar. In Latin, as in other languages, 'many things (as Maffei says[1]) had two names: one of which was used by educated persons and by writers, the other was current among the lower orders and in common use.' Thus in an elevated style a writer or speaker would use *os, equus, fimus, pumilio, pulcher, ruber, percutere, ducere:* but in familiar conversation, or in works *sermoni propiora,* the corresponding terms, *bucca, caballus, lætamen, nanus, bellus, russus, batuere, menare,* would be employed[2]. So Varro tells us that what the inhabitants of towns call *quiritare,* the country people called *jubilare,* that where the former said *pellicula,* the latter said *scortum*[3]. Pliny calls *conterraneus a castrense verbum,* Gellius says the same of *copior*[4]; and we know that Livy was reproached with his Patavinity. But when Maffei would infer from such facts as these that there was a dialect spoken by the lower orders of ancient Italy, resembling the modern Italian rather than the Latin[5], his reasoning has just as little weight as his proofs of the use of articles and

---

[1] 'Di molte cose v'eran due vocaboli; un dei quali si adoprava dalla gente colta e dagli scrittori, l'altro era proprio della plebe ed usuale.' *Verona Illustrata,* part I. col. 313. [For a list of plebeian Latin words, see Diez, *Rom. Gramm.,* vol. i. p. 7—28.]
[2] These instances are given by Maffei.
[3] De L. L. vi. 68, vii. 84, ed. Müller.
[4] Plin. *Præf. ad Nat. Hist.,* § 1. Gellius, xvii. 2.
[5] See his entire argument, col. 312—20. Maffei's conclusion is rejected as absurd by Tiraboschi, *Storia della Litteratura Italiana,* Preface to tom. iii. part I.; by Pignotti, *Storia di Toscana,* vol. ii.: *Dell' Origine e Progressi della Lingua Italiana;* by Diez *Poesie der Trouba-*

THE ORIGIN OF THE ROMANCE LANGUAGES. 15

auxiliary verbs in ancient Italy[1]. There is no doubt that
Latin writers sometimes prefix the pronoun *ille* to a noun,
much in the same way that the Italian uses its definite
article, there is no doubt that they sometimes used *habeo*
and a past participle, after the manner of the modern
conjugation with *avere*; but these are anomalous instances, not rules; they are only the rudiments and germs
of a system which had not then come into being; and
notwithstanding these idioms the Latin had no articles,
and no active conjugation with auxiliary verbs. The
very examples cited by Maffei make against him: for we
find that the purest and most elegant writers of Latin
did not avoid his plebeian words, and that they used
them moreover with the Latin terminations and inflexions. Instead therefore of producing an exclusively
plebeian word with an Italian termination, he quotes
from Lucretius, Horace, and Juvenal such words as
russus, bellus, and *caballus* with a purely Latin form.
There can be little doubt that the state of the Latin
language in ancient Italy exactly resembled that of the
English in most parts of England, and that of the
French in Paris and its neighbourhood: viz.,—that the
language spoken by the whole population was the same
in its structure and form, but that the upper and educated
classes spoke it without solecisms, and coarse or vulgar
expressions, while the lower orders and the country people used an ungrammatical, homely, and sometimes anti-

---

dours, p. 286; and by other writers. See also Hallam's *Middle Ages*,
ch. 9, part I. vol. iii. p. 320.

[1] Ib. col. 318, 319. By the same mode of reasoning it might be
shown that the Greek, which sometimes said καλύψας ἔχω, βεβουλευμένως
ἔχω, used auxiliary verbs. See Matthiæ's *Gr. Gr.*, § 559.

quated mode of diction. It would be easy to make in English a list of passages from writers on style who give cautions against the use of plebeian expressions: and to collect a series of double synonyms, of which one is suited to a serious, poetical, and lofty, the other to a ludicrous, familiar, or humble style. This, according to Maffei's way of reasoning, would be a proof of the existence of two languages in England, one spoken by the upper, the other by the lower classes. The orthography of the Latin, as of all other languages before the use of printing, was completely unfixed, and from the practice which prevailed in ancient, as it prevails in modern Italy, of representing the exact sounds of the voice with letters, (instead, like English and French, of often making a word an arbitrary symbol to represent a sound,) many peculiarities of local pronunciation were introduced by the stone-cutters into public and private monuments: but there is no trace of the existence in ancient Italy of a language spoken among the lower orders, differing from the Latin in its grammatical structure, of a *patois* or *dialetto*[1], standing to the Latin in the same relation as the Provençal or Gascon to the French, as the Catalonian to the Spanish, as the Genoese, Mantuan, or Bolognese, to

[1] We have no word in English to express the idea signified by these words, of an unwritten language spoken by the inferior classes, differing in structure or in origin from the national or common language. The Welsh, the Gaelic, and the Irish, as spoken in Wales, Scotland, and Ireland, are indeed properly *patois* like the Bas-breton: but the provincial languages of Norfolk, Somersetshire, Yorkshire, and Scotland, cannot in strictness be so called, as they have the same inflexions as the written English, though they contain many peculiar words not generally understood. A Norfolk or Yorkshire peasant would understand a play of Shakspeare, or a speech made in pure English, but a Provençal learns French as he would learn Spanish, and there are translations of

the Italian: which are languages with different inflexions and syntax, and the one is not intelligible to a person acquainted with the other, although both belong to the same stock. But the language popularly spoken in Tuscany has the same inflexions and grammar as the pure Italian, the κοινὴ διάλεκτος of Italy, though it may contain many words peculiar to itself[1]; and such, I conceive, was the relation which the plebeian language of Rome bore to the style in which Cicero addressed the senate, or composed a philosophical treatise. It was only a less perfect, refined, and correct form of the self-same Latin language. Without further discussion, therefore, we may reject, as wholly destitute of evidence, the theory of Maffei, which finds the Italian, and of Perticari[2], which

---

Tasso into Venetian, Milanese, Bolognese, and other Italian dialects. The definition of *dialetto* in the *Vocab. della Crusca*, viz.,—'Spezie particolare di pronunzia di alcun linguaggio,' is very imperfect. The *Dictionnaire de l'Académie* defines *patois* to be 'langage du peuple et des paysans particulier à chaque province.' Baretti, in his Italian and English Dictionary, explains *dialetto* to be 'a manner of speech peculiar to some part of a country, yet all using the same radical language.' The latter limitation is probably true of the word *dialetto*, as used in Italian: but it does not appear to apply to the French term *patois*: for the Basque in Navarre, or the Bas-breton in Britany, would, I conceive, be properly termed *patois*, though they belong to a different stock from the French and Spanish.

[1] See the *Lamento di Cecco di Varlungo*, a pastoral poem in the language of the Tuscan peasants. Some remarks on the much controverted point of the relation of the Tuscan to the written Italian, and the other Italian dialects, will be found in note (A.) at the end.

[2] The following statements of Balbi, in his *Atlas Ethnographique*, agree nearly with Perticari's theory; tab. xii., par. 161. 'Latine. C'était la langue écrite et commune au beau monde de l'Italie et de tout le vaste empire romain; elle était très différente de la *lingua plebria* ou *rustica*, parlée dans les campagnes de la péninsule, et par les personnes des classes inférieures dans les Espagnes, les Gaules, et autres provinces.' Ib. 102: '*Romane* ou *Romana rustica* parlée dans

c

finds the Provençal, in the dialect of the lowest classes of ancient Italy[1].

§ 4. The extension of the Latin language over the countries of Western Europe occupied by the Romans, is a fact more easily proved[2] than accounted for. As the native tribes of Italy, Gaul, and Spain, yielded successively to the Roman arms, so their multifarious dialects gave way before the language of their conquerors. In many instances the language of conquering nations has disappeared, or left only faint traces of its existence in the native dialect of the country. Thus the Normans adopted the language of their subjects and neighbours in Northern France[3]; and the English tongue, though com-

---

[1] les beaux temps de Rome par les basses classes de la société dans tout le midi de l'Europe romaine; la Grèce et quelques autres pays exceptés. Après avoir subi des modifications plus ou moins considérables, *la romane paroît encore subsister* dans les dialectes vulgaires qu'on parle dans une grande partie de l'Espagne, de la France, de la Suisse, et dans quelques cantons de l'Italie.' For a similar view of this subject in a more recent work on the modern European languages see note (B.) at the end.

[1] On an assertion of Niebuhr's, with respect to the mention of a *lingua volgare* subordinate to the Latin, by Priscus, in relation to an embassy which took place in 448, A.D., see note (C.) at the end.

[2] See Raynouard, vol. i., p. 1—6. 'Exploratum est (says Muratori) per universam Italiam, Galliam, et Hispaniam propagatum ita fuisse Latinæ linguæ usum, ut non docti tantum viri, sed et plebes et rustici denique omnes eamdem usurparint.' *Antiq. It. Med. Ævi,* Diss. 32, vol. ii., p. 1014 A. On the universality of the Latin language in Gaul, see *Histoire Littéraire de la France,* vol. vii., avertissement, § 1. The universal prevalence of the Latin language is proved by the use of the word Latin for language generally, in old French and Italian: see Orell, *Alt-franzôs. Grammatik,* p. 28. *Vocab. della Crusca* in v. On the universality of the Latin language in Spain, see Mayans i Siscar, *Origenes de la Lengua Española,* vol. ii., p. 20.

[3] On this change of language see Gibbon, c. 60, note 17. Gley, *Langue et Littérature des Anciens Francs,* p. 275. Raynouard, *Obser.*

pletely subverted by their influence, nevertheless retains in substance its original Saxon character. But the Latin, having at the same time the advantages accruing from the influence of government, which imposed on the governed the necessity of understanding it[1], seems like the Greek, to have propagated itself by a sort of magical power among the inhabitants of Western Europe[2]. In Italy the Etruscan disappeared before it under the early emperors, and every trace of that singular language has been lost except the inexplicable inscriptions: the Oscan and other dialects of the native Italian tribes underwent the same fate[3]: the Celtic was forgotten in Gaul and Spain, and was only preserved among the inhabitants of

---

vations sur le Roman de Rou, p. 16—21. Heeren, Ueber den Einfluss der Normannen auf die Französische Sprache und Litteratur, Werke, vol. ii., p. 307—9.

[1] The Romans used their own language in all acts of the government even in Greece (see Raynouard, vol. i., p. 2, 4), and did not, like the Austrians and the French in Italy, employ the language of the conquered nation. The Latin however did not supplant the Greek either in Greece or in Magna Græcia; and in the former country it was not constantly used as the language of government, as we know from the many extant Greek inscriptions relating to public matters which belong to the time of the Empire: but it was introduced by the influence of government into Asia Minor, Syria, and Constantinople: see the *Quarterly Review*, vol. xxiii., p. 142.

[2] 'The facility with which they were thus moulded into Greeks is a characteristic of the Pelasgian tribes, and a main cause of the dissolution and extinction of the nation. It is natural to view it as resulting from the affinity between the two races, which yet were not on that account the less essentially different: and such I believe to have been the case; yet we may observe *a magical power exercised by the Greek language and national character over foreign races that came in contact with them, even where no such affinity can be conceived*.' Niebuhr, *Hist. of Rome*, vol. i., p. 50.

[3] On the extension of the Latin in Italy, see Lanzi, *Saggio della Lingua Etrusca*, vol. i., p. 27.

Armorica[1]: the Iberian gave way in Spain, and only lived in the modern Basque among the mountaineers of the Pyrenees: the Ligurian became extinct on the shores of the Mediterranean. The use of the Latin language gradually became as universal over Western Europe, as the dominion of the Roman laws and political institutions. As this language had been spread by conquest, so it was destined to be destroyed by conquest; and when the Teutonic races of the Herulians, Goths, Lombards,

---

[1] On the diffusion of the Latin language in Gaul, see Bonamy, *Mémoires de l'Acad. des Inscriptions*, vol. xxiv., p. 687—94. The Celtic however still lingered in some of the Eastern and Southern parts in the third and fourth centuries. Alex. von Humboldt has the following remarks on this subject: 'I believe (he says) that we must look into the character of the natives and the state of their civilization, and not into the structure of their language, for the reason of this rapid introduction of Latin among the Gauls. The Celtic nations with brown hair, were certainly different from the race of the Germanic nations with light hair, [see Niebuhr, vol. ii., n. 1100;] and though the Druid caste recals to our minds one of the institutions of the Ganges, this does not demonstrate that the idiom of the Celtic belongs, like that of the nations of Odin, to a branch of the Indo-Pelasgic languages. [This affinity has now been proved by Dr. Prichard.] From analogy of structure and of roots, the Latin ought to have penetrated more easily on the other side of the Danube, than into Gaul; but an *uncultivated state, joined to great moral inflexibility,* opposed probably its introduction among the Germanic nations.' *Personal Narrative*, vol. vi., p. 249, note. Although it may be true that the Celtic is inferior in natural capacity to the Teutonic race, yet the reason why the Latin made no way in Germany, is, that the Germans were not subjugated and their country occupied by the Romans. It is certainly difficult to explain how the Romans should have completely eradicated the Celtic language from a large part of Gaul, while the same causes which appear at that time to have produced so great an effect, have during the last eight or nine centuries produced so little effect, among the Celts of Britany, Wales, Scotland, and Ireland. In Cornwall alone the Celtic language has become extinct, and that within less than a century.

THE ORIGIN OF THE ROMANCE LANGUAGES. 21

Burgundians and Franks, successively overran the West of Europe in the fifth and sixth centuries, and established themselves in it as rulers by the power of the sword, it was to be expected that the language of the conquered people would undergo great changes; such as in England and Scotland were produced by the invasion of the Normans, and in Greece by the irruption of the Sclavonic tribes. If the relative numbers of the invaders and the native population had been reversed, if the Teutonic armies had formed a large majority, instead of a small minority of the entire nation, the Latin would probably have become extinct; as the Celtic in England disappeared before the Saxons and Angles, who not only vanquished but exterminated the ancient Britons. As it was, the numbers of the natives were too large to allow of the extinction of their language[1]; while the conquerors would naturally be as little willing to yield the use of their native tongue, as to surrender any other of the privileges of conquest. But as it was necessary that the two parties should communicate with each other, the one in order to give, the other in order to receive commands; the less numerous party abated something of their privileges, and

---

[1] 'Tunc (says Muratori, speaking of the Lombard invasion of Italy) immanis turba promiscui sexus, Germanicam linguam a teneris unguiculis edocta, in Italiam effusa est, et provinciis fere universis dominari cœpit. Didicere illi quidem debellatæ gentis linguam, utpote dulciorem, et nimis altis radicibus stabilitam; nam ut ut exhausta habitatoribus tunc Italia fuerit, *longe tamen major Italicorum superstitum quam Langobardorum novorum hospitum numerus fuit*. Didicerunt, inquam, sed ita ut nova ipsi quoque vocabula in sermonem Italicum intulerint, et ad immutandam gravius quam antea pronuntiationem et desinentiam Latinarum vocum, inscitia potissimum ubique grassante, operam suam et ipsi contulerint.' *Antiq. It. Med. Ævi*, vol. ii., p. 1014 A. And on the numbers of the German invaders of Italy, see ibid., p. 1100 A—p. 1103 B.

submitted to attempt to explain themselves in the language of their subjects. Being, however, more versed in war than in letters, they used a form of speech which instead of faithfully imitating the Latin only approximated to it[1], and by introducing the use of articles and auxiliary verbs, by destroying the inflexions of cases which was too complex a system to be easily learnt, and by infusing a number of Teutonic words, they formed a hybrid lan-

[1] The following account of this change is given by Sismondi. 'Ignorant les uns et les autres tout principe de grammaire générale, ils ne songeaient point à étudier la langue de leurs ennemis; ils s'accoutumaient seulement à entendre réciproquement le jargon dans lequel ils cherchaient à se rencontrer. Ainsi nous voyons encore aujourd'hui des gens du peuple transportés dans un pays étranger, se faire avec ceux dont ils ont besoin, un patois de convention qui n'est le leur, ni celui de leurs hôtes, mais que tous deux comprennent, et qui empêche tous deux d'arriver, à la langue de l'un ou de l'autre. Ainsi dans le bagnes de l'Afrique et de Constantinople des esclaves Chrétiens de toutes les parties de l'Europe mêlés avec les Maures, n'ont point enseigné à ceux-ci leur langage, et n'ont point appris celui des Maures; mais ils se rencontrent avec eux dans un jargon barbare qu'on nomme *langue franque;* il est composé des mots romans les plus nécessaires à la vie commune dépouillés des terminaisons qui marquent les temps et les cas, et unis ensemble sans syntaxe. Ainsi dans des colonies d'Amérique, les planteurs s'entendaient avec les nègres dans la langue Créole, qui est de même le Français mis à la portée d'un peuple barbare, en le dépouillant de tout ce qui donne de la précision, de la force, ou de la souplesse.' *Littérature du Midi,* vol. I. p. 19, and compare p. 33. 'The Moravians have translated the Bible and a book of hymns into the *Talkee-talkee,* or negro language, of which they have also composed a grammar. It is curious that this patois of the blacks, though it includes many African words, should have for its basis the English language, *pared of inflexions,* and softened by a multitude of vowel terminations.' Bolingbroke, *Voyage to Demerary,* cited in the *Quarterly Review,* vol. xliii. p. 559, where specimens are given of a similar negro corruption of the Dutch language, in which the inflexions are also obscured. On the change of the Latin into the Romance language of France, see also *Histoire Littéraire de la France,* vol. vii. avertissement p. 28. And compare Brere-

guage, generated from the corruption of the Latin, and differing essentially from its parent, though still retaining a strong resemblance to it[1].

It is likewise to be remembered that in contending with the language of the Teutonic invaders, the Latin enjoyed the advantage which is derived from the possession of a classical literature and a high cultivation, both of grammatical form and rhetorical style; an advantage which was wanting to the German language, when the Goths, Lombards, Vandals, Franks and Burgundians overran the Western Empire. The maintenance of the Roman law in its original form, and of the constitution and worship of the Roman church also tended to uphold the Latin language, and to preserve it from oblivion. If these circumstances had been reversed, if the Germans with a cultivated language and literature, and a code of laws already written in their native tongue, had overrun a less civilized people, (which was the case with the Latin, when brought in collision with the Celtic, Iberian, Etruscan, etc.) the probability is, that not even the large numbers of the native Roman population would have saved their language from almost total destruction[2].

From what has been said, it follows, that the change

---

wood's *Enquiries touching the Diversity of Languages*, c. 5. Wachsmuth's *Europäische Sittengeschichte*, vol. i. p. 254.

[1] The following conceit of an Italian writer cited by Galvani, *Osservazioni sulle Poesie dei Trovatori*, p. 20, correctly expresses the origin of the modern languages. 'La lingua latina ... della gravidezza dei linguaggi barbari partorì la nostra volgare, e ne morì a mezzo il parto.'

[2] On the difficulty of eradicating a language, particularly a cultivated language, with a literature, see Heeren's Essay *Ueber die Mittel zur Erhaltung der Nationalität besiegter Völker: Historische Werke*, vol. ii. p. 17 sqq.

undergone by the Latin, in consequence of the Teutonic invasion, was three-fold: viz.—*a change of structure*, affecting the terminations and inflexions of nouns, participles, and pronouns, and the conjugations of verbs: *a change of syntax*, including the introduction of new idioms; and *the introduction of numerous foreign terms*, relating in great part to military and political subjects[1]. On the two first of these changes, which alone concern the grammar of the Romance tongues, I shall hope to be able to give a satisfactory account in the course of the present work: the latter, which is a question of etymological research, scarcely admits of being treated in a connected form, though a discussion of it might lead to highly interesting

---

[1] 'In comparing (says Gibbon, speaking of the Lombard kingdom in Italy) the proportion of the victorious and vanquished people, the change of language will afford the most probable inference. According to this standard it will appear that the Lombards of Italy, and the Visigoths of Spain, were less numerous than the Franks or Burgundians; and the conquerors of Gaul must yield in their turn to the multitude of Saxons and Angles, who almost eradicated the idioms of Britain. The modern Italian has been insensibly formed by the mixture of nations; the awkwardness of the barbarians in the nice management of declensions and conjugations reduced them to the use of articles and auxiliary verbs, and many new ideas have been expressed by Teutonic appellations. Yet the principal stock of technical and familiar words is found to be of Latin derivation.' *Decline and Fall*, c. 45. This passage appears to me to contain a just view of the origin of the Italian: but although the French has departed further than the Italian or Spanish from the Latin, I am not aware that it contains a greater number of Teutonic words. Moreover, the confusion and loss of cases gave rise not to the use of *articles*, but to that of *prepositions*, to express the relation previously signified by the inflexion. Savigny, *Geschichte des Römischen Rechts im Mittelalter*, vol. i. c. 3, p. 181—2, infers from the difference of the legal relations, that in Northern France the Franks settled in large numbers, and expelled the chief part of the natives, while in Southern France their number was smaller, and most of the Romans were spared.

results, as regards the history both of nations and languages[1].

By this change the Latin language of Western Europe passed from the *synthetic* to the *analytic* class: that is to say, instead of declining nouns and conjugating verbs by the inflexion of their terminations, it resolved the ideas into their component parts, and expressed them by means of prepositions and of participles with auxiliary verbs: as will be explained in detail when we come to examine those parts of speech. It has been supposed by some writers that this grammatical system was transferred from the Teutonic to the Latin language; and that the Germans, accustomed to analytical forms in their own tongue, copied them faithfully in the jargon which they produced by literally translating German thoughts into Latin words. But this hypothesis, though it affords an easy solution of the problem, is not entirely consistent with fact. The ancient German or Gothic was undoubtedly a synthetic language, like the Greek; and at the time when the Teutonic tribes settled over the Western Empire, it had as yet made but little progress to the adoption of analytic forms. It still used the inflexion of cases; it had no indefinite article, and of the definite article it made little use; nor does it exhibit more than the rudiments of conjugation by auxiliary verbs[2]. Consequently, although there appear to be some few instances (which will be pointed out hereafter) of German idioms having been adopted into Romance languages, yet we must seek some other explanation of the new character assumed by the Latin at the time of the German con-

---
[1] See note (D.) at the end.
[2] Schlegel, *Observations*, p. 19, 21, 34, 87.

quest. This explanation is doubtless to be found in the remark of Schlegel, that ' when synthetic languages have at an early period been fixed by books which served as models, and by a regular instruction, they retained their form unchanged: but when they have been abandoned to themselves, and exposed to the fluctuations of all human affairs, they have shown a natural tendency to become analytic, even without having been modified by the mixture of any foreign language[1].' He illustrates this position by the history of the German language, ' which, not having been fixed by any artificial means till the beginning of the sixteenth century, had full liberty to follow its natural course; and the progress which it made during that time towards analytical forms, by losing part of its synthetical forms, is immense[2].' It cannot be doubted that the natural tendency of language is to substitute analytical for synthetical forms: but this principle being admitted, there are two ways of accounting for the predominance of the latter in the Romance languages. One is that adopted by Diez, who, without going to the same length as Maffei, thinks that the familiar language of the people had adopted a number of analytical forms, and that the German influence only increased and hastened the disposition to change which already existed in the popular Latin. And he cites as a parallel instance the modern German; which, as the language of the educated classes, retains the use of cases; while in the mouths of the lower orders the cases are supplanted, as in Dutch, by a preposition or pronoun[3]. But although there might be strong reason, on the

---

[1] Schlegel, *Observations*, p. 18. [2] Ibid. p. 19.
[3] *Poesie der Troubadours*, p. 288—90.

ground of analogy, for accepting this explanation, still there is no historical evidence in its favour: on the contrary, we know that not only compositions meant for general perusal, but that private letters, such as those of Cassiodorus, were, either at or immediately after the settlement of the Goths in Italy, written in a Latin, which, however impure or inelegant, retains its synthetic character as strongly as that of Ennius or Lucretius. Notwithstanding the powerful tendency which may exist to break down synthetic forms, it may perhaps be conjectured with some reason, that as the Latin had a fixed classical standard, it would have retained its grammatical character unchanged in Italy, Spain, and France, as it has in the mouths of the people in some parts of Hungary, if the German invasion had never taken place. The explanation of Schlegel, that the change produced in the Latin was purely the effect of the German conquest[1], seems therefore preferable. The conquerors, not understanding the complicated and refined system of in-

[1] 'Les conquérans barbares (ils adoptèrent eux-mêmes ce nom qu'ils croyoient honorable, puisqu'il signifioit l'opposé de romain) trouvant dans les pays conquis une population toute latine, ou, selon l'expression du temps, *romaine*, furent en effet forcés d'apprendre aussi le latin pour se faire entendre, mais ils le parloient en général fort incorrectement; surtout ils ne savoient pas manier ces inflexions savantes, sur lesquelles repose toute la construction latine. Les Romains, c'est-à-dire les habitans des provinces, à force d'entendre mal parler leur langue, en oublièrent à leur tour les règles, et imitèrent le jargon de leurs nouveaux maîtres. Les désinences variables étant employées arbitrairement, ne servoient plus qu'à embrouiller les phrases: on finit donc par les supprimer et par tronquer les mots. *Voilà ce qui distingue les dialectes romans, dès leur origine, de la latinité même la plus hérissée de barbarismes.* Mais ces désinences supprimées servoient à marquer d'une manière très-sensible la construction des phrases, et la liaison des idées; il falloit donc y substituer une autre

flexions on which the Latin language depended, naturally sought to express their ideas by the more circuitous but less artificial method of analysis; according to which each phrase is, as it were, built up of the single ideas which compose it, instead of their being all expressed by the modifications of one word. It was in this way that the Normans mutilated the Anglo-Saxon inflexions, and produced the modern English; and that other nations have, as Sismondi expresses it[1], by a mutual compromise formed a sort of neutral language, which properly belongs to neither party, but is the language of the one or the other, deprived of its characteristic forms. By degrees the Germans, forming a small minority of the entire nation, disused their own language, even among themselves[2]: and the native population, forced to adapt themselves to the habits and convenience of their masters, and actuated by the disposition just noticed to analyse grammatical forms, substituted the several Romance languages for the ancient Latin.

§ 5. It is natural to suppose that the mode of speech formed by the process just described would be unsettled and fluctuating, and would vary in different parts of western Europe, according to the greater or less purity of the Latin spoken by the natives, the different proportions of the natives and invaders, and the different Teutonic dialects spoken by the latter: while it would

méthode, et c'est ce qui donna naissance à la grammaire analytique.' Schlegel, p. 24.

[1] See above, p. 22, note.

[2] German, however, was still used in the French court at the end of the ninth century: Thierry, *Lettres sur l'Histoire de France*, p. 43, 220. See also Schlegel, p. 101. Bonamy, *Mém. de l'Acad. des Inscriptions*, vol. xxiv. p. 657.

preserve a general resemblance on account of the similarity of the causes which produced it. In the mean time the Latin retained its place in literature, in legal instruments, and in the service of the church, not only on account of its superior cultivation, but as being the language of the clergy, who were then the only depositories of learning. The invaders indeed for some time continued to use their native tongue: but the mass of the people or the *Romans* (as the subjects of the empire were called, in Gaul, Spain, and Italy[1]), spoke a mixed dialect, which (as distinguished both from the Latin and Teutonic) was thence called *lingua Romana*, and from being the lan-

[1] Ducange in *barbarus* and *Romani* shows that Roman was a general name of Roman provincials as opposed to the barbarians. Galvani, *Osserv. sulla Poesia dei Trov.* p. 433-7, has some remarks on the opposition of the Roman and Latin. The title of king of the Romans was even applied to the head of the Gothic kingdom in Spain by an Arabian historian (Gibbon, c. 51, vol. vi. p. 478), in the same way that the Anglo-Saxons and Normans of England are called Britons; and that Machiavelli, in his *Discourses on Livy*, speaks of the taking of Rome by the French. See also Sismondi, *Litt. du Midi*, tom. i. p. 200, ed. J. Perticari, *Difesa di Dante*, c. 12, says, that the 'lingua romana' was 'veramente degnissima di tal nome; perchè in Roma è ancora parlata quasi intoramente, dopo il giro di 800 anni.' The inhabitants of Gaul and Spain however were probably quite ignorant what language was spoken at Rome, when they called their vulgar tongue the *lingua Romana rustica*. Smollett, above quoted, p. 64, says that it was called Romance from its great affinity to the Latin; which comes nearer to the truth. The right explanation is also given by Wachsmuth, *Athenæum*, vol. i. p. 301. After speaking of the *Lingua Romana rustica* he says: 'The origin of the appellation *Romana* appears to have been, that the inhabitants remembering that they had been from an early period distinguished from the Germans by their language, thought less of pure Latinity than of the political dominion of the Roman people: whence it arose that the natives, as opposed to the Germans, were called *Romani*, (Menage, *Orig. de la Langue Fr. in Roman*,) and France itself had the epithet *Romana*, (Liutprand, l. I. *Franciam quam Romanam vocant*.)'

guago of the rural population, *lingua rustica Romana*, or simply *lingua rustica*. This was a general term for all the varieties of language formed by the union of the Teutonic and Latin[1]. The language used by Lewis the Germanic in the oath of 842, and by Charles king of France in the treaty of 860, is called *lingua Romana*[2]. In the acts of the council of Tours, A.D. 813, the bishops are warned, 'ut—homilias quisque aperte transferre studeat in rusticam Romanam linguam aut Theotiscam, quo facilius cuncti possint intelligere quæ dicuntur.' A monk of Bobbio who wrote an account of the miracles of St. Columbanus about 950 A.D., describes a mountain near Bobbio thus, 'Alter vero qui est ad lævam nuncupatur rustica lingua Groppo altum,' i. e. *Groppo alto*[3].

The modern language spoken in Italy seems not to have been called *lingua Romana* in the middle ages, but to have been usually known by the name of *lingua vulgaris* or *volgare*[4], as opposed to the *lingua erudita*, the Latin: numerous instances however occur where that name is applied to the languages of France and Spain, to the

---

[1] See Schlegel, p. 40. Daunou, *Journal des Savans*, 1823, p. 80.

[2] Raynouard, vol. ii. p. 2, 8. Thierry, *Lettres sur l'Histoire de France*, p. 204-6. Rochefort, *Glossaire de la Langue Romane*, vol. i. p. xx, xxi. Muratori, *Diss.* 32, citing *Baluz. Capit.* vol. ii. p. 144.

[3] These passages are cited by Muratori, *Diss.* 32.

[4] See Muratori, *Diss.* 32, vol. ii. p. 1010, D. Learned writers at a later period have however given the name of *romanzo* to the Italian: Raynouard, *Gr. Comp.* p. 374. In the following extract from the *Tresor* of Brunetto, Dante's master, it seems that, 'Romance after the manner of France,' is equivalent to 'French.' 'Et se aucuns demandoit pourquoi chis livre est ecris en roumans selon la raison de France, pour chou que nous sommes Italien, je diroie que c'est pour chou que nous sommes en France; l'autre pour chou que la parleure en est plus delitable et plus commune a toutes gens.' Cited in Ginguené, *Hist. Litt. d'Italie*, vol. i. p. 369.

Provençal, the French, the Spanish, and the Portuguese[1]. This community of appellation does not afford any reason for supposing that the corruptions of the Latin in the different parts of western Europe were identical: there was a sufficient resemblance in their character, in the circumstances under which they had arisen, and in the classes of persons by whom they were spoken, to warrant their being included under a common name, in spite of minor differences. At the same time it cannot be doubted that the differences between them were not at first so great as they are now, and that in their early youth the children more resembled their common parent and one another[2]: as the English and Scotch, which were formed independently under the same circumstances have a closer resemblance both in words and structure, the nearer they approach their respective sources[3]. This is particularly seen in the French language, which formerly used the masculine and feminine terminations in *o* and *a*, since modified into *e*, as in the article *lo* for *le*, *Cellas*,

[1] See Ducange in *Lingua Romana*, romancier, romanites, romane, romanire, romanum, romancium, romantium. Muratori, *Diss.* 32. Raynouard, *Gr. Comp.* p. 371-4. The modern Latin languages of Walachia and Switzerland, although they have departed widely from the original type, are called in those countries by the name of Romance, viz. *linguaig romansch* or *rumonsch*, and *limba romanesca*. See Diefenbach, *Ueber die Romanischen Schriftsprachen*, (Leipzig, 1831,) p. 21.

[2] 'Naturam enim ac genium linguarum considerans, quæ sensim mutationem patiuntur, veri simile reor, Italici populi linguam, quo propius accessit ad fontes sive ad sæcula latinitatis eo minus tum verbis tum modis dicendi a Latina matre potissimum sua dissensisse.' Muratori, vol. ii. p. 1037, C.

[3] Willan, in *Archæologia*, vol. xvii. p. 164. On the independent origin of the Southern English and Scotch, see Jamieson, *Dissertation on the Origin of the Scottish Language*, p. 24, 25 (profixed to his *Dictionary*).

CHAPTER I.

Fontanas, Ferrerias, names of places, afterwards changed into *Celles, Fontaines, Ferrières*[1]. The affinity indeed was so great that a person who spoke the vulgar Roman dialect would probably have been able to make himself understood in any part of western Europe: as we find it narrated by a monkish writer that in the reign of Charlemagne an Italian priest, who happened to meet a Spanish pilgrim in Germany, understood the conversation of the Spaniard *as being an Italian*[2]; whence it is evident that the Italian and Spanish were not then so

---

[1] See Raynouard, *Gr. Comp.* p. xii. Diez, *Poesie der Troub.* p. 325. The final *a* has in French passed into the *e muet*, as *musa, muse, domina, dame*, etc. In *la* however (which in old French was sometimes made *le*, Rayn. in *J. des S.* 1820, p. 109) *ma, ta,* and *sa*, it was retained. On *le* for *la*, see Orell, ibid. p. 7—9.

[2] Mabillon, *Act. SS. Bened.* sec. 3, Part II. p. 258, correctly explained by Raynouard, vol. i. Introd. p. xvi. *Gr. Comp.* xxix. and after him by Perticari, vol. i. p. 305. The remarks of the critic of Perticari, in the *Florence Antologia*, No. III. p. 350, that perhaps the pilgrim could talk Italian, or the monk understand Spanish, are untenable; for it is distinctly said that the priest, as being an Italian, understood the language of the Spaniard ('quoniam linguae ejus, eo quod esset Italus, notitiam habebat:') plainly implying that he understood it, not as having learned it, but in his character of an Italian. Schlegel, p. 50, remarks that this statement affords no proof of the identity of the languages then spoken in Italy and Spain, as even now an Italian and Spaniard understand one another tolerably without an interpreter. The general resemblance of these two languages is indeed so great, that a Venetian writer of the sixteenth century, introduced into a drama a Spanish character speaking his native language: thus putting the Spanish on the same footing with an Italian *dialetto*. See Gamba, *Serie degli Scritti Impressi in Dialetto Veneziano* (Venice, 1832), p. 75. Mr. Planta, in his *Paper on the Romansh Language*, says, that he had heard it stated as a fact, that two Catalonians travelling in the Grisons, found to their surprise ' that their native tongue was understood by the inhabitants, and that they could comprehend most of the language of the country.' *Philos. Transactions*, vol. 65, p. 154.

different as not to be mutually intelligible to natives of both countries. As has been already observed, M. Raynouard does not adopt the absurd fancy that the Romance or the Italian existed as the language of the lower orders of ancient Italy, in a shape little different from that which they bore in the thirteenth century: his theory is, that the Latin, by the influence of the Germans, was corrupted into an uniform language, called the Romance, spoken for some centuries, and at least as late as the reign of Charlemagne, over the whole of western Europe: that this language is preserved unchanged in the Troubadour poetry and the early literature of Provence: and that it was gradually modified into the Italian, Spanish, Portuguese, French, modern Provençal and their various dialects, all of which he believes to have been derived indirectly indeed from the Latin, but directly from the Romance, and to have retained with different degrees of fidelity the forms of that language.

On the first statement of this hypothesis, it is obvious to enquire in what manner M. Raynouard understands that an uniform language arose on the ruins of the Latin. Languages may be diffused by colonisation or conquest; as the Greek was propagated in Asia Minor, Africa, Italy, Sicily, and Gaul; as the Latin in Gaul and Spain; as the Spanish and English in North and South America and the West Indies; but where were the conquests or the colonies of the Provençals? Or does he suppose that the Romance was diffused from Provence by the influence of the Troubadour literature? Nations however do not learn languages from poets, least of all from foreign poets; and some other cause must be found for the propagation of the Provençal language than the fame

D

of the Provençal minstrels[1]. If on the other hand, M. Raynouard does not suppose that the Romance was diffused from Provence as from a centre, he must conceive that the Romans over the chief part of Italy, Sicily, Sardinia, Corsica, Gaul, and Spain, when invaded at different periods by different Teutonic races, agreed without communication to corrupt the Latin into the self-same language; but unless he here calls in the assistance of a miracle, and supposes that as at Babel the tongues were confounded, so after the invasion of the Germans they were made uniform, it is difficult to understand how he accounts for such a prodigy. If he means that the Romance was spread over western Europe from a common centre[2], he is contradicted by history, which records no movements of population capable of bringing about this effect; if he means that accidentally all the natives of Italy, Gaul, and Spain, coincided in forming one and the same new language, he supposes an agreement to which no parallel can be furnished, and which is utterly incredible.

§ 6. The proofs of the original coincidence of the modern Romance languages with the Provençal, which M. Raynouard collects with great industry and learning, and which will be presently examined in detail, are of two kinds. 1. Words and forms in which the Italian,

---

[1] Muratori, *Diss.* 33, says, that the few words which came from Provence into Italy, were indeed used by some writers, but not adopted by the people. On the small influence of literature on the language of the lower orders, see *Philol. Museum*, vol. ii. p. 248.

[2] It would seem that this is M. Raynouard's meaning, as in the *Journal des Savans*, 1820, p. 672, he states, that *nessuno* was received into the Italian from the Trouvères, that *adesso*, was taken from *ades* as used by the Troubadours and Trouvères.

Spanish, and French agree with the Provençal, but in which the Provençal agrees with the Latin. 2. Words and forms in which the Italian, Spanish, and French agree with the Provençal, but in which the Provençal disagrees with the Latin. Of these two kinds of proofs, the first is obviously open to the following objection. Everybody admits that the Italian, Spanish, Provençal, and French, were derived from the Latin: M. Raynouard's position is that the Provençal, under the name of the Romance, was intermediate between the Latin and the other modern languages. Now in order to support this assertion, it behoves him to show forms in those languages which can only be accounted for on the supposition of such an intermediate language, and could not have been directly derived from the Latin. Instead of confining himself to this species of proof, he often alleges forms in Italian, Spanish and French, which he derives from the Provençal, but which may just as well be referred to the Latin, and by no means necessitate the hypothesis of a transition language. Whenever the Provençal form is not a necessary condition for the existence of the Italian, Spanish, or French form, the coincidence of the two goes for nothing in proof of the interposition of the Provençal between the Latin and the modern language, or at most is only consistent with it. M. Raynouard might have put his argument in this shape: part of the Italian, Spanish, and French languages can only be accounted for on the supposition of the Provençal having succeeded the Latin; the other part, though consistent with the supposition that those languages immediately succeeded the Latin, is equally consistent with the supposition that they did *not* immediately succeed it. Without making this distinction, M. Raynouard is liable to the objection that a large part of his proofs are good for nothing, which may induce an inconsiderate reader to condemn the whole because the majority are untenable. He himself clearly points out this distinction in some passages of his treatise, which will be hereafter noticed[1]: nevertheless he has not kept it constantly in view, and has often alleged in proof of the derivation of the modern Latin languages from the Provençal, facts which can be equally well accounted for on the supposition of their being all parallel languages derived from a common source.

The second class of proofs above mentioned refers to words, forms, and idioms, in which all the modern languages differ from the Latin; such as, the use of articles, and the disuse of cases, the formation of nouns from the accusative of Latin nouns of the third declension, the use of affirmative expletives, which afterwards became negative, as the derivatives of *mica, res, passus,* etc.; the introduction of foreign words, as the adverb *tosto, tost,* quick; the derivatives of the German *herberge, frisch, reich, mark, helm, fein, lassen,* and many others which occur in all the Romance languages[2]. The argument founded on these facts is, however, one which may as well be employed against M. Raynouard's theory as in its support: for why does the agreement of the Provençal with the Italian, Spanish, or French, in forms or words not traceable to the Latin, prove that the latter languages borrowed them from the Provençal rather

---

[1] *Gram. Comp.* p. 70, 265.
[2] See note (D.) at the end.

than the converse? All we know is, that the Latin disappeared as a living language from western Europe soon after the sixth century, and that a new form of speech was substituted in its place; which, as far as we can learn from the earliest monuments of it, had a different character in Spain, in Italy, in Northern and in Southern France: in these several Latin dialects we find numerous forms, idioms, and words, not borrowed from the Latin, but corresponding or identical with one another. On what ground are we to conclude, from the mere fact of agreement and apart from historical evidence, that one of these dialects in particular made the innovations in question, and afterwards communicated them to the others? The Provençal may have had a literature and a standard of composition before the others, but there is no reason to suppose that as a language it existed before them[1]. No error indeed has been more frequent among speculators in language, nor is there any which it requires greater vigilance to avoid, than the confusion of cognate with affiliated languages. Where we see in two languages corresponding forms or words, nothing is easier, or apparently safer, than to derive one from the other. Thus if we find that the Greeks said βοῦς, Foῖνος, Foῖκος, φάω, λέγω, that the

---

[1] Specimens of Italian forms, chiefly names of places, occurring in documents of the eighth and following centuries, are collected in Muratori, *Diss.* 32. The language of the notaries, which, as Muratori has shown, was evidently not a spoken language, is an unquestionable proof of the disuse of the Latin soon after the invasion of Italy, Spain, and Gaul. Schlegel, p. 5, calls the Provençal the eldest daughter of the Latin: an assumption for which there appears to me to be no ground, if it means that the Provençal existed as a spoken language before the other Romance tongues.

Romans said *bos*, *vinum*, *vicus*, *faor*, *lego*: it is immediately concluded that the latter were borrowed from the former: and a Latin lexicographer would think that he had not performed his duty unless he had duly registered the Greek as the originals of the Latin words. In like manner a German etymologist will inform his readers that *werk* is derived from Ϝέργον, and *wein* from Ϝοῖνος. But what evidence have we that these words were not separately derived from a common source; and that the Latins might not have used *vinum* and *bos*, the Germans *werk* and *wein*, if the natives of Greece had never developed their language, and had been crushed in their germ by a barbarous immigration? It is on this mistaken principle, that Dr. Johnson has arranged the etymological part (which however he chiefly borrowed from others) of his English dictionary. Whenever he is at a loss for an etymology, he sets down the corresponding word in Dutch or German, or he derives an English from a German word[1]; and sometimes he even makes a parallel increased form the origin of the English word[2]: as if we had not only borrowed our radical words, but even our formations from our neighbours! In kindred languages derived from a common stock, there is always a correspondence both of roots and formations; more or less close, according to the length of time since

[1] 'From *are*, an eagle, I believe our word *eyrie* derived; Johnson derived it from *ei*, an egg, properly *ey*, German: but I do not believe there is a word in the English language, (unless very modern,) of German origin.... The words which we have in common with the Germans are not borrowed from them, but drawn from a higher source.' Herbert's *Icelandic Poetry*, p. 121, note.

[2] For instance, he derives the word *manikin* from *manniken* Dutch. See *Phil. Mus.* vol. i. p. 680.

they parted from the parent-stem, and the various disturbing causes to which both or either have since that divergence been exposed. It is therefore of no avail, in proof of a derivation or dependence, to show a scheme of parallel forms, idioms, and words, in several languages: they may have arisen from a common source under similar circumstances; and we may be led to mistake for cause and effect, what in truth are only similar effects of the same cause. Now such, as I conceive, is the case of the Romance languages: they all owed their origin to the same cause, viz. the permanent subjugation by Teutonic races of a people speaking Latin; and there is nothing in their character which cannot be explained without supposing a nearer affinity. They have just the amount of resemblance which might have been expected in languages derived from the same original, and just the amount of difference which might have been expected in languages formed under similar circumstances independently of each other:

> Facies non omnibus una,
> Nec diversa tamen, qualem decet esse sororum.

A comparison of the analogous forms in cognate languages is calculated to throw light both on their relation to each other, and on the causes to which their affinity is owing: as the sculpture of the Greeks may be illustrated by comparing it with their poetry, and their poetry by comparing it with their sculpture. The mistake too often committed with respect to languages consists, not in comparing them, but in making a wrong use of the comparison, by discovering parentage where there is only fraternity: as any one would err who should derive the sculpture of the Greeks from their poetry, or their poetry from their sculpture; the truth being that they are both the products of the national taste and genius of that people, which they serve in common to illustrate.

M. Raynouard, in answer to some remarks of Schlegel on the independent origin of the Romance languages, says that 'if each nation had formed its language separately, doubtless one of those languages would have presented several essential and indispensable forms which the other languages would have wanted, such for instance as the use of a passive voice, as in Latin[1].' This example is unhappily chosen. There is no part of the Latin language which was more likely to disappear under the German influence than the formation of a passive voice by inflexion. The Germans themselves made the passive by means of auxiliary verbs; and would therefore according to their way of speaking Latin doubtless imitate their own idiom. The passive voice of the Latin verb had already degenerated from its original model, and the Greek system of inflexion had been much encroached upon by the formation of some tenses with auxiliary verbs introduced by a foreign influence at some early period of the Latin language[2]. The inflexions of the Latin are precisely that part of it which was mutilated by the German influence; and there is only one instance in which any trace of them

[1] 'Si chaque peuple avait composé son idiôme Isolément, sans doute quelqu'un de ces idiômes eût offert plusieurs formes essentielles et indispensables qui ne se fussent pas trouvées dans les autres idiômes, telles par exemple que de conserver un passif ainsi que les Latins,' etc. *Journal des Savans*, 1818, p. 591.

[2] See above, p. 10[1]. Müller's *Etrusker*, vol. i. p. 23. *Philol. Mus.* vol. i. p. 660.

THE ORIGIN OF THE ROMANCE LANGUAGES. 41

has been preserved. But in this instance, viz. the retention of the nominative and accusative cases, all the languages do *not* agree; for we find that while this inflexion was preserved in the languages of *oc* and *oïl*, there is no trace of its having ever existed in Italian and Spanish[1]. This therefore is an example, in respect of a rule which M. Raynouard himself calls fundamental, of the occurrence of an essential form in some of those languages which is absent in others.

When we come to the detailed examination of the corresponding forms in the Romance languages, it will be shown that there are many traces of the Latin preserved in the Italian and Spanish which have been lost in the Provençal; and consequently could not have been preserved in those languages if they had been derived from the latter in which those features of the model had been obliterated. There are however other difficulties of a more general nature to which M. Raynouard's theory gives rise, and of which it affords no explanation. If the Romance of the Troubadours was once the universal language of western Europe, which was afterwards modified into distinct dialects; there appears to be no reason why any one of these dialects should be more like it than another. Now there is no doubt, and it is distinctly admitted by M. Raynouard[2], that the modern Provençal

---

[1] See below, ch. 2, § 2.

[2] 'Il (l'idiôme provençal) a peu varié depuis les troubadours': says M. Raynouard, in the *Journal des Sav.* 1818, p. 589. See him also in *Journal des Sav.* 1824, p. 92—7, in a review of a dictionary of the Limousin patois, and Ibid. p. 174—80, in a review of a Languedocian dictionary. In p. 96, he points out some words in Low Limousin which occur in the language of the Troubadours, and not in the other Romance languages.

has a far closer resemblance than any other modern language to the Romance of the Troubadour poetry: especially if we take specimens of that language as it existed about the eleventh century[1], at which time the Italian and Spanish had been completely fixed in their present form. But if the Romance, as used by the early Provençal poets, was once the language of Italy and Spain, there is no reason why the Italian and Spanish should have departed from it so much more widely than the modern Provençal. It seems far more natural to suppose that the Troubadours wrote in the language of their country, the *langue d'oc*, which was from the beginning distinct from the Italian, and the Spanish, and the *langue d'oil*, (although it resembled the latter much more closely than the others,) and that the modern Provençal has arisen from the natural development of it, in the same way that the modern French has been developed from the language of Villehardouin and the Trouvères.

Another important fact, directly opposed to the theory of an universal Romance language, is the vast number of modern Romance dialects which prevail in France, Spain, Switzerland, the Tyrol, Italy, and the neighbouring islands. The patois of the *langue d'oil* in Northern France and Flanders[2]: of the *langue d'oc* in Southern

[1] See a relation of the arrival of Charles, Duke of Savoy, at Nice, in 1488, in the *langue vulgaire*, published in Durante, *Histoire de Nice*, vol. ii. p. 182—4. (Turin, 1823.)

[2] Champollion-Figéac in Balbi's *Atlas Ethnogr. du Globe*, tab. 12, enumerates the following dialects of the French. 1. Picard. 2. Flemish. 3. Norman. 4. Walloon or Rouchi: spoken in Picardy, Normandy, French and Dutch Flanders, and the Dutch provinces of Namur and Liege. 5. French Breton. 6. Champenois. 7. Lorrain and Bourguignon. 8. Franc-comtois. 9. Neufchâtelois. 10. Oz-

France, Savoy, Piedmont, the Grisons, and the county of Nice, are very numerous, and are distinguished by important differences[1]. In Spain there are the dialects of Leon, the Asturias, Aragon, Andalusia, Murcia, Galicia, Catalonia, and Valencia: the two latter of which, as well as the language of the Balearic islands[2], resemble the langue d'oc more than the Castilian or written Spanish[3]. The islands of Corsica and Sardinia appear to possess native dialects different from any other Romance tongue[4]. In Italy not only are the languages of the northern and

---

léanais. 11. Angloin. 12. Manceau: spoken in a part of Britany, in Champagne, Lorraine, a part of Burgundy, in Franche comté, the Swiss canton of Neufchâtel, the Orleanese, Anjou, and Maine. See also Raynouard, *Journal des Sav.* 1818, p. 282. *Mélanges sur les Langues*, (Paris, 1831,) where numerous specimens of the different French *patois* are collected, and Adelung's *Mithridates*, vol. ii. p. 578 —07. [Compare Burguy, *Grammaire de la Langue d'Oïl* (Berlin, 1853), vol. i. p. 14.]

[1] There are several dictionaries of different dialects of the langue d'oc; two are mentioned above, p. 41[2]. There are also two dictionaries of the Eastern Provençal, published in the last century, and a more recent work published at Marseilles in a cheap form. There are likewise a few books in the same language; particularly some poems by M. Diouloufet of Aix, and a poem in the Nice dialect, (which partakes more of the Genoese,) by M. Ranchez of Nice. A curious specimen of the popular Provençal may be seen in Mr. Hayward's *Translation of Faust*, p. 286, ed. 2.

[2] Bastero, *Crusca Provensale*, p. 21, quoted by Diez, p. 5.

[3] On the relation of the Valencian and Catalonian to the Provençal, see Raynouard, vol. 1. Intro. p. xiii.; *Gr. Comp.* p. xxxviii. In the Universities of Vicenza and Vercelli, the schools were divided into four universities of nations, as follows. 1. French, English and Normans. 2. Italians. 3. Provençals, Spanish, and Catalans. 4. Germans. Savigny, *Gesch. des R. R.* c. 21. On the Catalonian language and literature, see Janhart de Passa, *Recherches Historiques sur la Langue Catalane*, in *Mélanges sur les Langues*, p. 297—431.

[4] Diefenbach, *Ueber die Jetzigen Romanischen Schriftsprachen*, p. 21, (Leipzig, 1831,) states that he was informed by a Sardinian of good

southern districts distinguished from each other by certain broad marks of difference, but almost every town which was once independent has a dialect of its own, differing from the common or written Italian, both in its inflexions and its terms[1]. Muratori says, that there is scarcely a city of Italy which is not distinguished from others by its pronunciation, the sound of its accents, the terminations of its words, and its peculiar forms. Much more does the dialect of one province differ from that of another; sometimes there is such a difference that even the Italians of other provinces, although they speak the common language, can with difficulty understand each other[2]. How are diversities of this kind to be reconciled with the theory of an uniform language, formed on the ruins of the Latin? Is it to be supposed that these irregularities and discordancies grew up spontaneously in

authority that, 'besides the language of foreign introduction, the Catalonian and Italian, there are in Sardinia three Romance dialects, one verging towards the Spanish, another towards the south Italian, the third still a kind of *Romana rustica* closely resembling the ancient Latin both in forms and words. This latter is still spoken in about twenty-four villages in the interior of the country.' See Adelung's *Mithridates*, vol. ii. p. 528—34. Niebuhr, vol. i. p. 144, says, that 'specimens of the Sardinian language from the civilized districts exhibit peculiarities which are more than varieties of dialect, and indicate a Romance language of a distinct kind.'

[1] The literature of the Italian dialects is very rich, and there are few of any importance (except that of Genoa,) which have not their dictionary. Thus dictionaries have been published of the Sicilian, Neapolitan, Venetian, Bolognese, Ferrarese, Veronese, Mantuan, Brescian, Bergamasque, Milanese, and Piedmontese dialects. See Adelung's *Mithridates*, vol. ii. p. 496—528; [and concerning the dialects of northern Italy with consonant terminations, Biondelli, *Saggio dei Dialetti Gallo-Italici*, 2 vols. 8vo. Milan, 1853.]

[2] *Dissert.* 32, vol. ii. p. 1038, A. See also Denina, *Observations sur les Dialectes, particulièrement sur ceux d'Italie. Mémoires de l'Acadé-*

the midst of an universal Roman language, as the multifarious Christian sects arose out of the bosom of the universal Roman Church?' Such a hypothesis would be directly opposed to all experience. The progress of language is to widen the dominion of prevailing analogies; to enlarge rules, and to diminish anomalies: to root out what is local, partial, and peculiar: to carry the speech of the towns into the country: to abolish provincialisms: and to spread the language of literature and of educated persons in the place of dialects less cultivated and less generally understood. Thus the English gradually encroaches on the Welsh, along the borders of Wales; thus the Gaelic and Irish are slowly giving way in Scotland[1] and Ireland[2], and the Cornish language, though spoken in the memory of living persons, has been completely extirpated in Cornwall. The diffusion of the Latin over Italy, in the place of the Etruscan, the Oscan, the Umbrian, the Ligurian, and other native dialects, has been already noticed. Much easier however is this process when the inferior dialect is threatened by a language

---

mie de Berlin, 1797. *Classe des Belles Lettres*, p. 64—90, and Baretti's *Account of Italy*, vol. ii. c. 30. There is also the Romanee language of Walachia, on the origin of which see the *Wiener Jahrbücher*, vol. 46, p. 77—88. [Diez, *Rom. Gramm.* vol. i. p. 89.]

[1] Johnson, *Journey to the Hebrides*, p. 277, speaking of the Highlanders, says, 'Of what they had before the late conquest of their country, there remain only their language and their poverty. Their language is attacked on every side. Schools are erected, in which English only is taught, and there were lately some who thought it reasonable to refuse them a version of the holy Scriptures, that they might have no monument of their mother tongue.' See also note (E.) at the end.

[2] On the measures taken by the government to diffuse the English and to extinguish the Irish language in Ireland, see Anderson, *Historical Sketches of the Native Irish*, sect. 3.

of the same family; as was the case with the propagation of the Attic Greek in the age of Philip and Alexander; and such is the case with the French, the Italian, and the Spanish, as they come in contact with the dialects spoken in the countries where they are the ruling languages[1]. As the progress of civilization is to destroy local usages and laws, to break down distinctions both of place and rank, and to fuse large bodies of men into an uniform and compact whole; so the progress of language is to substitute one polished idiom in the place of numerous uncultivated dialects. In supposing, therefore, that the multiplicity of Romance dialects which now prevail over western Europe, were capricious aberrations from a single type, as established after the disturbance of the German invasion, and that their difference, having once been almost imperceptible, became such as we now see it[2], M. Raynouard makes a supposition at

[1] Mr. Marshall, in explaining his reasons for making a collection of the Provincialisms of Yorkshire, has a remark which applies to this subject. 'Finding (he says) in this particular instance, a declining language which is unknown to the public, but which, it is highly probable, contains more ample remains of the ancient language of the central parts of this island, than any other which is now spoken, I was willing to do my best endeavour towards arresting it in its present form, before the general blaze of fashion and refinement, which has already spread its dawn even over this secluded district, shall have buried it irretrievably in obscurity.' *Rural Economy of Yorkshire*, vol. ii. p. 302.

[2] 'Anche senza prova di fatto la ragione fa congetturare, ch' essendovi fra gli antichi Italiani minor cultura e minor commercio, la differenza tra le loro favelle dovea essere maggiore di quella che è ai nostri tempi.' Niccolini, *Discorso*, etc. p. 22, note. See also Lanzi, vol. i. p. 24. 'The little connection there is in mountainous countries between the inhabitants of the different vallies, and the absolute independence of each jurisdiction in this district, which still lessens the frequency of their intercourse, also accounts in a great measure for the

variance with all analogy, and represents the stream of language as flowing back upon its source.

Perticari attempts to get rid of this difficulty by saying, that as the empire of Charlemagne was partitioned, so the common Romance language was divided into dialects, as languages follow the government[1]. But if languages follow the government, how came the universal Romance language to be formed? When the East and West Goths, the Lombards, Burgundians, and Franks, had separate and independent empires, how could an uniform language arise through their influence? And if each of these several states had a peculiar dialect, it surely will not be contended that Charlemagne by uniting them into one empire, could during his lifetime have removed all these varieties, and established a common mode of speech. There is scarcely any change which requires[7] more time than a change of language. Obedience to foreign laws may be enforced after the loss of a battle: outward observance of a new religion may in a short time be brought about by persecution or conquest; but no terror can inculcate the use of a new language, even if there were any motive for introducing it: for its use does not depend on the mere desire to use it, but is the result of early and long-continued habit. All explana-

---

variety of secondary dialects subsisting in almost every different community or even village:' says Mr. Planta, *Philos. Transactions*, vol. lxvi. p. 144, speaking of the Romance of the Grisons.

[1] 'Ma intanto quella lingua, che prima era una, si divise in molte: perciocchè le lingue seguono le condizioni de' governi. E come per la novità de' feudi e de' baronaggi quel francese imperio si squarciò a brani così il *comune romano* anch'esso fu partito nel Limosino, nel Provenzale, nell' Italico, nel Vallone, nel Catalano, ed in altri.' Perticari, *Difesa di Dante*, c. 11.

tions therefore which suppose sudden and extensive revolutions of language produced by the mere influence of government, unassisted by the mixture of population, are liable to strong objections[1]. It would moreover be easy to show that the Romance dialects have not always followed the government; for instance, the French of Dutch Flanders has existed not in consequence but in spite of the government. If Perticari had said that the Romance languages followed the *original* government, that is, the number and influence of the German invaders, who first occupied the country when its inhabitants spoke Latin, he probably would have been much nearer the truth.

Nevertheless, when it is said that the natural course of things is, that differences of dialects are softened down; it is necessary to distinguish between changes arising from the natural development of a language, and from the introduction of new or foreign words, and those caused by the fresh creation of separate forms and analogies, so as to give rise to a new dialect. If there is a nation speaking the same language, which by colonisa-

---

[1] As to the small influence of government in producing changes of language, see Prichard on the *Eastern Origin of the Celtic Nations*, p. 8. 'The pertinacious adherence of mankind to their mother tongue, (says Mr. Anderson, in his work on the Irish language,) might be verified by a number of remarkable proofs. "It is a curious fact, (says a writer in the *Statistical Account of Scotland*, vol. xx. p. 400,) that the hills of King's seat and Craigy Barns, which form the lower boundary of Dowally (parish in Perthshire) have been *for centuries* the separatory barrier of the English and Gaelic. In the first house below them, the English is and has been spoken, and the Gaelic in the first house, not above a mile distant, above them." In different parts of Ireland something similar to this will be found. It is said, that on crossing the river Barrow, a very striking difference is observable; on the eastern bank, English is spoken, and Irish scarcely known; a little

tion or conquest forms two new societies, the languages of those three nations, which at first were identical, will become continually more and more unlike one another, and their common stock, in proportion as the time elapsed since their separation increases. Analogies which one nation will extend, another will narrow or even disuse: in one language the exception will supplant the rule, in another the rule will swallow up all exceptions: different words will be contracted; different contractions will be used: different modes of forming new derivatives will be followed; accidents of literature, taste, form of government, manners, foreign influence and intercourse, will variously affect the growth of the respective languages of each nation. Thus the Portuguese of Brazil has become in many respects different from that of the mother country, chiefly by the introduction of many new words[1]: and the language of the North American states would, within no short time, have differed widely from that of England, in using many peculiar idioms, in introducing new words, and attaching different senses to the same words, (the grammatical forms and syntax remaining indeed the same;) if the frequent and rapid communication between the two countries, and the mutual influence of their literature had not kept up an uniform standard of composition. In like manner I conceive that the Italian and Spanish, and the languages of *oc* and *oïl*, being together with their dialects formed independently by the German working on the Latin, had in their origin fundamental differences, but still bore a strong likeness to

way interior it is quite the reverse.' *Hist. Sketches of the Native Irish*, p. 105.

[1] See Balbi, *Atlas Ethnogr.*

each other: as years rolled on, each language assumed a more peculiar form by dealing differently with the wreck which it had saved from the Latin: by altering more or less the original forms, and by following different principles of inflexion. In this respect languages are like human beings: the older they become, the more strongly marked are their distinctive features. The same would doubtless be the course of the several dialects of each language: every dialect would doubtless assume in the process of time a more distinct and individual character. But there is nothing in the development of language, independently of political circumstances, which leads to the arbitrary creation of separate dialects distinguished by their inflexions and forms: on the contrary, the influence of government and literature tends always to spread the use of the language of the ruling classes and the writers, to the prejudice of local dialects: an effect which in modern times has been immensely assisted by the use of printing, and the facilities given to the circulation of newspapers and books, and to the carriage of persons. It seems to me, therefore, that although the difference of actually existing dialects is increased in the lapse of time, yet that dialects are not formed by mere caprice, without external and political influence: and that the spontaneous generation of the countless Romance dialects now spoken in Europe from an universal language, which has existed since the extinction of the Latin, is just as improbable as the spontaneous generation of insects and reptiles.

§ 7. Having offered these general considerations on M. Raynouard's views with regard to the origin of the modern Latin languages, I shall proceed to a detailed

examination of his proofs: for which purpose it will be
necessary to repeat at length the principal parts of his
Romance Grammar, as the language to which it refers,
and the rules which it contains, are not generally known,
like those of the living languages to which it is allied.
But before this comparison is begun, it is first necessary
to determine what name shall be given to the language
which is to serve as the standard of comparison. 'There
is (as Schlegel has remarked) some difficulty in finding a
proper designation for the language of the Troubadours.
The names of Provençal, Limousin, and Catalonian,
which have been applied to it, are too narrow, as they
only comprehend one of the districts where it was
spoken, and as its use extended over a much wider
territory. On the other hand, the name of *Romance* is
too indefinite[1].' M. Raynouard constantly applies the
name of Romance to the language of the Troubadours:
and M. Champollion-Figéac, who has since discussed this
subject, adheres to his use of the word, and makes the
Romance language a common term for the dialects of
Provence, Dauphiny, the Lyonese, Auvergne, Limousin,
Languedoc, Gascony, and Catalonia[2]. In the following
pages, however, I shall attempt to show that although

---

[1] *Observations*, p. 40. See also Biester on *Oc* and *Oyl*, *Philol. Mus.* vol. ii. p. 340.

[2] *Charte de Commune en Langue Romane*, (Paris, 1820,) p. 7—18. M. Roquefort has published a dictionary of the ancient French language, which he has entitled '*Glossaire de la Langue Romane*.' As well might the author of an Anglo-Saxon dictionary call it a dictionary of the Teutonic language. M. Roquefort has, however, full as much right to call the ancient langue *d'oïl*, as M. Raynouard has to call the ancient langue *d'oc*, *the* Romance language. Compare Berrington's *Literary History of the Middle Ages*, p. 397. [Concerning the use of the word *Romance*, see Diez, *Rom. Gramm.* vol. i. p. 72.]

the ancient language of *oc*, the language spoken in Southern France and Catalonia, was *a* Romance language, it was not *the* Romance language : that it was merely one of the dialects arising out of the change produced in the Latin by the Teutonic invasion[1]. Nor does M. Raynouard merely employ an ambiguous, and therefore an inconvenient term : but he founds an argument in favour of his theory upon that ambiguity; when he attempts to show that the Italian, the Spanish, and the French, were once identical with the Troubadour language, because they were all called Romance languages[2]. In this mode of reasoning, however, he appears to me to have committed the same error as a person who having undertaken to write a history of trees, and described those kinds, such as the ash and the oak, which are deciduous, should thence conclude that the ilex and the olive are deciduous, because they are also trees. The language of Southern France was doubtless a Romance language, as were the languages of Northern France, Spain, Italy, Savoy, and parts of Switzerland and the Tyrol. But it does not follow that what is true of the language of

[1] 'It is generally admitted that the word *Romance* was first employed to signify the Roman language as spoken in the European provinces of the empire; and that in its most extensive sense it comprised all the dialects of which the basis was the vulgar Latin, whatever might be the other materials which entered into their construction. The name was therefore equally applicable to the Italian, the Spanish, and French, and was sometimes, though incorrectly, applied to the vulgar languages of other countries.' Ellis, *Specimens of Early English Romances*, vol. i. p. 1. See also Walter Scott's article on Romance, near the beginning, in the *Supplement to the Encyclopedia Britannica*. A passage occurs in *Giraldus Cambrensis*, where the common English is called Romance. See Ritson's *Ancient English Romances*, vol. i. p. 12—18.
[2] *Gr. Comp.* p. 371.

Southern France is also true of the Spanish or Italian, because they were all three Romance languages, any more than it follows that lions ruminate, as well as oxen, because they are both animals. There is perhaps no name for the language in question which is wholly unexceptionable: nevertheless the appellation Provençal, as Diez remarks, deserves the preference. The historians of the Crusades apply the term *Provincia* to all the south of France, distinguishing the inhabitants of the northern and southern parts of that country by the names *Francigenæ* and *Provinciales*: an ancient Grammar of the *langue d'oc* is called *Donatus Provincialis;* and Dante, as well as a contemporary biographer of a troubadour, speaks of the Provençal language[1]. It may be moreover remarked, that although it might be inconvenient to give the name of Provençal to the language of Catalonia, the examples cited by M. Raynouard are almost without exception taken from the poems of troubadours who were strictly natives of Provence, in the extended sense of that word.

[1] Diez, *Poesie der Troubadours*, p. 5—12.

CHAPTER II.

Formation of the Romance Articles and Nouns from the Latin.

§ 1. ARTICLES.

THE utility of articles, and especially of the definite article, is so obvious, that there is no wonder that they should be gradually introduced by the effort which is constantly perceivable in language, to analyse and separately to express every idea. Thus we know that in the early Greek language there were no definite articles: but in the interval of time which elapsed between the ancient epic poets and the first prose writers, the pronoun ὁ had become a definite article. The same transfer of the German demonstrative pronoun *der*, and of the Anglo-Saxon pronoun *that*[1], to the sense of a definite article, likewise took place in the gradual development of the language, and without external influence. In those languages likewise the numeral *one*, by a similar process of abstraction, obtained the sense of the indefinite article. It is probable that the sudden change which the Latin underwent in this respect, at the time of the German invasion, was the consequence rather of the

[1] See Rask, *A. S. Grammar*, § 146.

tendency just described, than of the imitation of the Teutonic idiom. It seems more than doubtful whether the use even of the definite article had at that era been introduced into the Teutonic languages: and it is probable that we shall most nearly approach the truth, if we suppose that when the Latin was by that event put into a state favourable to a new development of its grammatical forms, it obtained the use of articles, and adopted for them those words which appear naturally to suggest themselves as most convenient for this purpose. Hence *unus* was taken as the indefinite, and *ille* as the definite article: and their forms and inflexions underwent those changes which will be explained when we speak of the formation of the modern nouns.

The following scheme exhibits the structure of the Provençal definite article: the masculine singular (as will be shown below) is formed from the Latin accusative *illum*, by rejecting either the first or the last syllable: the masculine plural is partly formed from the Latin nominative, partly from the accusative: *els* and *los* being made out of *illos*; *ill* and *li* from *illi*: the feminine plural is formed from the Latin accusative *illas*. The genitive, dative, and ablative cases have completely disappeared, and their forms are replaced by the use of prepositions; *de* being prefixed in order to give the sense of the genitive and ablative, *a* (from *ad*) of the dative, and *a* (from *ab*) of the ablative[1]. It will be observed that in the masculine plural, *de li* and *de los*, *a li* and *a los*, the forms derived from both the Latin nominative and accusative, are placed after the preposition: in general, however, as

---

[1] See below in these prepositions.

will appear when we come to the nouns, the prepositions govern the Provençal accusative.

	SINGULAR.		PLURAL.	
MASC.	FEM.	MASC.		FEM.
El, lo	ill, la	Ill, li, els, los		las
de lo, del	de la	de li, de los, dals, des		de las
a lo, al, el,	a la	a li, a los, als, as		a las¹.

Vol. i. p. 38—44. *Gr. Rom.* p. 13—24.

All the modern Latin languages have formed their definite article from *ille*, and exhibit nearly the same modifications as those which appear in the Provençal. *El*, which is the common Spanish form, occurs in old French and Italian: *lo* also occurs in old French, as well as *del*, *al*, *dels*, *als*, and *els*, from which have been formed by the suppression of *l* or its change into *u*, so prevalent in that language, *deu*, *du*, *au*, *des*, *aux*, and *ès*: *los* and *las*, by changes likewise of frequent occurrence, became *les*. It should be observed that the Spanish exhibits no trace of *li*, (from *illi*,) and the Italian no trace of *los*, (from *illos*,) and that the Italian made the feminine plural *le*, (from *illæ*,) whereas the Spanish agreed with the Provençal in forming it from *illas*. These characteristic differences will be again adverted to, when we speak of the nouns. (*Gr. Comp.* p. 2—19.)

Several modern grammarians have thought that the articles in the Romance languages have supplied the place of the Latin inflexions of the nouns to which they are prefixed. Thus the Italian grammarians call their articles *segnacasi*; and M. Raynouard says, that 'the

[1] I have not inserted the mere varieties of orthography, as *elh* for *el*, *ill* for *il*, etc. See *Gr. Rom.* p. 79—116.

use of articles has delivered the modern languages from the slavery of the Latin declensions, without diminishing the clearness of the expression.' (Vol. i. p. 44.) This is, however, an erroneous view of the subject. The use of the Latin nominative and accusative has been supplied by a certain collocation of words, of the genitive, dative, and ablative, by prepositions. Neither of the articles has any influence whatever in giving to nouns the meanings expressed by the Latin cases. In languages which have both cases and articles, the article is as much inflected as the noun to which it belongs.

§ 2. FORMS AND INFLEXIONS OF NOUNS.

We come now to the nouns, which we shall consider under the heads of their form, their mode of declension, their gender, and their derivative terminations; and by these means be enabled to judge how far the changes which they underwent in the several modern languages support M. Raynouard's theory with regard to the universal prevalence of the Provençal, and the derivation of the other Romance languages from it as a common type.

The entire confusion of cases which prevailed in the Latin language after the German invasion, may be seen in many legal instruments of the middle ages; and although we may concede to Muratori that the Latin of the notaries was not a spoken language, still it is impossible to conceive that charters and deeds would have been composed in a barbarous and ungrammatical jargon, when the pure language was current in any part of the community. The following extract from a Pisan deed of sale, of 720 A.D. may serve as a specimen of this language. 'In nomine Domini dei nostris Jesum Christi, regnante domno nostro Liutprand rege, anno hoctavo sup die quartam kalendis Februari, per inditione tertia, constant me Sundualdo, vir honorabilis, hac dies arvitrium bono meo voluntatis ... eniente, neque aliquis mo suadente, nisi bono animus meus, vindedisse et vindedi, tradedisse et tradedi tivi Filicausi modictatem de casa meas infra civitatem cum gronda sua livera tam solamentum sine grondas, etc[1].' In this language it is not always possible to distinguish between the proper terminations of the cases and the corruptions of a vicious pronunciation: thus in some of the above instances, as 'in nomine Domini nostris Jesum Christi,' 'hac dies' 'aliquis suadente,' 'bono animus meus,' 'de casa meas,' the Latin cases are used at random: in others however, such as 'sub die quartam,' 'per inditione tertia,' it is uncertain whether it is not the pronunciation which is in fault, and whether the final *m* was not dropped from *diem* and *indictionem tertiam*, as 'bono animus meus' probably meant 'bonum animus meus.' The omission of the final *m* and *n* occurs again in the same instrument in other words, as *ligname* for *lignamen*, *nove* for *novem*, *hanc cartula* for *hanc cartulam*, *venditionem a me facta* for *venditionem a me factam*, *dece* for *decem*, etc.

A rhythmical poem, written in vulgar Latin about 871 A.D. on the imprisonment of the Emperor Lewis II. by Adelchis duke of Beneventum, offers another speci-

[1] Murat. *Ant. It.* vol. iii. p. 1003.

men of the state of the ancient during its transition into the modern language[1].

> Audite omnes fines terræ orrore cum tristitia
> Quale scelus fuid factum Benevento civitas.
> Lluduicum comprenderunt sancto pio Augustio[2].
> Beneventani se adunarunt ad unum consilium.
> Adalferio loquebatur, et dicebant principi:
> 'Si nos eum vivum dimitemus, certe nos peribimus.
> Celus magnum præparavit in istam provintiam:
> Regnum nostrum nobis tollit; nos habet pro nihilum:
> Plures mala nobis fecit: rectum est ut moriad[3].'
> Deposuerunt sancto pio de suo palatio.
> Adalferio illum ducebat usque ad pretorium, etc.

These verses offer numerous instances of the confusion of cases: but *Lluduicum sancto pio Augustio, Adalferio loquebatur, deposkerunt sancto pio, Adalferio ducebat*, appear to be corruptions by pronunciation of *sanctum pium Augustium, Adalferium* and *sanctum pium*: as in the same poem '*leto animo* habebat de illo *quo fecerat*' is put instead of '*letum animum* habebat de illo *quod fecerat*[4],' not by a confusion of the ablative and accusative cases, but by the corruption of the termination of the accusative. So in the following instances collected by M. Raynouard, (vol. i. p. 18—22,) from Italian, Spanish, and French instruments of the middle ages, the accusative case is probably

---

[1] Murat. *Ant. It.* vol. iii. p. 711. An explanation of the circumstances which occasioned this popular poem is given by Siamondi, *Litter. du Midi*, tom. l. p. 29.

[2] *Augustio* is a conjecture mentioned by Muratori. The MS. has *Augusto*. In the first line, for *errore* I have written *orrore*, i. e. *horrore*.

[3] That is, *moriat*, for *moriatur*.

[4] Muratori mistakes the meaning of this line, in supposing *habebat* to be here put for *abibat*.

CHAPTER II.

everywhere meant, though its characteristic letter is often dropped for facility of pronunciation.

'Ab hodiernum die: absque ullo dolo aut vim: ad die presente: ad ipso rio; adversus apostolico viro: ante valneo et orto: contra hoste barbaro: cum omnes res ad se pertinentes: cum pectus inscium: de quam præfatam portionem; ex successionem: infra vallo: intra comitatu nostro: per mandáto suo: per arte: pro panem: pro supradictas sex uncias: pro mercedem animæ meæ: propter amorem dei et vita æterna: sine præmium: sine rixas: usque memorato loco: versum palude: ubi nepte mea instituemus abbatissam: bona intentione monstrant mihi e faciunt Saracenis bona acolhenza.' The tendency to the use of the accusative case in particular appears in many places: thus in two sentences cited by M. Raynouard, 'Si aliquas causas adversus istud monasterium ortas fuerint:' 'ipsas monachas vel earum abbate (for abbatem) debeant possidere:' so a charter of 761 A.D. begins thus: 'Regnante domno Desiderio et Adelgis viros excellentissimos reges,' and a Lucchese plea of 853 A.D. as follows: 'Dum ap (i. e. ab) celsa potestatem Domni nostri Illudovici magni imperatoris directi fuissent Johannem venerabilem sancte Pisensis ecclesie episcopus, necnon et Adalpertum Marchionem, seu Gausbertum Vassum et ministrum minor ipsius imperialis potestatem, et conjuncti fuissent hic civitate Luca,' etc[1].

---

[1] Muratori, *Ant. It.* vol. iii. p. 167. See other specimens of this language in Muratori, *Diss.* 32, vol. ii. p. 1025 E—1048. Muratori argues with considerable force and ingenuity that the language of the notaries was never a spoken language, but was a barbarous jargon made in imitation of the old Latin, by illiterate scribes: he says justly that there is no dialect spoken by any class of persons, which does

The ancient system of cases being thus completely confounded, we need not be surprised to find that in the Italian and Spanish languages the nouns were formed, not from the nominative, but from some inflected case of the Latin word. In nouns of the first and second declension this fact cannot be perceived, as the Italian and Spanish *musa* and *muro* might come from either the nominative, accusative, or ablative cases of the Latin *musa* and *murus*. The nouns of the third declension which increase in the genitive case, furnish a criterion for ascertaining this fact: and from the following table it will be seen that not only the Italian and Spanish, but also the Provençal and French nouns, take the increment of the genitive, and consequently are not derived from the Latin nominative.

not observe some rules of grammar. This is undoubtedly true : a language without a grammar is not a language; unless there were some rules settled by general usage, people could not understand one another. But this does not appear to be precisely the case with the Latin of the notaries: although there is often a confusion both of number, gender, and tense, yet the chief confusion is that of the cases or inflexions of nouns and participles. The most probable explanation of this matter seems to be that the Latin of the early Italian deeds is the tradition of the corrupted language caused by the influence of the German on the Latin : that although the people in the eighth and ninth centuries may have spoken a language like the Italian, yet the Latin was not yet considered a dead language to be learned from books, and that the notaries who could not use the vulgar dialect, wrote in the jargon which they received by oral communication from those who spoke the bastard Latin which had sprung from the invasion. The verses which are cited in the text moreover exhibit the very same character of style as the legal instruments; and to them Muratori's remark with respect to the notaries does not apply : for they must have been written in a language intelligible to the public. [Additional examples of the accusative swallowing up the other inflected cases in low Latin are given by Diez, *Romanische Grammatik*, vol. ii. p. 10—14.]

CHAPTER II.

	Latin.	Italian.	Spanish.	Provençal.	French.
B	plebs	plebe	plebe	plob	
C	dux	duca	duque	duo	duo
D	laus	lode			
G	lex	legge	ley	leg or ley[1]	loy
N	caro	carne	carne	carn	carn[2]
	natio	nazione	nacion	nacion	nation
	virgo	vergine	virgen	virgen	
R	genus	genere	genero	goure	genre
T	salus	salute	salud	salut	salut
NT	gigas	gigante	gigante	gigant	géant
V	nix	neve	nieve	nev	nief

The above instances show that the derived nouns exhibit all the different increments of the Latin genitive: the following nouns from the Italian and Spanish are arranged according to the termination of the nominative, in order to show the diversity of forms derived from Latin nouns having the same termination in the nominative, which, if they had all been derived from that case, would have been impossible.

	Latin.	Italian.	Spanish.
as	Leonid-as	Leonid-a	Leonid-as
	Nai-as	Nai-ade	Nay-ada
	libert-as	libert-ate	libert-ad
	eloph-as	elef-ante	elof-ante
	v-as	v-ase, v-aso	v-aso
ax	p-ax	p-ace	p-az
	Astyan-ax	Astian-acte	Astian-ax

[1] The final g easily passes into y: thus the Anglo-Saxon ænig, blodig, dreorig, become in English any, bloody, dreary. etc. see Grimm, D. Gr. vol ii., p. 802—806.

[2] The old French used carn (Gr. Comp. p. 63,) which it afterwards changed into charn, char, and chair, the latter probably in order to distinguish it from char from the Teutonic car. It also used nief, neif, and noif for neige.

FORMS AND INFLEXIONS OF ROMANCE NOUNS. 63

	Latin.	*Italian.*	*Spanish.*
er	magist-er carc-er pat-er Jupit-er	maest-ro carc-ere pad-re Giove	maest-ro carc-el pad-re Jupit-er
es	fid-es her-es Cer-es interpr-es lim-es sp-es	fid-e er-ede Cer-ere interpr-ete lim-ite sp-eme	fe Cer-es interpr-ete lim-ite
is	cin-is fin-is Nere-is l-is	cen-ere fin-e Nere-ide l-ite	 fin Nere-ida l-id
ix	nutr-ix St-yx n-ix	nutr-ice St-ige n-eve	nutr-iz Est-ige n-ieve
ynx	l-ynx sph-ynx	l-ince sf-inge	l-ince esf-inge
o	ord-o serm-o	ord-ine serm-one	ord-en serm-on
on	horiz-on Cle-on phænomen-on	orizz-onte Cle-one fenomen-o	horiz-onte Cle-on fenomen-o
os	fl-os b-os os	fi-ore b-ove osso	fl-or b-oy, b-uey hueso
us	popul-us virt-us pal-us gen-us gr-us l-ans Selin-us lep-us	popol-o virt-ute pal-ude gen-ere gr-ue (grù) l-ode Selin-unte lep-re	puebl-o virt-ud pal-ude gen-ero lieb-re

These examples prove incontestably that the Italian and Spanish nouns are not formed from the Latin nominative; it now remains to ascertain from which of the remaining cases they were formed. The Provençal nouns above cited might have been formed from either of the oblique cases by simply rejecting the termination, thus *duc* or *nazion* might have been equally formed from *duc-is, duc-i, duc-em*, or *duc-e, nation-is, nation-i, nation-em,* or *nation-e,* by simply omitting the termination *is, i, em,* or *e;* any one of which might be supported by examples. Many of the Spanish terminations, as *luz, lid, margen, ley,* are of the same nature: others, however, end with a vowel, which is universally the case with the Italian nouns. On comparing these vowel terminations with the Latin cases, it will appear that there is little resemblance between the terminations of the modern nouns and those of the Latin genitive and dative cases: and that the forms in question are evidently derived from either the accusative or the ablative. Of these two cases the preference might seem due to the ablative, as it accounts for most of the forms, derived both from the second and third declensions of Latin nouns: thus *modus,* abl. *modo, modo* Ital. and Span.; *lignum,* abl. *ligno, legno,* Ital., *leño* Span.; *limes,* abl. *limite, limite* Ital. and Span. These, and nearly all other instances of Italian words derived from Latin nouns of the second and third declensions, exhibit the precise form of the Latin ablative[1]:

---

[1] Galvani, *Osserv. sulla Poesia dei Trovatori,* p. 515 n., considers the Latin ablative as the type of the Italian nouns: 'Dal sesto caso dei nomi (he says) si formano quasi tutti i nomi volgari.' The same is also the opinion of Diefenbach, *Ueber die Romanischen Schriftsprachen,* p. 119. Schlegel, *Observ.,* p. 38, says that 'il est incontestable que

FORMS AND INFLEXIONS OF ROMANCE NOUNS. 65

and the Spanish for the most part, though often without the final vowel. Nevertheless, it seems to me certain that the Italian and Spanish nouns were formed not from the ablative, but from the accusative case, as I shall now attempt to show.

In the first place, it may be observed that the nominative and accusative are more easily confounded than the nominative and the other cases; as the accusative merely signifies the government of a verb or preposition, without those additional meanings expressed by the genitive, dative, and ablative. It is natural that the termi-

dans l'italien la plupart des mots sont formés de l'ablatif latin.' Maffei does not decide between the ablative and the accusative: 'Siccome non era possibile (he says) che la gente idiota senza studio di grammatica regolarmente secondo la varia esigenza dei verbi usasse le inflessioni dei nomi, e dovea quasi sempre valersi dell' accusativo, o dell' ablativo, cosi da quei due casi venne l'Italico.' *Verona Illustrata*, P. I. c. 316. M. Raynouard remarks, vol. i., p. 38. 'Une observation me semble décisive pour nous convaincre que les noms romans ont été formés du nominatif et principalement de l'accusatif des Latins. Par ce système toutes les difficultés s'expliquent, tandis que les autres cas, tels que le génitif et l'ablatif, n'offrent pas le même avantage.' Diez, *Poesie der Troubadours*, p. 294, shows briefly, but convincingly, that the Italian nouns were formed from the accusative, and not from the ablative of the Latin. Sismondi, *Litt. du Midi*, vol. i., p. 15, has the following remarks on this subject: 'Elle (la grammaire) n'a dans aucune des langues du midi conservé les cas dans les noms; mais choisissant entre les terminaisons diverses du mot latin, elle a fait le mot nouveau avec le nominatif en italien, avec l'accusatif en espagnol, avec une contraction qui s'éloigne de tous deux en francais.' He then adds in a note: 'cette règle doit s'entendre surtout du pluriel.' It will, however, be shown below, that the formation of the plural is governed by different principles from the formation of the singular noun. Burguy, *Grammaire de la Langue d'Oïl*, vol. i., p. 22, thinks that the Romance nouns were formed, not from any determinate case of the Latin noun, but from the root, denuded of any characteristic termination.

F

nations denoting the subject and object of a verb should be confounded, especially by ignorant or unobservant persons. Thus in vulgar English, *him says, her says,* and *them say,* are of frequent occurrence; and the use of *lui* and *lei* (the modern objective cases) for *egli* and *ella* is established in the most correct Italian. The proneness of the Low Latin to the use of the accusative case, where the ancient language would have required the nominative or the ablative, has been already pointed out in numerous instances.

The supposition that the Italian and Spanish nouns and participles were formed from the Latin accusative by rejecting the final consonant, and changing the final *u* into *o*, accounts for all the phenomena, with a few exceptions of little importance. The omission of the final *m* is paralleled by *meco, sette, nove, dieci, undici, dodici, cento, amava,* Ital.; *migo, siete, nueve, diez, once, doce, ciento, amaba,* Span.; from *mecum, septem, novem, decem, undecim, duodecim, centum, amabam*. In the fourteenth century the Latin words *pax tecum, Te Deum, regnum tuum, flagellum Dei, gaudeamus,* were commonly known in Italy by the corruptions *pasteco, tadeo, regnontuo, flagellondeo, galdeamo*[1]. The elision of the final *m* in Latin proves that it had a dead sound[2], which was easily lost: and the interchange of the forms *cum* and *con* in ancient Latin (as *coneo* and *coeo* for *cumeo*) prove the close affinity between the sounds of the Latin *um*

---

[1] See Perticari, *Scrittori del Trecento,* L 1, c. 12.
[2] What Quintilian calls a *mugiens sonus:* ' Quid quod pleraque nos illa, quasi mugiente littera cludimus M, qua nullum Graece verbum cadit.' xii. 10, 31. On the elision of the final m in Latin, see Schaller's *Latin Grammar,* vol. i., p. 12. Engl. Transl.

and *on;* which last (as will be shown below) was probably the transition between the Latin *um* and the modern *o*. The change of the final *u* into *o* also occurs in the first persons plural of Italian and Spanish verbs: as *fummo, amiamo, temiamo, sentiamo,* Ital.; *fuimos, amamos, tememos, sentimos,* Span. The change of the short Latin *u* into *o* in the interior of Italian words, is likewise of frequent occurrence[1]. It is, moreover, a circumstance of some weight as regards this question, that in the Sicilian dialect the masculine termination is not *o* but *u*: thus *campu, funnu, (fondo,) arcu, argentu, cornu, corpu, capu*. It is true that the Sicilian often changes the Latin *o* into *u*, as in *maggiuri, minuri, inferiuri, funte,* from *major, minor, inferior, fons:* but in many other instances, as in *cornu, corpu,* just cited, it does not;

---

[1] Both in Italian and Spanish the Latin *u*, when long by nature, is with few exceptions retained unchanged: as *musa, palude, muro, uso, duro,* etc. In Italian, when it was long by position, it is occasionally retained: as *ultimo, gusto;* but usually changed into *o*, as *sepolcro, polvere, mondo, molto, nozze, mosca, sommo, sotto, giorno, bocca, rotto, colto,* etc. The short *u* was almost invariably changed into *o*, as *popolo, noce, croce, Tivoli,* etc.: though in some few cases it was not changed, as *numero, furore, subito, due, lupo.* The Italian *o*, formed from the Latin *u*, is shut like *torn*, but if not thus changed it is open, like *thorn*. Hence *volto* from *vultus* is not pronounced like *volto* from *volutus*. In Spanish the *u* long by position has sometimes been retained, as *mundo, sumo,* and sometimes been changed into *o*, as *boca, soto;* the short *u* (except in terminations where it is changed into *o*, as *Dios, Carlos, huebos, amamos,* etc.) has usually become *ue*, as *pueblo, nues;* probably, however, the *u* was first changed into *o*, and then the *o* was changed into *ue:* as *bueno, cuello, fuego, fuente, muerte, suerte,* etc. came from *bonus, collum, focus, fons, mors, sors.* In like manner the Italian made *nuora* from *nurus;* that is, *nurus, nora, nuora,* like *uovo, nuovo, ruota, buono, fuoco,* from *ovum, novus, rota, bonus, focus,* etc. Compare Diez, *Rom. Gramm.,* vol. i., p. 152.

and it seems that in Italian *u* has more frequently passed into *o* than the converse[1].

The supposition that the Italian and Spanish nouns were derived from the Latin ablative, does not account for many of the forms.

1. Although the derivation from the ablative explains such words as *popolo, collo*, Ital.; *pueblo, cuello*, Span.; from *populo, collo*; it does not explain such words as *mano, canto*, Ital. and Span., from *manu, cantu*: whereas the other hypothesis equally well explains *mano* from *manum*, as *populo* and *pueblo* from *populum*. It is true that *mano* might come from *manu*, as well as *gielo* and *yelo* from *gelu*: but the very object of the derivation from the ablative is to obtain the *o*, without having recourse to the supposition of a change of letters.

2. Where the Latin nominative of a neuter noun increasing in the genitive case ended in a vowel, as *poema, idioma, diadema*, the termination remained unchanged in the Italian and Spanish; but where the nominative of a masculine or feminine noun increasing in the genitive case ended in a vowel, the increment of the genitive was adopted, as *nazione, nacion, imagine, imagen, sermone, sermon*, Ital. and Span., from *natio, imago, sermo*. Now if the modern nouns had been formed from the ablative, *poema* would have become *poemate*, as *sermo* became *sermone* and *sermon*, Ital. and Span.: whereas, if they are

---

[1] See Pasquilino, *Vocabolario Siciliano*, Palermo, 1785, 4to. The dialect of Corsica likewise makes the final masculine vowel *u* and not *o*, see Micali, *Storia degli Antichi Popoli Italiani*, vol. ii. p. 54, note. On the occurrence of the final *u* in other modern Italian dialects, see Lanzi, *Saggio di Lingua Etrusca*, vol. i. p. 342, note, ed. 2.

derived from the accusative, this difference is explained, as neuter did not, like masculine and feminine nouns, take the increment of the genitive in the accusative case.

3. The Latin neuter nouns, indeed, increasing in the genitive case, whatever may be their termination, furnish a test, an *instantia crucis*, by which to try whether the modern nouns were formed from the ablative or accusative: for if they were formed from the ablative, they ought to exhibit the augmentative syllable of the genitive case; whereas, if they were formed from the accusative, they ought not. *Comes* made in the accusative and ablative cases *comitem* and *comite*, from either of which *conte* and *conde* might be formed: but the accusative and ablative of *tempus* were not *tempore* and *temporem*, but *tempore* and *tempus*: so that we are enabled to distinguish which of these cases was the type of the modern form. Now from the following table of neuter nouns of the third declension, and their modern derivatives, it will be perceived that the derivatives in no instance assume the augmentative syllable which characterizes the ablative case.

Latin.	Italian.	Spanish.
abdomen	addome	abdomen
acumen	acume	
æramen	rame	alambre
albumen	albume	
cacumen	cacume	
caput	capo	cabo
carmen	carme	
certamen	certame	
cetus (from κῆτος)	ceto	
corpus	corpo	cuerpo
crimen	crime	crimen

CHAPTER II.

Latin.	Italian.	Spanish.
examen	esame / sciame	examen / exambre
flumen	fiume	flumen[1]
foramen	forame	foramen
gravamen	gravame	gravamen
jus	gius	
lætamen	letame	
latus	lato	lado
legumen	legume	legumbre
ligamen	legame	
litus	lito or lido	
lumen	lume	lumbre
marmor	marmo	marmol
nomen	nome[2]	nombre
numen	nume	numen
opus	uopo	huebos[3]
pectus	petto	pecho
pignus	pegno	
piper	pepe	
pondus	pondo	
semen	seme	semen
stamen	stame	estambre
stercus	sterco	
stramen	strame	
sulphur	solfo	
tempus	tempo	tiempo
velamen	velame	velamen
vellus	vello	vello
vimen	vime	vimbre
volumen	volume	volumen[4]

[1] *Flumen* occurs in the *Vida de S. Domingo*, v. 229. Sanchez, *Colleccion de Poesias Castellanas Anteriores al Siglo XV.*, vol. ii., p. 30.

[2] The Provençal likewise made *lum* and *nom* from *lumen* and *nomen*, although in masculine and feminine nouns it adopted the increment of the genitive.

[3] See Sanchez, *ibid.*, vol. i. Index in *huebos* and *huevos*.

[4] The French has evidently formed its nouns in the same way as

In these words the Italian, in order to avoid a consonant termination, rejects the last letter of the Latin accusative, and where the termination includes *u*, it changes that vowel into *o*. In this manner *acumen, flumen*, become *acume, fiume*, etc.; as *fenomeno, lessico*, are formed from *phænomenon, lexicon, forse* from *forsan, amme* from *amen*, in Dante, (*Paradiso*, xiv. 64:) and *latus, sulphur, marmor, caput*, become *lato, solfo, marmo, capo*. The Spanish is less regular, but in no word does it assume the increment of the genitive: like the Italian it changes *us* and *ut* into *o*, (with the exception of the old word *huebos* from *opus*); but the termination *en* it sometimes exhibits entire, as *examen, volumen*, and sometimes changes it into *re*, as *lumbre, nombre*[1]. In *marmor* the Italian rejects the final *r*, the Spanish softens it into *l*.

the Italian and Spanish: thus from *caput, chap,* or *chef,* from *carmen, charme,* from *corpus, corps,* from *nomen, nom,* from *pondus, poids,* from *stamen, étaim,* from *tempus, temps*: in some of which words the final Latin *s* is still preserved. From *marmor* and *sulfur* it has likewise made *marbre* and *soufre*; but in these words the formation from the uninflected case is not so obvious. [For modern Romance nouns, formed with these terminations, see Diez, *Rom. Gramm.*, vol. ii., p. 308—10.]

[1] The old Spanish said *nome, lume*, etc. Rayn. *Gr. Comp.* p. xxxiv. It will be observed, however, that now all words from neuter nouns in *en*, which have not retained that termination unchanged, end in *re*; as *enxambre, legumbre*, etc. There are likewise the forms *sangre, hombre*, and *hambre*, from the masc. and fem. *sanguis, homo*, and *fames*. This termination has been caused by the easy transition of the liquids into one another, and has originated thus: *homine-m, homne*, (which form occurs, Sanchez, vol i., p. 300,) *homre, hombre; sanguine-m, sangne*, (which occurs in the *Sacrificio de la Misa* 16, Sanchez, vol. ii., p. 183,) *sangre; lumen, lumne*, (by transposition, used in old Spanish, Sanchez, vol. i., p. 396,) *lumre, lumbre*. So in Italian *anima, anma, alma, arma,* (see Marrini on the *Lamento di Cecco*, p. 176,) and in Spanish *fémina, marmor, carcer, arbor*, became *hembra, marmol, carcil, arbol;* in French

CHAPTER II.

In the following words the Italian, and sometimes the Spanish, adds a vowel to the Latin accusative case:

Latin.	Italian.	Spanish.
animal	animale	animal
cor	cuore	cuer
ebur	eburo	
fel	fielo	fiel
fulgur	folgore	
lac		leche
mel	miele	miel
nectar	nettare	nectar
os	osso	hueso
sal	sale	sal
tribunal	tribunale	tribunal
vas	vase or vaso	vaso

That in these words the final *e* is euphonic, and is not the *e* of the Latin ablative, is proved by *cuore, cuer, ebure, fiele,* and *miele,* which if they were derived from the ablative would be *cuorde, cuerde, ebore, felle,* and *melle.* The Spanish *fel, miel,* etc., indeed, prove nothing either way, as they might be curtailed from the ablative: but *leche* is evidently formed from *lac* with an euphonic vowel,

---

ordine-m became *ordre, pampinus pampre, altare* first *alter,* (*Gr. Comp.* p. 35,) then *auter,* then *autel;* in Provençal *femina* has become *frema,* i. e. *femna, frema, frema.* The *b* in *lambre, hombre,* etc. is inserted on account of the difficulty of pronouncing a liquid following m: as in *hombro,* Span. from *humerus; comble, chambre, humble,* and *nombre,* French, from *cumulus, camera, humilis,* and *numerus:* in Greek γέμβρος (for γάμρος) from γάμος, παρμίμβλωσι for παρμελάλωσι, μεσήρβρινος for μεσημβρινός, ἤμβροτον for ἤμορτον (i. e. ἤμορτον, ἤμροτον, ἤμβροτον,) etc. So in English *ramble* and *tumble* correspond to *rammeln* German, and *taumeln* German, *tommelen* Dutch: *Hamblet* for *Hamlet, Hambleton* for *Hamilton:* *solemn* and *damned* were formerly written *solempne* and *dampned:* '*fimble* hemp' for '*female* hemp' occurs in Tusser, c. 45, § 8, etc.

FORMS AND INFLEXIONS OF ROMANCE NOUNS. 73

since if it came from the ablative it would be *lette*, like the Italian *latte*. That the final *e* is here only euphonic, and was added in order to avoid the consonant termination, is also shown by the circumstance that when the neuter noun ended in *a*, the form of the Latin nominative or accusative was preserved without alteration, as in the following words:

Latin.	Italian.	Spanish.
ænigma	enimma	enigma
anathema	anatema	anatema
axioma	assioma	axioma
baptisma	battesmo[1]	bastismo
chrisma	cresima and -esimo	crisma
clima	clima	clima
diadema	diadema	diadema
diploma	diploma	diploma
dogma	domma	dogma
drama	dramma	drama
epigramma	epigramma	epigrama
idioma	idioma	idioma
problema	problema	problema
psalma	salmo	salmo
sagma	salma	salma
sophisma	solfisma *or* -mo	sofisma
spasma	spasimo	espasmo
systema	sistema	sistema
thema	tema	tema
theorema	teorema	teorema

That in these words (which passed into the Latin from the Greek) the inflexion of the genitive case was not forgotten, and that they would have been *anatemate*, *idiomate*, etc., if the Latin accusative had been *anathematem, idiomatem*, appears from the Italian form *stimati*,

[1] The reason of the change of the final *a* into *o* in neuter nouns is explained below under the head of the genders, ch. II. § 8.

from the plural *stigmata*. In the words of most frequent use, the final *a* has been changed into *o*, on account of the gender.

There are a few words in which the Italian form exhibits the increment of the Latin neuter noun: as *numine, esamine, crimine*, where *nume, esame, crime*, are the more common forms[1]; *vimine* also occurs, as well as *vime*, the form used by Dante. But in the words *fulmine, genere, latte*, and *pettine*, there is no variation: in the latter word, the preference of the genitive form seems to have been due to a desire of avoiding a confusion with *petto* from *pectus*. *Estiercol*, Spanish, is derived from some inflected case of *stercus*.

The Italian appears at first sight to offer some instances of the formation of nouns from the Latin nominatives of the third declension, as *uomo, ladro, margo, imago*: but it is evident that these are modern forms which have undergone different modifications, and that the original words were *homine*, or *uomine, ladrone, margine, imagine*[2]. The Italian, however, sometimes

[1] Also *ulcero* from *ulcus*, where *ulcera* (from the plural) is the more common form: on the origin of *ulcera* see below, ch. II. § 3.

[2] The original form of *uomo* was probably *homine*, regularly formed from *hominem*. This form is still extant in the plural *uomini*, anciently *homini*. It then became *omin* or *omen*, a form preserved in the Milanese dialect. *Omen* was then shortened into *ome*, by the rejection of the final *n*, like *volume* from *volumen*, etc. above p. 70,) and *ome* became *omo* or *uomo*, as in many other words where the termination vacillates between *e* and *o*. Thus *cespite* and *gurgite* were first contracted into *cespe* and *gurge*, (which last occurs in Dante,) and then changed into *cespo* and *gorgo*. (See Castelvetro on *Bembo*, vol. ii. p. 18.) The same explanation applies to *margo* and *imago*: which originally were doubtless *margine* and *imagine* (the common forms,) contracted into *image* (which occurs in Dante,) and *marge*, and then the terminations were confounded. The word *ladro* shortened from

preserved the Latin nominative in proper names, as *Peleus* in the early writers, *Feton, Semiramis, Minos*, in Dante[1]: in some names likewise there are two forms, one from the nominative, and the other from the accusative: as *Plato, Platone, Cato, Catone, Pluto, Plutone*[2]. The Spanish presents several instances of the Latin nominative in proper names; as *Jupiter, Palas, Apolo, Fenix, Carlos*, etc.: and has also retained it in the single word *dios*[3]. But with these exceptions there is not (as far as I am aware) in either language any noun or participle which has retained the termination of the Latin nominative.

It may therefore, I conceive, be laid down as the general result of the above remarks, that Italian and

ladrone, (*ladrone, ladron, ladro*,) furnishes another instance of the rejection of the final *n*. Words in constant use like *nomine*, were most liable to contraction: thus *mulierem* has now become *moglie*, though the form *mogliere* occurs in ancient writers; and *sanguine* has been contracted into *sangue*: the Spanish still has *sangre*, (see above, note, p. 71.) See Schlegel, p. 36: 'Ces mots, qui reviennent sans cesse dans le langage populaire, ressemblent à la petite monnoie d'argent: elle perd son empreinte à force de passer d'une main à l'autre, tandis que les gros écus la conservent.'

[1] See Perticari, *Difesa di Dante*, c. 13.
[2] See Castelvetro on *Bembo*, vol. ii. p. 17.
[3] Whence it has formed the fem. *diosa*, a goddess. *Coms* from *comes* in Provençal, (*conte* Ital., *conde* Span., *comte* French,) affords an instance of the preservation of the Latin nominative in a masculine noun of the third declension. In the *Poeme sur Boece*, v. 34. Coms fo de Roma, and v. 108—40. Molt fort blasmava Boecis sos amigs, Qui lui laudaven dereer eux dias antix, Qu'el era coms, molt onraz e rix: Raynouard in both places translates *consul*. Perhaps *count* (*comes*) is the word meant. The French has likewise retained the ancient form of the nominative in some proper names, as *Charles, Hugues*, (instead of *Challon, Hugon*, which were the ancient accusative,) though it now has universally adopted the form of the Latin accusative.

Spanish nouns and participles are formed from the Latin accusative: sometimes retaining it unaltered, as *poema*, *diadema*, Ital. and Span.; *semen, volumen*, Span.; sometimes by rejecting the final consonant, as *musa, limite, amante, gente, nume, fiume, marmo;* sometimes by rejecting the final consonant and changing *u* into *o*, as *modo, amato, mano, solfo, capo, corpo, cabo, cuerpo:* and the Spanish sometimes by rejecting the final syllable, as *imagen, trinidad, luz*[1].

On comparing this system of forming nouns and participles from the Latin with that prevalent in the other Romance languages, it will appear that there was an important and fundamental difference between the method adopted by the Italian and Spanish on the one hand, and the Provençal and French on the other. It has been shown above that the Provençal and French nouns adopt the increment of the Latin genitive[2], and so far all the four languages agree. The Provençal, however, in forming its nouns and participles from Latin forms in *us*, sometimes preserved the termination of the Latin nominative entire, as *us*, (for *uns*,) *mieus, Deus*, or where *us* was preceded by a consonant, it omitted the *u* and preserved the *s*, as *philosophs, bels, amics, fers, amatz*, from

---

[1] *Spems* in Italian is evidently *spem*, the accusative of *spes*, as *ren* in Provençal (like *rien* in French) is the accusative of *res*, both which forms occur. This explanation accounts for the double form *spems* and *spene*, since the final *m* was in Italian (as has been already shown) often changed into *n*. *Aria* likewise, as will be explained below, comes from *aëra*: as also *lampara* Span., from *lampada;* (on the change of *d* and *r*, as in *fedire* for *ferire, rado* for *raro*, Ital. see Muratori, *Ant. It.* vol. ii. p. 532, A. vol. iii. p. 1090, A.: so in English paddock is *parrock*, (*parruc*, A. S.) whence *park* is contracted: see *Archæologia*, vol. xvii. p. 138.) [See Diez, *Rom. Gr.* vol. L p. 219.]

[2] Above, p. 62.

philosophus, bellus, amicus, ferus, amatus. By analogy this termination was then transferred to all nominatives, even to those which were not terminated with *s* in Latin, as *amors, talens, valors,* to comparatives, as *maiers, mielhers,* and even to infinitives used substantively, as *sabers, plazers.* This analogy was not, however, extended to Latin substantives in *a,* to the definite article, or to personal pronouns.

Pursuing this system of imitating the terminations of the Latin cases, the Provençal rejected the final *s* from its accusative singular, the only oblique case which it preserved from the Latin: and in the plural number formed the nominative without, and the accusative with the *s*. The following example, therefore, may serve as a general type for the declension of Provençal nouns and participles, and at the same time by the comparison with the Latin show the reason of the changes.

	SINGULAR.			PLURAL.	
	Lat.	*Prov.*		*Lat.*	*Prov.*
Nom.	amicus	amics		amici	amio
Acc.	amicum	amic		amicos	amics'

The Provençal has moreover a declension of proper names founded on the same principles, and in which the traces of the Latin are more distinctly visible. These nouns sometimes made the nominative sing. in

[1] These are traces of the rule with regard to the final *s* not applying to nouns where it was not present in Latin: thus *paire, maire, hom,* from *pater, mater, homo,* sometimes have the *s* and sometimes have it not. Thus *el drax,* nominative plural, i. e. *e li dracs,* (*dracones,*) *Gr. R.* p. 100; whereas *lo drac,* nominative singular, p. 141 (*draco*): according to the rule these forms ought to be just reversed: but from the same translation of the *Apocalypse* in which these forms occur, *Johans,* nominative singular, i. e. *Johannes,* p. 141. See Diez, *Poesie der Troubadours,* p. 296.

s or *es*, and the accusative in *on*, the final *n* of which might be omitted, when the Provençal accusative became the same as the Italian and Spanish form. Thus we find, nom. *Aimes, Hugues, Odiels*; acc. *Aimon* or *Aimo, Ugon, Odilo*, (*Gr. Comp.* p. 85, 86.) This declension has probably preserved the intermediate steps between the Latin and the common Provençal form: viz. *campus, campes, camps : campum, campon, campo, campe, camp.*

The declension of the nouns is further illustrated by a comparison of the Latin and Provençal possessive pronouns, (*Gr. R.* p. 96—114.)

SINGULAR.

	MASC.			FEM.	
Lat.	*Prov.*		*Lat.*		*Prov.*
meus	meus, mos		mea	}	mia, mieua, ma
meum	meu, mon		meam		
tuus	teus, tos		tua	}	tua, tieua, ta
tuum	teu, ton		tuam		
suus	seus, sos		sua	}	sua, sueua, sa
suum	seu, son		suam		
noster	nostres		nostra	}	nostra
nostrum	nostre		nostram		
vester	vostres		vestra	}	vostro
vestrum	vostre		vestram		

PLURAL.

	MASC.			FEM.	
Lat.	*Prov.*		*Lat.*		*Prov.*
mei	mei, meu	}	meas		mias, mieuas, mas
meos	mos, meus				
tui	tei, teu	}	tuas		tuas, tieuas, tas
tuos	tos, teus				
sui	sei, seu	}	suas		suas, sueuas, sas
suos	sos, seus				
nostri	nostre	}	nostras		nostras
nostros	nostres				
vestri	vostre	}	vestras		vostras
vestros	vostres				

FORMS AND INFLEXIONS OF ROMANCE NOUNS. 79

With all classes of nouns except those ending in *a*, and another kind to be mentioned below, the Provençal exactly imitated the Latin declension in *us*, in making the nominative singular, and the accusative plural in *s*, and the nominative plural and the accusative singular without *s*. With those ending in *a*, however, it preserved the Latin nominative singular unchanged, but formed the plural of all cases after the Latin accusative, as *musas, domnas, mias*, etc.

In the declension of its adjectives the Provençal observes the same rules, founded on the same reasons.

Thus *bons*, good, is declined as follows:

	Singular.			Plural.
Nom.	bons *or* bos	bona	bon	bonas
Acc.	bon	bona	bons	bonas

Gr. R. p. 42.

Past participles of verbs are declined in the same manner: thus

	Singular.			Plural.
Nom.	amatz	amata	amat	amadas
Acc.	amat	amata	amatz	amadas

Gr. R. p. 200.

Some adjectives, however, are common to both genders, and these in the singular number omit the *s* in the accusative case, but in the plural preserve it for both the cases. *Grans*, great, will furnish an example of this declension.

	Singular.	Plural.
Nom.	grans	grans
Acc.	gran	

The reason of this difference is obvious, viz. that whereas the Latin adjectives which took a feminine termination, ending in *us*, made *i* in the nominative plural; those which did not take a feminine termination ending in *ens, ans, is*, etc. made *es* in the nominative plural, though they made *em* in the accusative singular: consequently the Provençal, after the model of the Latin adjective, omitted the *s* in the accusative singular, but preserved it in the nominative plural.

The present participles of verbs active were declined on the same principle, only they showed in the accusative case the letter of the increased genitive: as

Singular.	Plural.
Nom. amans	amans or -anz *for* amants
Acc. amant	

Gr. R. p. 197.

The acc. singular is often written without the final *t*, as the Provençal used *mon* for *mond* from *mundus*, and generally omitted the final *d* or *t* after *n*: thus *chant*, the first person of the present indic. of *chantar*, became *chan*, *atend* from *atendre* became *aten*, *sent* from *sentir* became *sen*, etc. (*Gr. R.* p. 209.)

In old French the same system of declension is observed, as M. Raynouard has shown by a multitude of examples, which prove beyond a doubt the retention in that language of the same two Latin cases. Thus in the nom. singular, 'Qui ere *amirals* des galies:' '*Johans* li *rois* de Blaquie venoit;' '*Nus* n'est joyeux com *Thiebaus*,' (i.e. Thiebauds, Theobaldus); 'Que ce fut la *flors* des barons¹.' In the acc. singular, 'del plus bas *enfern*;' '*Ested e ivern* tu as fait.' Nom. plural, 'Celui cui li *Franc* avoient chacié de Constantinople;' 'tout mi *penser* sont à ma douce amie;' 'dont li *nom* ne sont mie en escrit.' Acc. plural, 'Li rois mande *ses arcevesques, Ses* meillors *clercs* et *ses evesques*;' 'sur les *chevels* de mun chief;' 'Sire Deus de *vertuz*,' (i. e. *vertutz*.) *Gr. Comp.* p. 71—84.

The old French likewise, as well as the Provençal, extended this inflexion to the infinitives of verbs, when used as substantives: thus in the nom. singular, 'Si la blonde savoit Com li *departirs* m'ocira:' but in the acc. singular, 'mainte larme i fu plorée de pitié al *departir* de lors pays.' (*Gr. Comp.* p. 96.)

The same inflexion of proper names as that above pointed out in the Provençal also occurs in the old French: thus *Hues, Pieres, Bueves* are nom. *Huon, Pieron, Buevon*, are acc. (*Gr. Comp.* p. 86, 87.)² Many traces of this ancient form of the accusative still appear in the modern French proper names; thus *Hugon, Pierron*, or *Perron, Odilon, Guyon*, (from *Guy*,) *Guillon*, (from *Guille* for *Guillaume*,) *Giraudon*, (from *Giraud*,) *Girardon*,

[1] In modern French the words *fils*, (from *filius*) *fonds*, (from *fundus*,) *lacs*, (from *laqueus*,) *tiers*, (from *tertius*,) and *Artus*, (from *Arturs*,) for *Arthur*, are remnants of this ancient form: also *corps, poids, temps*, (see above, p. 70, note ⁴) *choux*, (from *caulis*,) *puits*, (from *puteus*,) and proper names, such as *Charles, Hugues, Jules, Georges, Jacques, Louis, Villars* or *Villiers*, (from *Villarius*,) *Londres*, (from London, like *Havre*, from the German *hafen*.) Anciently the final *s* in these words was doubtlessly sounded, and *fils* nom. was distinguished from *fil* acc., to the ear as well as the eye.

[2] On the inflexions of the ancient French nouns, see also Raynouard, *Journal des Savans*, 1826, p. 297, 298; 1828, p. 136, 137. *Observations sur le Roman de Rou*, p. 48—58.

(from *Girard,*) *Morelon* or *Morlon,* (from *Morel,*) *Philippon,* (from *Philippe,*) *Vernon,* (from *Verne,*) etc.[1]

It is unnecessary to repeat any of M. Raynouard's instances of the declension of French adjectives, as it is a mere repetition of the declension of the substantives, (*Gr. Comp.* p. 129—36.)

The French also anciently used *mes, tes, ses,* formed from *mos, tos, sos,* in the nom. singular, and *mon, ton, son,* in the acc. singular: thus 'je suis ses fils, il est mes pere.' *Nostres* and *vostres* were likewise used as nom. singular, as ' sacés que *nostres* sires m'a pardonnez mes pechiez.' The latter forms have, however, been supplanted by the acc. *nostre* or *nôtre, vostre* or *vôtre,* and the former by the acc. *mon, ton, son.* (*Gr. Comp.* p. 162—170.)

The Provençal had a peculiar exception to the general rule with regard to the final *s,* for substantives ending in *aire, eire, ire,* which made the acc. singular, and the nom. and acc. plural, in *ador, edor,* and *idor.* Thus *trobaire, cantaire, amaire, entendeire, servire,* were nom. singular; but in the acc. singular, *trobador, cantador, amador, entendedor, servidor,* and in both cases of the plural, *trobadors, cantadors, amadors, entendedors, servidors.* (*Gr. R.* p. 33—5.) The reason of this singular declension is that these words, or the words from which the analogy was derived, were formed from Latin nouns in *ātor, ŭtor,* and *itor;* and in such words as *amātŏr, domĭtŏr, audītŏr,* in the nom. singular, the last syllable being short, the *o* was easily slurred over, and *ator, itor,* and

---

[1] [For a copious illustration 'of this subject,' see Burguy, *Gr. de la Langue d'Oïl,* vol. i. p. 03—98; Ampère, *Hist. de la Litt. Franc,* p. 48—89.]

itor, contracted into *aire, eire,* and *ire;* but in all the other cases, singular and plural, *amatōrem, amatōres, domitōrem, domitōres,* etc.; the *or* being long, it had a stronger hold on the tongue, and only the last syllable, according to the constant practice of the Provençal language, was omitted. In like manner the Italian has formed *lepre* from *lepŏrem,* eliminating the short *o,* but has preserved the long *o* in *lepore* from *lepōrem.* The following scheme, therefore, explains this declension.

	SINGULAR.		PLURAL.	
	Lat.	*Prov.*	*Lat.*	*Prov.*
Nom.	amatŏr	amairo	amatóres	amadors
Acc.	amatŏr-em	amador		

An analogous change may be observed in those Provençal comparatives which have been derived from the Latin. These form the nom. singular in *ers,* the acc. singular and nom. plural in *or,* and the acc. plural in *ors.* The reason of this change is, that in the nom. singular the final *or,* being short in Latin, lost its full sound of *o,* and became *er;* then, according to the analogy above explained, it took the final *s* in the nom. singular: but in the augmented cases the *or* being long, the vowel was not changed into the thinner sound of *e*[1].

This remarkable declension of nouns in *aire,* reappears in the old French: which in the substantives corresponding to the Latin nouns in *ator* and *itor* made the nom. singular in *eres, erres,* and *ieres*[2], but the other three

---

[1] So it may be observed in the declension of proper names, the Provençal changed the final *us* of the nom. into *es,* because it was short, but changed the final *um* of the acc. into *on,* because it was long.

[2] None of the Provençal examples cited by M. Raynouard, *Gr. R.*

cases in *eor* or *or*. Thus nom. singular, 'Dicx tu ies rois et *conseilleres*, et *gouvernieres*, et *jugieres*.' 'Couronés em-*pereres* i fu.' Acc. singular, 'il deguerpit Deu sun *faitor*.' Nom. plural, 'Vous estes dui *enchanteor*, et li nostre enemi sunt *jugeor*.' Acc. plural, 'Que il est dieu des *jongleors*, et dieu de tous les *chanteors*.' The modern French has formed these nouns from the ancient termination, not of the nominative, but of the accusative singular: thus from *empereor*, *chanteor*, came *emperor*, *chantor*, changed first into *emperour*, *chantour*, then into *empereur*, *chanteur*[1]. The word *troubadour*, from *trobador*, has never undergone the last change and become *troubadeur*. The modern Provençal on the other hand has formed all these nouns in *aire* from the termination of the nominative, as *chantaire*, *triounfaire*, *troumpaire*, etc.; but like the French it has lost the inflexion.

Of the distinction between the cases of comparatives derived from the Latin, there appears to be no trace in any Romance language except the Provençal. (*Gr. Comp.* p. 138.)

Now when we come to compare the system of formation and declension which has been just described, with

---

p. 39, take the final *s* after *aire;* the French nouns, however, take it invariably. *Gr. Comp.* p. 87—94.

[1] This series of changes may be observed in many other French words, thus *illorum*, *lor*, *lour*, *leur*; *morir*, *mourir*, *meurs*; *probus*, *prous* (whence *prouesse*,) *preux*, etc.: also in the substantives derived from Latin nouns in *or*, as *honor*, *honour*, *honneur*, etc., (see below § 3.) Some of these preserved the ancient termination unchanged, as *amour*, *labour*; in others it can be perceived in their derivatives, as *vigoureux*, *douloureux*, *rigoureux*, *savoureux*, etc.: *valeureux* has been formed after the termination *eur* came into use. *Soporeux* and *liquoreux* have preserved the Latin form in *or*. *Nous* from *nos*, *vous* from *vos*, *bouche* from *boca*, (*bucca*, Lat.) *mouvoir* from *mover*, *vouloir* from *voler*, are

that which prevails in the Italian and Spanish, we shall find the strongest and most marked dissimilarity.

1. In the first place there is no trace in the Italian and Spanish languages of any distinction of cases: whereas the Provençal distinguished between the nominative and accusative, both in the singular and plural, by at least four different manners: viz. the retention or omission of *s*, the change of *es* and *on*, of *aire* and *ador*, and of *ers* and *or*. Three of these methods of distinguishing cases likewise appear in the old French.

2. The Provençal in all nouns and participles derived from Latin nouns and participles in *us*, formed its derivative from the nominative by omitting the last but one, and preserving the last letter, as *amic-u-s*, *amics*; *amat-u-s*, *amatz*: the Italian and Spanish, on the other hand, formed their derivative from the accusative by preserving the last but one, and omitting the last letter; thus *amicu-m*, *amico*, *amatu-m*, *amato*[1].

instances of the change of *o* into *ou*; *le* from *lo*, *les* from *los*, *ce* from *eo*, of the change of *o* into *e*. [Compare Diez, *Rom. Gramm.* vol. i. p. 147.]

[1] M. Raynouard, having shown that the Italian formerly used *meo* for *mio*, goes on to say that 'the Romance (i. e. Provençal) pronoun *mos* was adopted and still exists in *Monsignor*. This remarkable vestige is a fresh proof of the ancient community of language.' *Gr. Comp.* p. 164. This vestige, which is certainly remarkable, proves no more than this: that the Italian, as well as the Provençal, corrupted the Latin *meum* into *mon*: the Provençal used it as an acc. case; in Italian it was the only case. Afterwards *mon* became *mo*, as in the ancient expressions *fratelmo*, *patremo*, *cuginomo*: see Menage *Etym. Ital.* in *cuginomo*. If M. Raynouard can show that the Italian, like the Provençal, used *meus* and *mos* in the nom. case, he will then indeed have gone far to prove a community of language. It is not improbable that in Italian, as it appears to have been the case in Provençal, (see above, p. 78,) the transition of *um* into *o* took place in this manner:

M. Raynouard himself, speaking of the strong resemblance which the Catalonian and Vaudois languages bear to the Provençal, remarks that their chief difference consists in their wanting the *fundamental* rule with regard to the final *s*. He then adds: 'it appears that this rule has never been able to cross either the Pyrenees or the Alps.' (*Gr. Comp.* p. xxxix.) By these words, M. Raynouard, if I rightly understand him, means to say, that the rules for the formation and declension of nouns and participles were originally different in the Provençal and French on the one hand, and in the languages spoken in Italy and Spain on the other. If this be so, his theory of the universality of the Provençal language must, according to his own admission, be considerably circumscribed.

It might, indeed, be argued, that as the Provençal and French, although they adopted as their type the accusative of Latin nouns increasing in the genitive case, yet retained the *s* of the nominative case of nouns and participles in *us*; so the Italian and Spanish, though they formed from nouns and participles increasing in the genitive, by taking the accusative case, yet formed from nouns and participles in *us*, by taking not the accusative but the nominative, with the rejection of the final *s*, which, we know, was often suppressed in Latin before a consonant[1]: thus *mondo, buono, amato,* would come from *mundu', bonu', amatu'*: and in some Italian dialects the final vowel is still *u* and not *o*[2].

viz. *um, om, on, o; amicum, amicom, amicon, amico*. The suppression of the final *n* is very frequent in the Provençal. *Gr. R.* p. 346. *Gr. Comp.* p. 163. So likewise in Italian *con il* and *non il* are contracted into *col* and *nol*, in German *von dem* into *vom*.

[1] See Lanzi, *Lingua Etrusca,* vol. i. p. 91.   [2] See above, p. 68.

FORMS AND INFLEXIONS OF ROMANCE NOUNS. 87

This hypothesis, however, would not account for such forms as *tenero, suocero, genero, ministro, maestro,* Ital. *tierno, suegro, yerno, ministro, maestro,* Span., etc., the originals of which have not *u* in the nominative case. We are, therefore, compelled to suppose that the Latin accusative was the universal type for the Italian and Spanish nouns. We know, likewise, from the Provençal and French form of the nominative case, that the final *s* had not been in the corrupt period of Latinity, dropped from the terminations of nouns even in conversation; although it was frequently elided before a consonant by the early Latin poets.

3. In forming the plurals of masculine nouns, the Provençal and Italian so far agree, that both follow the Latin nominative case in *i*: the Provençal rejecting, the Italian retaining, the final vowel. The Spanish, however, forms its masculine plural after the model of the Latin accusative, not of the Latin nominative, by adding *s*: thus the Italian and Provençal have *amici* and *amic*, like the Latin *amici*, the Spanish *amigos* like *amicos*: *desiderj, pensamenti,* Ital. *desir, pensamen,* Prov., but *deseos, pensamientos,* Span. The Spanish forms its masculine plurals simply by adding *s*, from the analogy of the acc. plur. of Latin nouns in *us*, while the Italian forms its masc. plur. in *i*, from the analogy of the nom. plur. of nouns in *us*. Thus the Italian says indifferently, *modi, mani, onori, poemi;* the Spanish *modos, manos, onores, poemas.*

4. In forming the plurals fem. of nouns and participles in *a*, the Provençal and Spanish agree in following the Latin accusative, and in simply adding *s*: thus *domnas, bonas, amatas,* Prov., *dueñas, buenas, amadas,* Span. Here,

however, the Italian disagrees, as it forms the plural in these instances from the Latin nom. in æ, which, not having any diphthongs, it changes into e; thus *donne, buone, amate, nuptiæ, nozze.*

The characteristic varieties of the several Romance languages in forming their masculine and feminine nouns from Latin nouns in *us* and *a*, are shown by the following scheme, which at the same time proves that each language derived its terminations directly from the Latin, and independently of any of its cognate languages.

	Lat.	Italian.	Spanish.	Prov.	French.
Sing.	caballus			cavals	chevals
	caballum	cavallo	caballo	caval	cheval
Pl.	caballi	cavalli		caval	cheval
	caballos		caballos	cavals	chevals
Sing.	musa			musa	muse (musa)
	musam	musa	musa		
Pl.	musæ	muse			
	musas		musas	musas	muses (musas)

It has been shown that the Italian and Spanish nouns were formed from the Latin acc. singular: and that the Provençal and French nouns also took the increment of the genitive case; the same languages (as is shown in the above table) also formed the plural of feminine nouns in *a* from the Latin accus., and the Spanish formed the plural of all nouns from the accusative. The same tendency to employ the accusative as a nominative case is also visible in the progress of the Provençal and French languages; and, when the distinction of cases was gradually given up, led to the disuse of the nominative, and the retention of the accusative form in each number. Thus in both those languages, the singular number of nouns ending with a consonant is now marked by the absence of a final *s*, and the plural by its addition: which is the rule observed in the ancient accusative cases of nouns, but in the nominative cases the rule was just reversed. The gradual progress of this change can be observed in the remains of the early Provençal literature, in which the distinction between the nom. and acc. is by no means constantly observed; and in almost every instance it may be seen that the disposition is to use the accusative and not the nominative as the invariable form. In general, the observation of the distinction of cases is in proportion to the antiquity of the writing: thus in the *Poeme sur Boece*, the earliest work in the Romance languages now extant, the rule as to the final *s* is constantly observed; in the *Nobla Leyczon* it is almost constantly neglected in the singular number. The same progress is also discernible in other parts of speech; thus *mon, ton, son, nostre* and *vostre*, sometimes occur as nominatives singular, and *mos, tos, sos*, as nominatives plural, although for the most part they are only accusatives: but this licence (as M. Raynouard states) rarely occurs in the compositions taken from the best and most ancient monuments (*Gr. R.* p. 116). It is not improbable that a similar change took place in the formation of the plural of Provençal nouns in *a;* and that at a very early period of that language, prior to the date of any remains of it which we possess, *muse* was the nom., and *musas* only the acc. case; so that there were two cases in the fem. as in the masc. plural. This proneness to abandon the nom. and employ only the acc. case, however prevailing, was not invariable; thus it has been already shown that, although the modern French forms, *empereur, chanteur,* etc. have been formed from the ancient acc. *empereor, chanteor*, and not from the ancient nom. *empereres, chanteres*, yet the modern Provençal forms *chantaire, triomfaire*, etc. have followed the analogy of the ancient nominatives *cantaire, amaire*, and not of the ancient acc. *cantador, amador*[1]. The Italian, moreover, although it completely deserted the traces of the Latin nominatives in the singular number, still retains their terminations unchanged in the plural. However it cannot be doubted that on the whole the Romance languages show a decided tendency to the accusative in preference to the nominative case; a tendency, likewise, pointed out above in some specimens of the Latin of the middle ages[2]: and it seems to me that this disposition affords a better explanation of the forms of the modern nouns than the remark of Schlegel that the oblique cases served as a type, because taken together they were more numerous, and therefore occurred oftener than the nominative[3]. All the cases except the nom. and acc. appear to have become obsolete at a very early period after the German invasion: and therefore this remark does not explain why, when only those two cases remained, the preference should, in almost every instance, have been given to that case which seems to have the less obvious claim. But although the existence of a disposition to abandon the subjective and

---

[1] See above, p. 84.   [2] See above, p. 58—61.

[3] 'Toutes les langues dérivées du Latin ont donné la préférence à un cas oblique quelconque. Et pourquoi? parce que tous les cas obliques pris ensemble étant d'un usage plus fréquent que le nominatif, la forme du substantif commune à tous ces cas s'étoit mieux imprimée dans la mémoire de ceux qui ne savoient pas le latin d'une manière savante.' *Observ.* p. 38. The same explanation is also given by Diefenbach, p. 119.

use the objective case as the invariable form, appears to me to be convincingly proved by a wide induction[1], I am unable to suggest any very satisfactory explanation of the causes which induced the mind to make this preference.

In explaining the formation of the Italian nouns from the acc. case, I had occasion to remark that when the final syllable was *um* or *us*, the last letter was rejected, and *u* became *o*; that where it was *em*, the last letter was rejected and the *e* retained. According to this hypothesis, there could be nothing arbitrary in the final vowel of the Italian nouns, and the harshness of a consonant termination was avoided, not by adding a vowel

---

[1] It may be observed that foreigners, in attempting to speak a language which they do not understand, almost always use the accusative as the nominative of the pronoun in speaking of themselves: e. g. *moi* in French, and *me* in English. The accusative seems to be more emphatic than the nominative, and to be preferred to it on that account: thus in French, where a stress is laid on the pronoun, the accusative case is invariably used: as *c'est moi, c'est toi*, and not *c'est je, c'est tu*; which the strict rule of syntax would require. Thus when Nisus, in *Virgil*, wishes to direct instant attention to himself, he exclaims,

    Me, me, adsum qui feci, in me convertite ferrum
    O Rutuli, mea fraus omnis, etc.

The West Indian negroes have made the same change in the pronouns, in their corruption of the English language: thus in a song written in the negro dialect of Jamaica,

    Peter, Peter, was a black boy;
    Peter *him* pull foot one day:
    Buckra girl, *him* Peter's joy;
    Lilly white girl entice him away.

(*Journal of a West India Proprietor*, by M. G. Lewis, p. 120). 'The negroes (the author of this song adds in a note) never distinguished between "him" and "her" in their conversation.' They have therefore not only abolished the distinction between the two cases by making the accusative serve for both, but they have also abolished the distinction between the two genders, by making the masculine serve for both.

after a consonant, but by suppressing a consonant after a vowel. M. Raynouard, however, takes an entirely different view of this subject. Conceiving that the Italian was derived from the Provençal, he represents the Italian nouns and participles as having been first reduced to the Provençal form, and then being augmented with a vowel, for the sake of euphony, in order to avoid a consonant termination. Hence he considers such words as *largo, porco, tardo, campo, carne, altare, toro, falso, furto, parte,* as formed by the addition of the euphonic *e* or *o*, from the ancient forms *larg, porc, tard, camp, carn, altar, tor, fals, furt, part:* he even goes further, and supposes that the anciont *e* has sometimes been changed into *o:* thus the original forms *diable, secle, sepulcre, nostre, vostre, clergue, evesque,* were, according to him, changed in Italian into *diavolo, secolo, sepolcro, nostro, vostro, cherico, vescovo.* In support of this assertion he cites the authority of Giambullari, a Florentine writer of the sixteenth century, who states that in ancient times most of the Florentine words ended with consonants, and that the Florentines, seeing the softness of the vowel terminations of the Sicilians, adopted the Sicilian rule. This ancient usage, he thinks, is preserved in many of the Italian dialects, which reject the final vowels, and have the same consonant terminations as in the corresponding words of the Provençal: and a remnant is retained by the written Italian, in the power of omitting the final vowel of certain words ending with a liquid. He further adds that Boccacio called his great collection of novels *Decameron,* without the final *e*, which was not added till afterwards: and that in a poem of Barsape, an early Milanese writer, the final *e* is never added to substantives in *on*, and is often wanting after those ending in *x*, as *pax, lux, verax*, which are now always *pace, luce, verace*[1].

To this doctrine I must object, in the first place, that the Provençal nouns were not as M. Raynouard represents them, but *largs, porcs, tards, camps*, etc., with the final *s*, the mark of the nominative, which there is no reason to believe ever existed in Italian. Moreover if the Italian nouns originally ended in consonants, and the final vowel was afterwards added for the sake of euphony, how comes it that attention should in almost all cases have been paid to the Latin termination, and that where the Latin accusative ended in *um* or *us*, the final vowel was *o*, where it ended in *em* or *en*, the final vowel was *e*? Is it conceivable that if the Latin terminations had been long cut off and forgotten, we should never (with a very few exceptions) find *monde* from *mundum*, or *monto* from *montem*?[2] Let us take ten Italian substantives which M. Raynouard has deprived of their terminations in order to exhibit their agreement with the Provençal forms, viz. *animal, cardinal, cristal, mal, metal,*

---

[1] See *Gr. Comp.* p. lx. lv.—vii. and for the consonant terminations of the Italian dialects, p. 307—409. He makes the same supposition with regard to the addition of the euphonic vowel to the Spanish nouns, ib. p. xxxv.

[2] Sometimes *e* is used for *o*, as in *stile* for *stilo* from *stilus, padrone* from *patronus*, and in the termination *iere* from *arius*: (see below, § 4,) sometimes *o* is used for *e*, as *vimo* for *vime* from *vimen, povero* from *pauper, lavoro* from *labor, albero* from *arbor, consolo* from *consul, rubero* from *ruber*: sometimes *a* is used for *e*, as *sirena* from *siren, duca* from *dux*. Some changes of final vowels produced by the genders will be explained below, § 3. *Duolo*, which Castelvetro *on Bembo, Prose*, vol. ii. p. 19, (Naples, 1714,) mentions as an irregular form, is probably not derived from *dolor*, but from the ancient Teutonic word *dol, suffering*, preserved in the Scotch *dule*. See *Meidinger in Dulden*. The Italian has *dolore*, regularly formed from *dolor*.

quintal, sal, senescal, signal, val, (*Gr. Comp.* p. 33,) and I will ask him to calculate how many million chances to one there are, that a person ignorant of Latin (which we must take to be the condition of his Romance euphonist) does not err in adding to these words their vowel terminations? Nor is this all: but we are called on to believe that where the Provençal had reduced the Latin *u* to the meagre sound of *e*, as in *diable, secle,* etc., the Italian retraced its steps and returned to the fuller vowel. The invariable progress of language is to shorten long forms, and to attenuate full sounds: and we would as willingly believe that the Tiber and Ebro in the middle ages ran up to their sources, as that the languages of Spain and Italy, having once been identical with the Provençal, returned to their present state. It cannot be doubted that when the practice had once been established, that all the Italian words ended with a vowel, the euphonic *e* and *o* were sometimes added to consonant terminations, and I have already had and shall hereafter have occasion to point out some instances, such as *speme, animale, sono, hanno,* etc., where the final vowel is plainly owing to the love of euphony[1]: the difference between my opinion and M. Raynouard's is, that what he considers the rule, I consider as the exception, and what he considers as arbitrary, I consider as regulated by fixed principles.

The argument which M. Raynouard founds on the absence of vowel terminations in the dialects of Upper Italy deserves a full investigation, as there can be no doubt that the lower orders and provincial districts com-

[1] See above, p. 72.

monly preserve the ancient language with the greatest
fidelity. In most of these dialects the nouns, verbs,
participles, prepositions, adverbs, and other parts of
speech, have not the vowel terminations which prevail
in the written Italian language, but follow the system
perceptible in the Provençal and French. Thus they
say *sacc, vin, bianch, nemic, fuog, bosc, mond, camp, nav,
paradis, abiss, sabbat, libertat, argent, digest, sacerdot, nativ,*
etc. Numerals from five to nine are *sinch, ses, sett, ott,
nov:* participles, present and past, and gerunds, *parland,
volend, tocat, fatt, miss, mort:* first persons of verbs, *perd,
parl, demand:* third persons of verbs, *dorm, pend, cognoss:*
adverbs and prepositions, *poc, quand, trop, ades, apress,
vers, mezz, inanz, altrament.* The examples collected by
M. Raynouard (from which the above words are taken)
refer only to the dialects of Piedmont, Engaddine in the
Tyrol, Milan, Bergamo, Mantua, Friuli, Ferrara, and
Bologna. It would require more local knowledge than
a foreigner can pretend to possess in order to trace the
exact line of demarcation between the Italian dialects
which have the vowel terminations, and those which
have not; but the following description may probably be
considered as an approximation to the truth. The dialects of the Provençal run into Piedmont both on the
west and north: in Piedmont, however, an Italian dialect
with consonant terminations begins, and it reaches through
part of the Grisons, over the districts of Milan, Bergamo,
Pavia, Parma, Brescia, Cremona, Mantua, Modena, the
Italian vallies of the Tyrol, Friuli, the territory of Tre-
viso, and those of Ferrara and Bologna. In the west
and east, it does not extend into the Genoese, Venetian,
Vicentine, Paduan, and Veronese territories: and towards

the south the vowel terminations first appear in Tuscany and Romagna. Throughout all the rest of Italy the vowel terminations are as prevalent in the local dialects and in the mouths of the lowest classes, as in the written language[1]: and, as far as our knowledge extends, have ever been so: the anonymous history of Roman affairs in the fourteenth century written by a contemporary in the Roman dialect[2], and the Chronicle of M. Spinello written in the thirteenth century in the Apulian dialect[3] precisely agree in this respect with the language of the present day. M. Raynouard's argument would have great weight, if over the whole of Italy the lower orders used a dialect which wanted the final vowels: in that case it might be said that the ancient language is always most faithfully preserved among uneducated persons, and in mountainous or secluded districts; and that the upper classes, from their love of a harmonious and flowing language, had softened the rough pronunciation of their forefathers. But this is not so: the lower orders of southern Italy and Sicily speak a language which even luxuriates in vowels beyond the written Italian: and although the vowel terminations may have been introduced among the upper ranks of northern Italy, there is no reason to suppose that they were not

[1] For an account of the dialects of Southern Italy see the *Foreign Quarterly Review*, vol. v. p. 158—90. [Compare the work of Biondelli, above, page 44, note [1].]

[2] This history (which contains the life of the celebrated Cola di Rienzo) is printed in Muratori, *Ant. It.* vol. iii. p. 251—548. It is written, according to Muratori, p. 240, 'vulgi Romani dialecto, quæ fortassis a Neapolitana eo tempore parum distabat.' See a passage of it rendered into the Roman of the present day in Perticari, *Dif. di D.* c. 36.

[3] Murat, *Script. Rer. It.* vol. viii.

always in use among the rudest peasants in the remotest corners of Tuscany[1], the states of the Church, of Naples, Calabria, and Sicily. It appears to me that the Italian[2] must be considered as divided into two principal dialects, one with vowel, the other with consonant terminations. The latter of these, (which closely resembles the French and Provençal) probably owed its characteristics to the same causes which gave a peculiar form to the latter languages; viz. the larger proportion of Germans who occupied Gaul and northern Italy, as compared with those who settled in southern Italy and Spain. The Lombard kingdom, which was the principal Teutonic establishment of Italy, had its head quarters at Pavia; and along the Alps and in the Tyrol[3], the Italians came in actual contact with a German population. Friuli, moreover, and the north-eastern angle of Italy, was the highroad by which armies of Germans continually poured into Italy. And generally it may be observed, that it was in the country lying between the Alps, the Apennines, and the Exarchate, that the German influence was most strongly felt[4]. It is remarkable, however, that

[1] Any body who has heard the harsh and guttural pronunciation of the peasants of Tuscany will not easily believe that considerable changes were introduced into their language for the sake of euphony.

[2] By the Italian I understand that language which makes the masc. plural in *i* and the fem. plural in *e*.

[3] M. Raynouard remarks that 'le voisinage et même le mélange de la langue allemande ont influé surtout sur la prononciation du patois d'Engaddine.' *Gr. Comp.* p. liii. Engaddine is the valley of the Inn on the west of the Tyrol. The language of the Sette Communi, a part of the Vicentine territory, is a nearly pure Teutonic dialect, as may be seen from the specimens of it given in Rose's *Letters from the North of Italy*, vol. i. p. 257—8, and in the *Journal of Education*, No. xii. p. 353.

[4] Few Germans established themselves in the Duchy of Rome

although the consonant dialect occupies so considerable a space in the north-eastern part of Italy, it misses the districts of Venice and Padua, as it does the two *rivieras* of Genoa on the west. Whether this is owing to the influence of the sea-coast in the formation of language (according to the opinion of some philologists[1]) or to the comparative exemption enjoyed by those countries from the inroads and dominion of the Teutonic races, (particularly in the case of Venice,) I shall not pretend to determine: certain, however, it is, that the dialects of these districts, though widely differing both from the written Italian and from one another, have not the chief part of the consonant terminations which distinguish all the other dialects of northern Italy[2].

The statement which M. Raynouard quotes from Giambullari's treatise on the origin of the Florentine language, seems at first sight to prove that the consonant terminations once extended so far south as the city of Florence, and therefore requires our attention. Giambullari was a Florentine, born in 1495, who in 1546 published the first work written by a Tuscan on his native tongue. In this treatise (composed in the form of a dialogue) he undertakes to refute the common

---

and the Exarchate, according to Savigny, *Gesch. des Röm. Rechts*, vol. i., p. 305.

[1] See Müller's *Dorians*, vol. ii. p. 468.

[2] The Venetian dialect is divided between the southern and northern dialects: thus it says, *amigo, capo, carne, carità, caratere, potente, abate, fiume;* but *carbon, corexton, fior, amorin;* and it omits the final *e* of the infinitive, and says *amar, perder, sentir*. See Boerio, *Dizionario del Dial. Veneziano*. Venice, 1829. A specimen of the Paduan dialect of the sixteenth century (which closely resembles the Venetian) may be seen in Sismondi, *Litt. du Midi*, vol. ii. p. 239, c. 15, ad fin.

opinion, that the Florentine or written Italian language, was a corruption of the Latin; and proposes to show that it was derived from the ancient Etruscan: which language he conceives to have been allied to the Hebrew and Chaldean. Having offered various proofs of the affinity of the Etruscan, Hebrew, and Florentine languages, he represents one of the interlocutors in the dialogue as quoting a sonnet written by a certain Agatone Drusi of Pisa, in which the poet says, that 'if his *grande avolo*, who was the first to join the Sicilian with the Tuscan mode of speech, had left any works, as he intended, he would be greater than all the modern poets, including Dante[1].' The person referred to (Giambullari proceeds to say) is supposed to have been named Lucio Drusi, who wrote a poem on virtue, and another on the life of a lover, which were lost in the sea as he was taking them to the king in Sicily. The writer then argues, that as this Lucio Drusi was not great, either in arms or learning, Agatone does not mean by *grande avolo*, 'the great man his grandfather,' but 'his ancestor beyond the fifth degree:' whence he reckons five generations, or one hundred and fifty years, from the time of

[1] Se'l grande avolo mio, *che fu'l primiero*
 Che'l parlar Sicilian giunse col nostro,
 Lassato avesse un' opera d'inchiostro,
 Come sempre che visse ebbe in pensiero,
 Non sarebbe oggi in pregio il buon Romiero,
 Arnaldo provenzal, nè Beltram vostro.
 * * * * * * *
 Non Brunellesco o Dante sarian letti.
 Chè la luce di questo unico sole
 Sola riluceria lungi e da presso.
 Giamb. *Origine della Lingua Fiorentina*,
 p. 243. ed Milan, 1827.

Agatone Drusi, and thus fixes Lucio Drusi in 1170
A. D., the tenth year of William, king of Sicily; the
latter is therefore the king who was so unfortunate as
not to receive the two poems. The date of L. Drusi
being thus ascertained, it is asked in what manner he
joined the Sicilian and Tuscan modes of speech: and
Giambullari answers this question by saying that 'the
ancient Tuscans ended most of their words with consonants, *as might be seen from the very ancient Etruscan
words before mentioned in the dialogue*, while the Sicilians,
on the other hand, ended them with vowels: that L.
Drusi (as it is said) began to soften that harshness, not
by adopting foreign words, but by adding vowels at the
end of all the Tuscan words. This custom (he continues)
did not please many persons in Drusi's lifetime, but after
his death the Tuscans began to follow the practice introduced by him, not only in poetry, but even in prose and
in conversation.' This is the substance of Giambullari's
argument; and in the first place it may be remarked,
that the proceeding by which the date of L. Drusi's
compositions is fixed, appears somewhat arbitrary: for
Agatone Drusi might have called his ancestor a great
man, especially as he doubts not of his superiority to
Dante, even if he had never been a great commander or
doctor[1]. But the statement which more concerns the
subject in question, viz. that the Tuscans formerly ended

[1] The existence of Ag. Drusi was at first doubted by Tiraboschi,
Stor. della Litt. Ital., tom. iv., lib. 3. c. 3 § 2, and after him by Pignotti,
Storia di Toscana, vol. iv. p. 68. Tiraboschi, however, in the later
editions of his work, showed that his former suspicion was unfounded,
but justly considered Giambullari's argument as to the antiquity of L.
Drusi as untenable. L. Drusi probably wrote in the last half of the
thirteenth century.

all their words in consonants, seems to me nothing more than an imagination of Giambullari, made in order to support his baseless speculations on the affinity of the ancient and modern languages of Tuscany. The expression in the sonnet refers, as I conceive, to the influence of the Sicilian poetry on the ancient writers of Tuscany, and to their imitation of the earliest Italian compositions in an elevated and refined style[1]: and not to any change in the structure of the Tuscan language. Giambullari, however, seizes on this passage, grafts on it a false interpretation, supported by a statement which he gives only as a report[2], in order to strengthen his proofs of a theory which now would on all hands be admitted to be utterly devoid of foundation: and he would have us believe that a certain Lucio Drusi, who wrote in the middle of the twelfth century two poems that were lost in the sea, persuaded the whole population of Tuscany to change one of the most important characteristics of their language. It has been said, that Augustus, though master of the Roman world, could not alter the meaning of a Latin word: how fortunate then was this obscure rhymer, whose example induced a whole nation, in an unlettered age, not merely to change the meaning of a word, but to remodel their entire language[3]! The stress

[1] See Perticari, *Difesa di Dante*, c. 4—7.

[2] *Dicono* adunque che Lucio, considerando la nostra pronunzia e la Siciliana, etc. p. 245.

[3] If the ancient Tuscan had really been characterised by consonant terminations, the attempt of any individual to change that characteristic would probably have been as successful as that of Frederic the Great to add vowels at the end of the German words, or of Dr. Murray to effect the same improvement in the English language. See the article on English orthography in the *Philol. Mus.* vol. i. The only instance of such a change with which I am acquainted, is in some of the negro

which M. Raynouard lays on this passage of a treatise evidently belonging to the infancy of philology, and abounding in the wildest dreams about the history and languages of Italy, would have reminded me of the eagerness with which a drowning man catches at a straw, if his views were not supported by so many other proofs of a more substantial character[1].

As to the practice of cutting off the final vowel after a liquid consonant in Italian, which M. Raynouard considers as a proof that the vowel was originally added for the sake of euphony, it is to be observed that the Italian writers, especially in poetry, assume the privilege of suppressing it, not merely where M. Raynouard supposes it to have been arbitrarily added, but also in cases where it has manifestly been retained from the Latin: thus the poets contract both *amore* and *amori* into *amor*, both *Romano* and *Romani* into *Roman*[2].

For example, in the verses of Dante:

Perchè i Pisan veder Lucca non ponno
Inf., c. 33, l. 30.
Poiche i vicini a te punir son lenti
ib. l. 81.

son is contracted from *sono* by the rejection of a final

corruptions of the English (see above, p. 22, note[1]); and this, we may be assured, was not made at the suggestion, or by the authority of any individual. Comp. p. 34, note[1].

[1] The same passage of Giambullari is likewise cited with approbation by Perticari, *Dif. di D.*, c. 20; who adds the equally unfounded supposition that the Sicilians derived their final vowels from the Æolic dialect of the Greeks inhabiting their island.

[2] 'E da sapere (says Castelvetro) che tutti i nomi i quali potevano nel numero minore lasciare la *e* o vero lo *o*, potranno similmente nel maggiore lasciare lo *i*.' Bembo, *Prose*, vol. i. p. 80.

vowel not traceable to the Latin, and evidently added for the mere sake of euphony: *veder* and *punir* are contracted from *vedere* and *punire* by the rejection of the final *e*, which appears unquestionably to be retained from the Latin, though this is denied by M. Raynouard: *Pisan*, however, contracted from *Pisani*, is evidently not formed, according to M. Raynouard's own view, by the rejection of an euphonic termination: so that his mode of accounting for the practice of the Italian writers in omitting final vowels is not applicable in all cases; and consequently there is no reason for supposing that those vowels which may be elided were originally added for the sake of euphony. M. Raynouard, likewise, mentions in proof of his assertion with respect to the recent addition of the final vowels in Italian, the name of Boccacio's collection of novels, which by the author was written *Decameron*, but was afterwards changed into *Decamerone*. This example, however, has no weight: *Decameron* was a Greek word which had not passed through the Latin into popular usage, but was first employed by Boccacio himself. If it had thus come into general use, it would doubtless, like *fenomeno* and *lessico*, have been modified into *Decamero*. As it was, Boccacio introduced it into Italian without any change, as Dante employed many uncommon proper names with their consonant terminations, as *Minos, Semiramis, Empedocles, Austeric*, etc. The vowel terminations of the Italian nouns were, however, as firmly and universally established in the times of Dante and Boccacio as at the present day. As to the peculiarities of Barsape, mentioned by M. Raynouard, they may probably be referred to the dialect of his native city, from which this early Milanese writer had perhaps not quite emancipated himself: nevertheless the language of this poet (in Perticari's opinion) little differs from that of the early classical writers of Italian[1].

It appears, therefore, that there is no ground for assenting to M. Raynouard's conclusion that the final vowels in Italian were arbitrarily added, at a recent date, for the sake of euphony. Indeed it appears to me that the written remains of that language, so far as they reach, afford every reason for believing that the prevalence of vowel terminations was one of its earliest characteristics: in the Latin documents of Italy, which are of an earlier date than any compositions in the Romance languages, whenever any Italian word or name is accidentally inserted, it almost invariably exhibits the vowel termination, even in charters belonging to the northern states[2]: whence it seems to me much more

[1] *Dif. di Dante*, c. 20.
[2] For example, the names *Petro, Martino, Geminiano, Benedicto, Domminico, Bonoaldo, Raginberto, Lanfranco, Sigefredo, Ingelberto*, some of which are of Roman, others of German origin, occur in a document of Lemonte near Lake Como, A.D. 882: and another of Modena, about 980 A.D. published in Muratori, *Ant. It.* vol. iii. p. 747, 793: and see other instances, from deeds, of the use of the vowel terminations in Italian, during the tenth and eleventh centuries, in Murat. *Diss.* 32, vol. ii. p. 1030, B.—1037, D. Muratori, vol. ii. p. 1047, B. cites the following verses, which were inscribed in the ancient cathedral of Ferrara:

>Il mile cento trempta cinque nato
>Fo questo templo a Zorzi consecrato.
>Fo Nicolao scolptore
>E Glielmo fo lo autore.

If this inscription was not set up in the year 1135 A.D. its date, probably, is not much later. A diploma of Roger, Count of Calabria and Sicily, in 1122 A.D., published in Ughelli, *Italia Sacra*. tom. viii. Part I. col. 201, contains many Italian words with vowel terminations.

probable that the dialects of upper Italy originally had vowel terminations, and afterwards lost them, than that the dialects of southern Italy, having originally wanted them, afterwards added them for the sake of euphony.

The impossibility of the derivation of the Italian and Spanish languages from the Provençal is evidenced not only by the retention of the final vowels from the Latin which the Provençal had thrown away, but by the contraction or alteration of many Latin words in the latter language, which the former languages exhibit in a completer and less altered state. But if they had come from the Latin through the medium of the Provençal, this difference could not have been perceptible: the water must have tasted of the impure channel through which it had passed.

Latin.	Provençal.	French.	Italian.	Spanish.
medicus	metge[1]		medico	medico
lingua	lengua	langue	lingua	lengua
sæculum	segle	siècle	secolo	siglo
oculus	huel	œuil	occhio	ojo
auricula	aurelha	oreille	orecchia	oreja
diabolus	diable	diable	diavolo	diablo
latro	lairon	larron	ladrone	ladron
pater	paire	père	padre	padre
pavor	paor	peur	[2]	pavor
frater	fraire	frère	frate	fratre
mundus	mon	monde	mondo	mundo
nepos	nibot	neveu	nipote	nepote
undecim	unze	onze	undici	once

[1] In this list both the Provençal and French masculine nouns are exhibited without the final *s*, as the object is merely to compare the internal changes in the words.

[2] The Italian has not preserved the word *pavor*. *Paura*, like the Spanish *pavura*, is a fem. substantive in *ura*, formed from the verb *pavere*: see below, § 4, on the termination *ura*.

CHAPTER II.

Latin.	Provençal.	French.	Italian.	Spanish.
sol	solel	soleil	sole	sol
spes	esper	espoir[1]	speme	
eleemosyna	almorna	aumosne	limosina	limosna
episcopus	evesque	evesque	vescovo	obispo[2]

[1] The French *oi* sometimes came from the Latin *e*, as in the terminations of verbs, avoir from aver, valoir from valer, etc. (*Gr. Comp.* p. 257—60), te toi; tres trois; tect-um, toit; mes, mois; sometimes from the Latin *i*, as digitus, degt, doigt, pix, peç, poix: sometimes from *o*, as gloria, gloire, vox, voix, Ambrosius, Ambroise: sometimes from *u*, as punctum point, unctum oint, jungere joindre; sometimes from *au*, as claustrum cloitre. In the two latter cases, *u* and *au* doubtless became first *o*, then *oi*.

[2] *Bispo*, the Portuguese form of *episcopus*, occurs in a Latin charter of Alboacem, a Moorish king of Coimbra, of the year 734. Rayn. vol. i. Introd. p. xi. At so early a period (as Schlegel remarks, p. 49,) were the peculiarities of the Romance languages developed. The genuineness of the document in question has, however, been doubted: thus Southey, *Chronicle of the Cid*, p. 406, has the following remarks on it. 'This charter, like the funeral urn of Achilles, the tomb of Alexander, and the relics of the archangel Michael, is the more to be suspected because it would be of such exceeding value, if genuine. It may be doubted whether a Moorish governor, at so early an age, would give charters in Latin, whether at any age he would use the sign of the cross for his mark, and whether the language into which the Latin is corrupted be not of a more modern complexion. But the exemption, if it be forged, could be of no use after Coimbra was recovered by the Christians: so that even in that case it is of very curious antiquity, and may truly state the laws to which the Christians were subject.' There does not, however, appear to be any reason why a Moorish governor should not have given a charter to his Christian subjects in the language which they understood, and which was at that time and long afterwards universally employed by all the Christians of western Europe for the composition of both public and private documents. As to the use of the cross, it is expressly mentioned in the charter that he employed it 'rogatu Christianorum,' in compliance with the wishes of the grantees: and there is no reason to doubt that so many years after the invasion of the Goths, a Romance language was currently spoken in Spain. Gibbon, c. 51, n. 187, citing the substance of this charter from Fleury's *Ecclesiastical History* says: 'I have not the original before me; it would confirm or destroy a dark

On comparing these instances it will be seen that in some cases the Italian and Spanish, and especially the former, do not exhibit the modifications of the Latin word which appear in the Provençal: in others, that the same Latin word has been modified differently in the three languages. The Provençal likewise admits many occasional contractions and changes which do not appear in the Italian: thus

Latin.	Provençal.	French.	Italian.	Spanish.
nox	nueyt or nueg	nuit	notte	noche
septimana	sotmana or semmana	semaine	settimana	semana

Another difference between the several Romance languages consists in prefixing the vowel *e* to words beginning with *s* followed by a consonant[1]; a practice which the Spanish always observes, the Provençal and French often, the Italian never. The following examples will illustrate the manner in which the Italian has avoided this change admitted by the Provençal.

Latin.	Italian.	Provençal.	Spanish.	French.
stare	stare	estar	estar	estre (être)
spiritus	spirito	esperit	espiritu	esprit
strata	strada	estrada	estrada	estrade
sperare	sperare	esperar	esperar	esperer
scutum	scudo		escudo	escu (écu)
sclavus	schiavo	esclav	esclavo	esclave
	stoppa	estopa	estopa	estoupe (étoupe)

suspicion that the piece has been forged to introduce the immunity of a neighbouring convent.' Gibbon, however, was prone to suspect fraud when ecclesiastics were concerned.

[1] Meidinger, in his *Teutogothic Dictionary*, p. 82, completely mistakes the nature of this euphonic vowel prefixed only to words beginning with *s* followed by a consonant, in calling it a 'particle,' and comparing it with significant prefixes, such as *ge* in High German, and *a* in Anglo-Saxon.

The Spanish has no word beginning with *s* followed by a consonant: invariably it prefixes *e* to avoid the concourse of consonants: the Italian, on the other hand, seems rather to seek this sound, since in some cases it even rejects an initial *e* before *s* with a consonant, as *state* for *estate* from *æstas*, *stimare* for *estimare* from *æstimare*, *sperto* for *esperto* from *expertus;* in some cases it prefixes *s* to a word beginning with a consonant, as *spergiuro* from *perjurus*, *sprofondare* from *profundus*, etc.; and the prefix *dis* is always curtailed to a simple *s*, as *spietato*, *sbarcare*, *scavalcare*, etc. It is to be observed, however, that although the Italian rather seeks than avoids the concourse of *s* with a consonant at the beginning of a word, yet when the preceding word ends with a consonant (which rarely happens) it prefixes the vowel *i*, as *con isdegno*, and not *con sdegno*.

The French seems originally to have had the same tendency as the Spanish of prefixing *e* to *s* followed by a consonant; but the tendency was not so strong as to make the practice universal, and many words were formed in it without this change. It is obvious, on looking through the two classes of words which have and which have not undergone this change, that the former belong to an early period of the French language, and that the latter are of a more learned and less popular character, and have been formed with a view of adhering closely to the Latin originals: thus *scapula, schola, spatha, spatium, spina, sponsus, stagnum, stannum, stabulum, status, stella, scabinus, schaum,* have become *espaule, escole, espée, espace, espine, espour, estang, estain, estable, estat, estoile, eschevin, escume*: while *scandalum, sculptor, statua, statutum, stipulatio, stratagema, structura, stylus,* have become *scandale, sculpteur, statue, statut, stipulation, stratagème, structure, style*. In some cases there is both an ancient and a modern derivative from the same Latin root: thus from *stomachus* is the old word *estomac*, but from *stomachicus* comes the modern medical term *stomachique*; from *studium étude*, but from *studiosus studieux*.

There are also many words in which the Italian has retained the Latin *p*, while the Provençal and Spanish have changed it into *b*, the French into *v*[1]: thus

Latin.	Italian.	Spanish.	Provençal.	French.
aperire	aprire	abrir	abrir	ouvrir
aprilis	aprile	abril	abril	avril
capillus	capello	cabello	cabel	cheveu
capra	capra	cabra	cabra	chèvre
capistrum	capestro	cabestro	cabestre	chevestre
juniperus	ginepro	enebro	genibre	genievre
opera	opera	obra	obra	oeuvre
sepelire	seppellire	sepelir	sebelir	en-sevelir
sapere	sapere	saber	saber	savoir
sapor	sapore	sabor	sabor	savour

In some cases, however, the Italian has changed the Latin *p* into *v*; as in *riva* from *ripa*, and in *povero* from *pauper*.

In the Provençal likewise may be discerned the tendency which has been very prevalent in the French, but of which there is scarce a trace in Italian and Spanish, of changing *c* before *a* into *ch*: thus from *cantare* the Prov. has both *cantar* and *chantar*, *chanter* French; from *cantio*, *canson* and *chanson*, *chanson* French.

The following differences have prevailed in the Romance

[1] See Rayn. *Gr. Comp.* p. xxvi., Grimm, *Deutsche Rechtsalterthümer*, p. 776. On this change in Spanish, see Mayans i Siscar, vol. ii. p. 146.

languages with respect to the changes undergone by the Latin *c* before vowels.

In Latin *c* before all vowels was equivalent to *k*; thus *ca, ce, ci, co, cu=ka, ke, ki, ko, ku*.

In Italian *c* has retained the sound of *k* before *a, o,* and *u*; as *caro, coro, cura*: but it has become *ch* before *e* and *i*, as *Cerere, cinque* (according to the English pronunciation, *cherere, chinque*[1]).

In Spanish, as in Italian, the *c* retains the sound of *k* before *a, o,* and *u*; but before *e* and *i* it has the force of *th*, as *Ceres, cinco*, (pronounced *theres, thinco*.)

The French *c* before *a* has usually become *ch*, as *carus, cher; caro, chair; camera, chambre; capra, chèvre; castanea, châtaigne; carmen, charme; caput, chef; calidus, chaud; calvus, chauve; caulis, choux; scabinus, eschevin; karr, char; bucca, bouche; musca, mouche,* etc. : before *e* and *i* it is pronounced like *s*, as *ceci*, (pronounced *sesi* :) before *o* and *u* it has (as in Italian and Spanish) retained the sound of *k*, as *comme, contre, couleur, col, corde, corps, culte, curé, courbe.* Not unfrequently, however, the Latin *c* has remained unchanged before *a*: but (as has been already remarked of the prefix *e* before *s* and a consonant) in words which belong to a later period of the language, and which have a more learned aspect; as *cadavre, calomnie, canal, candide, canon, capable, capituler, caractère, cataracte, catégorie,* etc. Sometimes there is a double derivative from the same word, as in the following examples:

[1] It will be observed that this statement only applies to the southern Italian dialect with vowel terminations: that of the north with consonant terminations, pronounces the *c* like the French. (See above, p. 95). In Tuscany the sound of *c* before *e* and *i* has been softened, so that it is pronounced like *sh* in English.

Latin.	Ancient French.	Recent French.
calx	chaux	calquer
canonicus	chanoine	canonique
capitulus	chapitre¹	capitule
captivus	chetif	captif
capra	chèvre	caprice
carbo	charbon	carbon
carta	charte	carte
causa	chose	cause

Chevalier and *chevalerie* were the ancient forms from *cheval* (*caballus;*) *cavalier* and *cavalerie* were probably borrowed from the Italian. From *canis* was formed *chien;* but from *canicula canicule;* from *candela chandelle*, but from *candelabrum candélabre*.

It is obvious that these diversities of pronunciation could not have been borrowed by the Romance languages from each other, or from any one common origin: but that they must have been produced by the separate workings of each, and by the different vocal organization of the populations by which they were spoken. Nor is there any reason to suppose that they were of recent introduction: for we know that at the Sicilian vespers the French were distinguished from the Italians by being made to pronounce the words *ceci* and *ciceri;* and consequently the characteristic peculiarities of the French and Italian pronunciation were as firmly established at the end of the thirteenth century as at the present day; and it will be observed that in the pronunciation of *c* before *e* and *i*, *both* these languages differed from the Latin; thus CECI according to the Latin pronunciation would be *keki*, according to the Italian *chechi*, according to the French *sesi*.

¹ *Chapitre* from *capitulus* like *épitre* from *epistola*, *titre* from *titulus*.

CHAPTER II.

§ 3. GENDERS OF NOUNS.

With regard to the genders of nouns, it may be observed that as the use of them, like that of cases, requires some knowledge and discrimination, they are naturally destroyed or confounded by the same causes which lead to the destruction of inflexions, and the substitution of analytic for synthetic forms. Thus the Anglo-Saxon genders were lost at the Norman conquest: and the English only retains the natural genders; that is to say, no nouns have any gender which do not designate male or female individuals[1]. The influence of

[1] This appears to me to be a correct statement of the English usage of genders: our language never marks genders except by the use of the pronouns *he* and *she*, the former of which refers to males, the latter to females: of the relative *who*, which refers either to males or females, and of *it* and *which*, which refer only to inanimate things. The neuter forms *it* and *which* are commonly used in speaking of brute animals, especially where the sex is not apparent, as in insects, fish, birds, etc.: but never in speaking of the human race, except sometimes of infants. Whenever *he* and *she* are applied to an inanimate thing, as to the sun, the moon, a country, or a quality of the mind, the object is personified: the same is also the case with a ship, which a sailor personifies, in order to represent it as an object of affection. In all cases where *he* or *she* is applied to an inanimate thing, it would be correct, though perhaps not so energetic or suitable to the expression, to employ the neuter pronoun. It appears to me, therefore, that the state of things which Grimm anticipates, viz. that ' the English language will at some future time limit the use of *he* and *she* to persons, and in all other cases employ *it*,' (vol. iii. p. 547,) has already arrived, and has indeed existed for some centuries. Our language has no grammatical genders: the masculine, feminine, and neuter pronouns are applied with reference, not to the noun itself, but to that which the noun signifies. Whereas in languages which have grammatical genders, the noun itself has a certain gender, without reference to the sex or animation of the object signified: thus in Greek παιδίον is neuter, πέτρα is feminine, and αἰγιαλός masculine, although a child is either male or female, and a rock and a shore are lifeless objects.

the German conquest on the Latin language, as in other
respects it was not so great as that of the Norman
conquest on the Anglo-Saxon language, so likewise in
respect of genders it did not produce so considerable a
change: but it left the masculine and feminine genders
of nouns, and only destroyed the neuter gender. In
all the Romance languages the Latin genders of nouns
were, for the most part, preserved unchanged, with this
general exception, that all the neuter nouns became
masculine[1]. The close coincidence of the inflexions of
masculine and neuter nouns in Latin, as *caballus* and
damnum, sol and *sal*, naturally led to this confusion[2].
The resemblance of these two genders, sufficiently great
in the Latin, was moreover increased by the changes
in the form of nouns which took place in the Romance
languages: for in the Ital. and Span. the forms in *us*
and *um* were identified by the use of the acc. case; since
caballum, damnum, or their derivatives in *o*, had the same
invariable termination; and in the Prov. and French the
general adoption of the Latin nom. terminations produced a similar identity, as those words became *cavals*
and *dans*. Hence in Ital. and Span. the nouns in *o*,
and in Prov. and French those in *s*, were together as
masculines generally opposed to feminine nouns in *a*.
Besides this universal change of neuter into masculine
nouns, there are, however, particular deviations in the
Romance nouns from the Latin gender; in some of
which the reason is apparent, in others it is more
obscure.

[1] Some pronouns in Provençal and Spanish preserved the neuter
form; see below, chap. 3.
[2] See Grimm, vol. iii. p. 542.

In the first place the Italian changed the gender of some nouns of the third declension, as *arbore, fronte, acre, carcere, cenere, fine, folgore, fonte, margine, ordine*, which it made both masculine and feminine[1]. Whereas in Latin the two first were always feminine, and the eight last always masculine. The Spanish, likewise, has changed the gender of several nouns of this declension: thus *carcel, fuente, leche, legumbre, miel, sal*, are feminine; *arte, dote, canal, mar, margen, orden, fuente*, are of both genders. In Provençal *carcer, dens, fons, mar*, are feminine; *arbre* is masculine. In French, likewise, many Latin nouns have changed their gender without any apparent reason, as *dent, font, mer, mode, obole*, have become feminine; *corn* in old French was masculine, (*Gr. Comp.* p. 65;) *cor* is now masculine, but *corne* is feminine; *arbre, art, été, ongle, salut, sort*, have become masculine; *hymne* is of both genders[2]. Moreover, in the Latin nouns making *orem* in the accusative singular, which the Provençal adopted without further alteration, than the addition of *s* to the truncated accusative, it changed the gender from masculine to feminine, except in those words which signified a male. Thus from the Latin *amor, color, dolor, dulcor, flos, honor, sapor, timor, valor*, were formed the Provençal *amors, colors, dolors, doussors, flors, honors, sabors, temors, valors*, feminine; *lavors*, however, from *labor*, retained its masculine gender[3]. The old French preserved the same terminations,

[1] Castelvetro *on Bembo*, vol. ii. p. 26.
[2] Grimm, vol. iii. p. 560, cites *souris* fem. from *sorex* masc. as an instance of this change of gender in French. *Sorex*, however, being the name of an animal, was doubtless of both genders, and perhaps the feminine was familiarly used in preference, as in *sus* and *canis*.
[3] The following Provençal passage from Dante's *Purgatory*, canto

but likewise changed the gender: thus 'la bonne *amor*,'
'*l'amors* que Diex m'a commandée,' 'de bone *amor*,'
'sous la *color* de pitié,' 'la *dolors*,' 'la *flors*,' 'dont la
tenors estoit telle,' 'une des plus altes *honors*,' (*Gr. Comp.*
p. 59—61, 84.) This termination in *or*, when the *s*
had been disused, and the form of the acc. had supplanted that of the nom., was in French successively
changed into *our* and *eur*: and, with the exception of
words such as *acteur, auteur, seigneur,* from *actor, autor,
senior,* etc. which are necessarily masculine, and the
forms *labour,* and *labeur,* from *labor,* and *honneur* from
honor[1], which have retained the Latin gender, this termination is always feminine. Thus *ardeur, clameur,
chaleur, couleur, douleur, erreur, fleur, fureur, horreur,*

26, as restored from the Mss. by M. Raynouard, *Journ. des Sav.* 1830,
p. 67—78, clearly exhibits this change of gender:

> Tan m' abellis vostre cortes deman
> Ch'ieu non me puesc ni-m voil a vos cobrire;
> Ieu sui Arnautz, che plor e vai cantan;
> Consiros vei la passada follor,
> E vol jauzen lo joi qu'esper denan;
> Aras vos prec, per aquella valor
> Que us guida al som sens freich e sens calina,
> Sovegna vos stonprar me dolor.

That is, literally translated: 'So much does your courteous demand
please me that I neither can nor will conceal myself from you. I am
Arnald, who weep and go singing. Grieved I see the past folly, and
I see with pleasure the joy which I hope for the future. Now I entreat you by that virtue which guides you to the summit without cold
and without heat, that you will remember to assuage my grief.' For
further details relating to this passage, see Raynouard, *Journ. des. Sav.*
ubi sup. [*Lexique Roman,* vol. i. p. xlii. Blanc, *Vocabolario Dantesco,*
Art. Tan m' abellis.]

[1] *Honneur* was, however, feminine in old French, as in one of the
instances above cited.

116   CHAPTER II.

humeur, liqueur, mœurs, odeur, pâleur, peur, pudeur, rigueur, rumeur, saveur, splendeur, sueur, terreur, torpeur, tumeur, valeur, vapeur, vigueur, are feminine, although the Latin nouns from which they were derived are masculine. In their derivatives from these same nouns, the Italian and Spanish have constantly preserved the masculine gender[1]. It is difficult to say what induced both the Provençals and French to change the gender of so many Latin masculine nouns in *or*: probably, however, it was the tendency to designate abstract qualities by feminine nouns, so observable in the Latin language[2], which led to the deviation in question.

Other variations of gender, of which we can trace the cause, arose from the changes in the terminations of nouns which took place in the Romance languages. Thus in the modern languages *o* was generally the masculine, and *a* the feminine termination; and hence many forms in *o* derived from Latin feminine nouns became masculine, and many forms in *a* derived from Latin masculine or neuter nouns became feminine. In this manner all Latin feminine nouns of the second and fourth declensions became masculine in Italian, as *il pero, il melo, il fico, il duomo*, except *la mano* from *manus*[3]. The same change has likewise been made in Spanish: which, however, has preserved the feminine gender of *manus*. On the other hand, some masculine and neuter nouns in *a* have become feminine, as

---

[1] *Flor*, however, is feminine in Spanish, and *flore* was sometimes made feminine in old Italian: Perticari, *Dif. di Dante*, c. 13, vol. i. p. 323.

[2] See Grimm, vol. iii. p. 631.

[3] Castelvetro *on Bembo*, vol. i. p. 19.

aria, (from *aëra*,) *cometa, cresima, flemma, salma,* Ital.; *asma*, Span.; *anagramme, énigme,* French[1]; *fantasima* and *tema* in Ital., have both genders. On the other hand, *baptisma, psalma, sophisma*, having retained their genders, became *battesimo, salmo, sofismo,* in Ital.; *bautismo, salmo,* in Span., while *stigmata* plural in Ital. became *stimati*. Sometimes, however, the Ital. noun not only formed its plural according to the regular analogy, but also preserved the Latin plural in *ora* or *a*, as *i corpi* and *le corpora, i tempi* and *le tempora, i prati* and *le prata, i corni* and *le corna, gli ornamenti* and *le ornamenta,* etc.; and as in these cases the plural in *a* became feminine, it was sometimes changed into *e*, the regular feminine plural, as *gli ossi, le ossa,* and *le osse, i legni, le legna,* and *le legne*[2]. In some cases, moreover, the neuter plural of the Latin became the feminine singular of the Italian noun, thus *arma, strata, spolia, insignia*[3], *fata*[4], *pecora, folia, vela, ulcera,* became in Ital. *l'arma, la strada, la spoglia, l'insegna, la fata, la pecora, la foglia, la vela,* (the sail,) *la ulcera*[5]: so likewise in Span. *arma, bona, claustra, dona, fata, folia, insignia, plana, pecora, signa, strata, vela, ulcera,* Latin, became *l'arma, la bona, la claustra, la dona, la fada, la hoja, la*

---

[1] Popular usage had already made this change in Latin, in some words: thus *schema* (σχῆμα) is made feminine by Plautus and Suetonius, *glaucoma* (γλαύκωμα) by Plautus, etc.; see Scheller's *Latin Grammar*, by Walker, vol. i. p. 474.

[2] Castelvetro, ib., p. 21.

[3] Castelvetro, ib., p. 35.

[4] Manage, *Etym. Ital.*, in v.

[5] The Italian, however, likewise had the form *ulcero*, irregularly formed from *ulcus*, (above, p. 74, note [1],) now obsolete. It likewise preserved *il velo*, for *the veil*.

insegnia, la laña, la pecora, la seña, la estrada, la vela, la ulcera[1]. In French, likewise, we find *dépouilles, dette, étude, fée, feuille, huile, idole, livre, pomme, ulcère*, of the feminine gender. In Italian the Latin *millia* has become *miglia*, in the sense of *miles*; from the feminine plural *miglia*, the masculine singular *miglio* has been formed. In Spanish the Latin *millia* has become the feminine singular *milla*, in the sense of a mile; which makes *millas* in the plural. So in English *kitten* the plural of *cat*, *chicken* the plural of *chick*, *twin* the plural of *two*, *stocken*, (*stocking*) the plural of *stock*[2], and *garden* the plural of *geard* or *yard*, have become singular, because the ancient plural termination in *en*, like the Latin neuter plural in *a*, is no longer understood[3].

From this comparison of the changes which have taken place in the Latin genders, it appears that though all the Romance languages agree in retaining the masculine and feminine, and rejecting the neuter gender, and in changing the neuter into the masculine, yet that the Provençal has introduced innovations from which the Italian and Spanish are free, and in which it agrees remarkably with the French; and that the Italian has retained vestiges of the Latin which do not appear in the Provençal. These facts therefore are inconsistent with the supposition that the Provençal was the most ancient form of the Italian and Spanish languages.

[1] See Sanchez, *Poes. Castell*, vol. i. p. 392, 380, vol. iii. p. 302, 430, vol. iv. p. 307. [Other examples are given by Diez, *Rom. Gr.*, vol. ii., p. 21.]

[2] See Johnson, in *stocking*.

[3] *Holstein*, the proper name, (whence *Holsteiner*,) has in like manner been corrupted from *Holsten*, the plural of *Holsts*: see Grimm's *Deutsche Rechtsalterthümer*, p. 310, note.

§ 4. FORMATION OF NEW ROMANCE NOUNS BY AFFIXES.

M. Raynouard enters into a long comparison of the terminations of substantives in the Romance languages, and shows a great resemblance between the Provençal and the others, whence he would, as usual, infer the derivation of the latter from the former. (*Gr. Comp.* p. 23—71.) These similarities may be reduced to three heads.

1. *Those in which the Provençal has preserved the Latin word unchanged*, such as *barba, herba, comedia, bestia, forma, pluma, persona, aurora, animal,* etc. The agreement of the other languages with the Provençal in these forms evidently furnishes no proof of their derivation from the Provençal, as the Provençal and Latin are here the same. M. Raynouard seems occasionally to forget that the presumption is in favour of the Latin, and that the burden of proof lies on him to show that the Italian and Spanish came not from the Latin, but from another modern language.

2. *Those terminations which were formed from the inflexion of the Latin nouns*, as has been above explained. There would be nothing singular in different nations forming new substantives from the inflected cases, when they were influenced by the same causes, even if the agreement was perfect, which, as we have shown, it was not: inasmuch as the Provençal and French retained the termination of the Latin nom., of which there is no trace in the Italian and Spanish. Hence the agreement of the Italian and Spanish with the Provençal in such terminations as *metal, val, man, mar, part, trinitat, magis-*

trat, fren, orient, argument, mes, fin, marit, titol, leon, amor, carn, etc., affords no argument in favour of the derivation from the Provençal, as they are merely Latin words deprived of their terminations, a process which each language could doubtless have performed for itself without the intervention of the Provençal. Nor is it by any means true that the terminations of nouns agree in the different Romance languages; for M. Raynouard has only produced this exact correspondence by cutting off the only characteristic peculiarity which belongs to each language, and leaving what they have in common, the Latin type. Thus when he has omitted the final *s* of the Provençal and French, and the final vowel of the Italian and Spanish nouns, which are their distinctive and proper marks, it is easy to say that *amor* and *metal* are the same in all the four tongues: whereas in fact the Provençal and French forms are *amors* and *metals*, the Italian *amore* and *metallo*, the Spanish *amor* and *metallo*.

3. *Those substantives whose termination does not agree with the Latin, but is the same in the Romance languages.* M. Raynouard himself perceives the difference between this and the other two classes, and the assistance which these examples afford to his argument, though he does not admit that the other forms are just as consistent with the falsity as with the truth of his theory. 'If (ho says) many of the terminations pointed out come from the Latin, by the preservation of the entire word, as *animal*, etc., or by the omission of the final syllable which marked the case, as *pont-em*, there are many others which do not come directly from the Latin, and which have been introduced into all these languages, and joined to words to which the Latin annexed another

termination, as cor*age*, longu*age*, linh*age*, mess*age*, omen-*age*, vi*age*, etc., sign*al*, belt*at*, agn*el*, ann*el*, ram*el*, vass*el*, caval*ier*, corr*ier*, camp*ion*, cubert*or*, mirad*or*, servid*or*, etc. How could these different languages have agreed in rejecting the original Latin termination, in order to substitute a new one? Is it not evident that for this process a common type was indispensable?' *Gr. Comp.* p. 70. Now with regard to the words in question, it is to be observed that they have not rejected the Latin termination and substituted another of their own, like *altitudo*, for which the Italian and French said *altezza* and *hauteur*, but they are derivatives from Latin roots adopted in the Provençal: thus from *cor, lengua, via, vas, bel, servir*, etc., were formed *cor-age, lengu-age, vi-age, vas-sel, bel-tat, servi-dor*: the Latin, however, had no such substantives formed from *cor, lingua, via, vas, bellus, servire*, etc. Consequently these are not words which have rejected the Latin in order to substitute a different termination, but they are now derivatives formed in the Provençal from roots of its own. In order, however, to ascertain how far this argument of M. Raynouard's avails in support of his system, it will be necessary to examine, at some length, the subject of the terminations of nouns in the Romance languages.

With this view I will in the first place set down the formative terminations of nouns which the Romance languages have borrowed from the Latin, but have subjected respectively to various modifications.

Aoo, fem., as in *farrago, imago, indago, sartago, virago, vorago*, etc. The Romance languages, in forming their nouns from the accusative case, have subjected this termination to nearly the same changes: thus from *imago* the Italian makes *imagine*, the Spanish *imagen*, the Provençal and French, by the rejection of the final *n*, *image*.[1] Of all the modern languages the Italian alone appears to have formed new nouns with the termination *agine*, or *aggine*, as *dappocaggine, fanciullaggine, fantasticaggine, infingardaggine, insensataggine, scempiaggine, sciaguratag-gine, seccagine*, etc.[2]

ANTIA, ENTIA. Feminine nouns having this termination in Latin were derived from participles or participial adjectives in *ans* or *ens*, as *abundantia, diligentia, obedientia, petulantia, sapientia*. The Romance languages varied these terminations as follows; *anza, enza* Ital. and Prov., *anza, encia* Span., *ance, ence* French. Sometimes all the languages agreed in forming new derivatives with these terminations, as *tardanza* Ital. and Span., *tarzanza* Prov., *tardance* French, *decadenza* Ital., *decadencia* Span., *descaienza* Prov., *décadence* French. Sometimes each language formed separate words of its own, not occurring in the others: thus, *mancanza, vicinanza* Ital., *échéance, bienviellance, jactance, nuance* Fr. Sometimes also the corresponding words are derived from the forms peculiar to each language; thus *fidanza* Ital., from *fidare*, but *fianza* Span., and *fiance* French, from *fiar* and *fier*. *Credenza* Ital., from *credere, credencia*, and also *creencia* Span.,

---

[1] The Italian, likewise, has used the form *image*, which it has likewise changed into *imago*, like *uome* and *uomo*, etc., see above, p. 74. *Image* occurs in Dante, *Purg.* xxv. 26; *Par.* ii. 131; xiii. 2; xix. 2; on which latter place Lombardi says, '*Image* qui come altrove, ad. opera alla francese, per *immagine*.' M. Rayuouard mistakes the form of this word by comparing it with the masc. termination in *aggio*: Gr. *Comp.* p. 31. See below, in this termination.

[2] See Diez, *Rom. Gramm.* vol. ii. p. 317.

from *creer, credence, créance*, and *croyance* French, from *croire; possanza* Ital., *pujanza* Span., *puissance* French[1].

ANUS, IANUS. In Latin this was properly an adjectival termination, as *Romanus, urbanus, Christianus*. As proper names were often inflected with it, adjectives of this form frequently were used substantively, as *Romani, Pompeiani, Christiani*, etc. In the Romance languages it is usually a substantive termination: in Ital. *ano*, in Span. *ano* and *an*, in Prov. *an*, in French *an, ain* and *en*. Thus from *paganus* the Ital. and Span. have made *pagano*, the Prov. *pajan*, the French *payen*. Many modern words have been formed in the several languages with this termination: thus *scrivano* Ital., *escribano* Span., *escrivain* French, *sagrestano* Ital., *sacristan* Span., *sacristain* French. *Parmigiano, partigiano, maomettano* Ital., *cormanos, lozano, mahometano* Span., *hautain, luthérien, magicien, mahométan, parrain, paysan, Péruvien, prochain* French[2].

ARIUS, ARIS. The first of these terminations was common to both kinds of nouns in Latin, though properly belonging to adjectives, as *armentarius, nefarius, senarius:* the latter was confined to adjectives, as *militaris, vexillaris*. From *arius* the Italian has modified the several terminations *ario, aro, aio, iero, iere*[3], the Span. *ario, ero, er:* the Prov. *ari, ar, er*, and *ier;* the French *aire, er, ier,* (*Gr. Comp.* p. 35, 48.)[4] *Aris* in Ital. and Span. becomes *are* and *ar:* the French confounds it with the derivatives of *arius* under the terminations *aire* and *ier*, as the Prov. confounds them under the termination

---

[1] Diez, *Rom. Gramm.* vol. ii. p. 357.
[2] Diez, ib. p. 310.
[3] See Castelvetro *on Bembo*, vol. ii. p 23, and above p. 93, note [?].
[4] See also Raynouard, *Obs. sur le Roman de Rou*, p. 10.

ar: thus from *falsarius, militaris, Januarius,* and *singularis,* the French made *faussaire, militaire, Janvier, singulier;* and from *scholarius* and *familiaris* the Prov. made *escolar* and *familiar, (Gr. Comp.* p. 35, 110.) The following table of some Latin words shows the relation which the modern terminations bear to the ancient one.

Latin.	Italian.	Spanish.	French.
denarius	danaro, danaio	dinero	denier
forrarius	ferraio	herrero	ferrier
granarium	granaio	granero	grenier
Januarius	Gennaro, Gennaio	Enero	Janvier
librarius	libraio	librero	libraire
primarius	primario, primaio, primiero	primario, primero	primaire, premier
scutarius	scudiere	escudero	escuyer

When these modifications had once been established, a great number of new substantives were formed with them in all the languages.

Italian.	Spanish.	Prov.	French.
cavaliere	caballero	cavalier	cavalier *or* chevalier [1]
corriere *or* -ero	corriere	corrier	courrier
destriere [2]		destrier	destrier
falconiere	halconero	falconier	fauconier
guerriero	guerrero	guerrier	guerrier
pensiere *or* -ero			
prigionere -ero	prisionero	presonier	prisonier
sparviere -iero		esparvier	espervier
straniere	extrangero	estranher	estrangor

This termination has been much used in all the languages for the formation of new nouns, and in particular it has been employed after the model of the Latin,

---

[1] See above, p. 111.
[2] *i. e.* dextrarius. See Muratori in v.

which made *librarius, lignarius, ferrarius, vestiarius, sellularius, lapidarius, ærarius,* etc. to form nouns which signify certain orders, professions, or trades. This may be observed in several of the modern words, such as *cavalier, courrier, fauconier*, already mentioned, and it may be further perceived in several forms common to the Ital. and Span., as *cameriere* Ital., *camerero* Span.; *caffetiere* Ital., *cafetero* Span.; *forastiere* Ital., *forastero*¹ Span., *banchiere* or *banchiero* Ital., *banquero* Span.; *carceriere* Ital., *carcelero* Span. In other cases these two languages have respectively forms of this kind peculiar to each, as *calamaio, masnadiere, condottiere, dardiero, girellaio*, Ital.; *agujero, mercadero, tintero* Span. The French nouns in *er* and *ier*, forming their fem. in *ère* and *ière*, are in great number, and comprehend most of the words signifying the persons belonging to different kinds of trades, professions, orders, etc., as *aumônier, banquier, boulanger, boucher, chancelier, contrebandier, cordonnier, cuisinier, douanier, fermier, huissier, héritier, mercier, meunier, rentier, roturier, sorcier, usurier,* etc. The French has likewise modern nouns in *aire*, as *sociétaire, fonctionnaire, factionnaire*².

The various modifications of the Latin *ministerium* (*menester* Span., *mistero*³, *mestieri, mestiere* or *mestiero*

¹ From the Latin *foras*; see Muratori in v.

² The French nouns in *aire* are probably of a later date than those in *er*, and the two classes appear to stand to each other in the same relation as those pointed out above, p. 108, 111.

³ Perticari, *Scrittori del Trecento*, lib. i. c. ii. vol. I. p. 58, who calls the ancient use of *mistero* for *mestiero* a 'bruttissima, anzi sacrilega permutazione,' does not see that *mistero* is nearer than the common form to *ministerium*, and that it was evidently corrupted into *mestiero* in order to avoid the confusion with *mistero* derived from *mysterium*.

Ital., *mestier* Prov., *métier* French) do not belong to the modern words formed with the termination *er* or *ier*, but are corrupted and contracted from the Latin word. *Bicchiere* Ital., and *picher* French, are derived from the German *becher*[1], (*beaker* Eng., *bicker* Scotch): *alfiere* Ital., and *alferez* Span., are said to be derived from the Arabic *alpheres*[2].

Aster. This termination had in Latin a diminutive force, which, as in many other instances, sometimes passed into a contemptuous sense, as *filiaster*, a stepson, *calvaster*, a little bald, *oleaster*, a wild, bad olive, *poetaster*, a worthless poet, etc.[3] Hence the Ital. and Span. have derived the termination *astro*, the Prov. and French the termination *astre*, which the latter has softened into *âtre*. Thus *figliastro* Ital., *hijastro* Span., *filhastre* Prov., *filastre* or *filâtre* Fr. The French and Span. have *marastre* or *marâtre* and *madrasta* for stepmother, which word does not occur in Italian. The French uses this termination as a diminutive, (like the English *ish*,) as *blanchâtre*, *bleuâtre*, *douceâtre*, *grisâtre*, *folâtre*, *jaunâtre*, *rougeâtre*, *saumâtre*, etc.[4] The Ital. and Span. sometimes give it an opprobrious force, as *filosofastro*, *medicastro*, *teologastro*, etc. which it likewise has in the French *acariâtre* and *opiniâtre*[5].

[1] See Menage, *Et. It.* in *bicchiere*.
[2] Menage in *alfiere*. [Compare Diez, *Rom. Gr.* vol. ii., p. 327.]
[3] See Grimm, vol. ii. p. 372.
[4] See Muratori, in *salmastro*, and Menage in *falcastro* from *falx*.
[5] Also in *marâtre*: 'L'opinion qu'en général on a des marâtres dont le nom seul parmi nous est devenu presqu'une injure, est justifiée par les faits.' Guerry, *Statistique Morale de la France*, p. 22. The word commonly used in French for stepmother is *belle-mère*, which also signifies mother-in-law: in Italian *suocera*, not having the termination in *astra*, has not, as far as I am aware, obtained a reproachful

ATIUM, as in *palatium*. In Latin, however, the more common form was *itium*, as *exitium, servitium*, being a neuter form of the fem. termination *itia*, as in *lætitia, sævitia*, which will be noticed under another head. From *atium* the Ital. made *agio*, forming *palagio* from *palatium*, as *servigio* from *servitium;* in other Ital. words likewise *t* was changed into *g*, as *stagione, ragione*, from *statio, ratio*. In all the Romance languages this termination has assumed nearly the same form: thus it is *agio* or *aggio* in Ital. *azgo* or *age* in Span.¹, *atge* or *age* in Prov., and *age* in French: and although it is of rare occurrence in Latin, has in all the modern Latin dialects served to form a great variety of new nouns. And from the Romance languages it was translated into Low Latin, under the neuter form of *agium;* thus from *maritagio* or *maritage* came *maritagium*, from *homagio* or *homage homagium*. If these words had been formed in Latin according to the true analogy, they would have been *maritatium* and *hominatium*. Sometimes, however, a Low Latin form in *aticus* corresponds to a Romance form in *agio* or *age*, as *formaticus* (cheese) to *formagio* and *fromage*², *hostaticus* to

furco, although the character of stepmothers in Italy (unless they have greatly improved since ancient times) is probably not at all superior to that of stepmothers in France. [Compare Diez, *Rom. Gr.* vol. ii. p. 363.]

¹ The Spanish varies more in this termination than the other languages: thus it had not merely *patronazgo* corresponding to *padronaggio* and *patronage*, but *ventaja* corresponding to *vantaggio* and *avantage*, *ultraje* corresponding to *oltraggio* and *outrage*. The popular dialect of Rome formerly made this termination in *ajo*, as *lennejo* for *linnaggio, dannajo* for *danneggio*, in the Roman history in Muratori, *Ant. It.* vol. iii. p. 399, 501. This, however, was rather a variety of orthography than of form, as *j* was pronounced hard as in French.

² See Menage in *formaggio*, Schwenck's *Etymological Remarks* in

ostaggio and *ostage*[1], *silvaticus* to *salvage* and *selvaggio*, (although the Ital. and Span. likewise have *selvatico*.) Many of the substantives formed with this termination run through all the languages, as the instances cited by M. Raynouard, *corraggio, lignaggio, messaggio, omaggio, viaggio* Ital.; *corage, linage, mensage, omenage, viage* Span.; *corage, linhage, message, omenage, viage* Prov.; *courage, lignage, message, hommage, voyage* French, (*Gr. Comp.* p. 31.) So likewise we find in Ital., Span., and French, *padronnaggio, patronazgo*, and *patronage, potaggio* and *potage, passeggio, pasage*, and *passagge, villaggio* and *village*, etc. In other cases, however, these forms occur only in two languages: thus the Prov. and French formed *auratge* and *orage* from *aura*: in Span. and Ital., however, there is no trace of this word. So in Ital. and French there are *beveraggio* and *breuvage, formaggio* and *fromage, ostaggio* and *ostage, rivaggio* and *rivage*, but there are no corresponding words in Span. Frequently each language has substantives of this form peculiar to itself, as *alegratge, agradatge* Prov., *appagaggio*[2], *fardaggio, farangaggio, figliuolaggio, parlagio*[3], *vasellaggio* Ital., *aguage, cabezage, cabestrage, pontage*, or *pontazgo, primazgo, serage, villanage*, Span., *arrivage, bocage, chauffage, cirage, étage, fermage, feuillage, ménage, mirage, nuage, ouvrage, ramage, ravage, roulage, rouage, tapage, tirage, triage* French. Sometimes one language has preserved the

---

Welcker's *Rhein. Museum*, vol. i. art. kāse. *Formaticus* for cheese occurs in a charter of the Ambrosian monastery at Milan, of 957 A.D. in Murat. *Ant. It.* vol. iii. p. 719, B. cf. 718, c.

[1] Muratori in v.
[2] A Sienese word from *opacus*: see Menage, *Etym. It.* in *abbacinare*.
[3] The name of the place where the Florentines anciently held their parliaments; see Perticari, *Dif. di Dante*, c. 36, vol. ii. p. 102.

Latin noun, where another has made a new form in *age*, thus *testimonio* Ital. and Span., but *témoignage* French: sometimes one language has used the termination *age*, where others have used different terminations: thus *schiavitù* Ital., *esclavitud* Span., but *esclavage* French, *vicinanza* Ital., *voisinage* French: *vecinad* is preserved in Span. from the Latin *vicinitas*; the other two words translated into Latin forms would be *vicinantia* and *vicinatium*. Sometimes again the corresponding words do not precisely agree, but appear to have been formed from similar roots variously modified in the several languages: thus *linguaggio* Ital. from *lingua*, *lenguage*, Prov. and *lengage* Span. from *lengua*, *langage* French from *langue*: so *maritaggio* Ital. from *maritare*, *maridage* Span. from *marido*, *mariage* French from *marier*; *danneggio*[1] Ital. *dommage* French; *redaggio* Ital. from *redare*, but *héritage* French from *hériter*; *pedaggio* Ital. *peage* Span. *péage* French; *romitaggio* Ital. from *romito* corrupted from *eremita*, *hermitage* French from *hermite*[2].

IA, ITIA. The first of these terminations occurs in the Latin words *gratia*, *inopia*, *miseria*, etc.[3] The Italian has preserved and used it in forming *pazzia* from *pazzo*,

---

[1] Dammaggio occurs in a Neapolitan sonnet of the thirteenth century, cited by Perticari, *Dif. di Dante*, c. 7, vol. i. p. 280, who calls *aggio* a 'Neapolitan termination.' It may prevail in the Neapolitan dialect, but it is common to all the Romance languages.

[2] The English having adopted the termination *age* from the Norman French used it as a formative termination, and added to it Saxon roots: thus *bondage*, *carriage*, *cottage*, *package*, *stoppage*, *stowage*, *steerage*, *thirlage*, *tillage*, etc. [Compare Diez, *Rom. Gr.* vol. ii. p. 287.]

[3] See Grimm, vol. iii. p. 607. The terminations are here classed with reference not to the Latin, but to the Romance languages; otherwise the terminations *antia* and *entia* above treated would come under the general head of *ia* (p. 122).

K

bizzarria from *bizzarro*, *signoria* from *signore*, *follia* from *folle*, etc. So likewise in the Span. *fulleria, fusileria, plumageria* and in the French *boulangerie, boucherie, seigneurie*. Sometimes the Ital. used the simpler form in *a*, as *lega* from *legare*, *tema* from *temere*. The Latin termination *itia* (e. g. *justitia, nequitia, mæstitia*) has in Ital. past into *izia* and *ezza*, in Span. into *icia* and *eza*, in French into *ice* and *esse*. Thus *justitia, tristitia* Latin *giustizia, tristezza* Ital. *justicia, tristeza* Span. *justizia, tristeza*, Prov. *justice, tristesse* French. *Paresse* Fr. from *pigritia*, like *noir* from *niger*, and *roide* from *rigidus*[1]. With regard to these two terminations from *itia* it is however to be observed that the former only occurs in words of Latin origin, as *justitia, militia, malitia, notitia*, etc. and that all the new nouns formed with this termination take the latter in *ezza, eza* or *esse*. The modern languages have formed in this manner a great variety of nouns which do not occur in Latin: thus they have all substantives of this form derived from *altus, largus, probus*, and from the words *fein* and *reich* adopted from the German (in Proven. *alteza, largueza, proeza, fineza, richeza, Gr. Comp.* p. 80). Sometimes they have made a new noun of this form where the Latin employed a different termination; thus *altezza, alteza* and *altesse* correspond to *altitudo*, *agrezza* to *acritudo, giovanezza* and *jeunesse* to *juventus, nobilezza, nobleza* and *noblesse* to *nobilitas, secheresse* to *siccitas, chaitiveza* in the *Poeme sur Boece*, v. 88, to *captivitas*. Sometimes the different languages have used the corresponding terminations for the same words, as in the instances mentioned above: sometimes some of the

---

[1] See Grimm, vol. ii. p. 329. [Burguy in *parece*.]

NEW ROMANCE NOUNS FORMED BY AFFIXES.   131

languages used the termination derived from *itia*, and some another termination : thus from the various derivatives of the German *frisch* [1] came *frescura* and *freschezza* Ital., *frescura* and *frescor* Span., *frescor* or *fraichor* Proven., *fraicheur* French. So *agrezza*, Ital., *aigrura* Span., *aigreur* French; *grandezza* Ital., *grandeza* Span., *grandeur* French; *frigidezza* Ital., *frigidez* Span., *froideur* French; *rigidezza* Ital., *rigideza* Span., *roideur* French; *tepidezza* Ital., *tibieza* Span., *tiedeur* French. *Lunghezza* Ital., corresponds to *longueur* French; the Span. uses the Latin *longitud*. From *fievole* and *faible* modified from *flebilis*, the Ital. and French have made *fievolezza* and *faiblesse* : the Span. has not this word [2]. Sometimes each language has forms of this kind peculiar to itself, as *ampiezza*, *amorevolezza*, *dappochezza*, *mattezza* Ital., *honradez*, *idiotez*, *insensatez*, *pobreza* Span., *chaitiveza* Proven., *ivresse*, *rudesse*, *souplesse*, *vitesse* French[3].

The fem. termination of nearly the same form, which prevails in the Romance languages, as *duchessa* Ital., *duquesa* Span., *duquessa* Prov., and *duchesse* French, is considered by Grimm as a lengthened form of the Latin *ix*, as in *netrix*, *piscatrix*, etc.[4] This view is liable to the objection that the Romance words formed from Latin fem. in *ix* have kept nearer to the Latin form, as the derivatives of *nutrix*, *cicatrix*, *calyx*, *matrix*. It seems therefore more probable, that the fem. termination in *issa*, as in the words *mantissa*, *favissa*, of more frequent usage in the Greek, as βασίλισσα, Κίλισσα, etc. was the origin of the Romance form.[5]

---

[1] See Muratori in *fresco*.
[2] [Diez, *Rom. Gr.* vol. ii. p. 280, 339.]
[3] [Diez, *Rom. Gr.* vol. ii. p. 276, 326, 344.]
[4] Muratori in *fievole*.
[5] Vol. ii. p. 328.

K 2

Inus. This is a termination of nearly the same kind as *anus*, and is chiefly confined to adjectives, as *caballinus*, *Latinus*, *marinus*, *masculinus*, *matutinus*, *peregrinus*, *supinus*, *vicinus*. It occurs, however, in substantives of the fem. and neut. gender, as *farina*, *medicina*, *rapina*, *ruina*, *salina*, *lupinum*, *salinum*. The Ital. and Span., which have made it *ino*, the Prov. and French, which have made it *in*, used it for the formation of substantives, as *festino* and *festin* derived from *festus*. (*Gr. Comp.* p. 50.) In Italian this termination is still in great use, with a diminutive sense, as *ragazzino*, *tavolino*, *bambino* from *bambo* (i. e. babe[1]). It likewise has a diminutive force in Spanish. The French has also used it for the formation of new words, but without a diminutive force, as *angevin*, *bavardin*, *chevrotin*, *diablotin*, *fagotin*, *patelin*, *Poitevin*, *bécassine*, *routine*: so also names of parties in the French revolution, *Brissotin*, *Girondin*[2].

Ista. This termination, introduced into the Latin at a late period from the Greek, has passed into the modern languages: thus *copista*, *legista*, *algebrista*, *cabalista*, Ital. and Span.; *copiste*, *légiste*, *algébriste*, *cabaliste*, *modiste*, *dentiste*, French.[3]

O, onis, masculine, as in *caupo*, *latro*, *sermo*, *commilito*, and in proper names, as *Scipio*, *Cæsio*, *Cæpio*, *Maro*. Hence the Ital. *one*, the Span. Prov. and French *on* (*Gr. Comp.* p. 56, 7). Thus *bastone* Ital., *baston* Span., Prov. and Fr.; *falcone* Ital., *halcon* Span., *falcon* Prov., *faucon*

[1] In Italian this termination has commonly a sense of tenderness, but sometimes the sense of contempt which belongs to diminutives: see Marrini on the *Lamento di Cecco*, p. 166. Payne Knight's *Essay on Taste*, p. 229. *Philol. Museum*, vol. ii. p. 670, 685.

[2] See Grimm, vol. iii. p. 700. [Diez, *Rom. Gr.*, p. 813.]

[3] [Diez, ib. p. 368.]

NEW ROMANCE NOUNS FORMED BY AFFIXES. 133

French; *millione* Ital., *millon* Span., *million* Fr.; *campione* Ital., *campeon* Span., *campion* Prov., *champion* French. Many of the modern nouns of this form are derived from a German root: thus *bastone* comes from *bat* or *bast*, *campione* from *kampf*, *spione* from *spähen*, to spy, *balcone* from *balk*, *marrone* from *marre*, a chesnut, *poltrone* from *polster*, *prigione* from *prisund*, *sperone* from *sporn*, *fellone* from *fell*[1]. *Antrustione*, *barone*, and *garzone*[2] have likewise German roots. In French it has been used for the formation of many words, as *aiguillon*, *caisson*, *chainon*, *brouillon*, *jambon*, *menton*, *monton*, *rejeton*, *téton*, *vallon*, *piéton*; and in this language it is sometimes a diminutive termination, as in *mignon*, *salon*, *ânon*, and in the familiar proper names *Alison*, *Lison*, *Robichon*, *Fanchon*, *Jeanneton*, *Louison*, *Gothon*, *Marion*, *Nanon*, *Ninon*, *Suson*[3]. In Italian likewise it frequently occurs, sometimes as a mere formative termination, as in *burrone*, *falcione*, *montone*, and other instances above cited, and sometimes with an augmentative force, as *donnone*, *salone*, *cavallone*. In Spanish,

---

[1] See Menage in *bastone* and *fellone*, Muratori in *spia*, *balcone*, *marrone*, *poltrone* and *poltrire*, *prigione* and *sperone*. I have not thought it necessary to repeat the Spanish and French forms of the words mentioned in the text.

[2] *Garzone*, according to Muratori, is derived from an ancient Frankish word, which is written *Gartio* in an Italian document of the ninth century. *Ant. It.* vol. ii. p. 1118, A—C. *Garzûne* in the *Nib. Lied*, v. 905, is probably borrowed from the Romance. In Low Latin a marquis is *marchio*, a noun of this form, and not *marchensis*, the form used in the Romance languages.

[3] Grimm, vol. iii. p. 705, is mistaken in supposing that the old French proper names in *on*, as *Charlon*, are of this form. They are the ancient accusative case from the nominative in *es* or *s*: see above, p. 81.

likewise, *on* is sometimes an augmentative: thus *hombron* from *hombre*, *calaveron* from *calavera*[1].

On the feminine termination *io*, *ionis*, and its use in the modern languages it is unnecessary to say any thing.

Or. This masculine termination is of two kinds; first, when it denotes qualities, as *amor*, *honor*, *color*, and secondly, when it denotes persons, as *imperator*, *lictor*, *possessor*. Among the modern languages, it has become *ore* in Italian, *or* in Spanish and Provençal, and in old French; in which language it has since been modified into *our* and *eur*. (*Gr. Comp.* p. 59—61, above, p. 84.) The modern languages have formed, with this termination, some new words corresponding to the former class of Latin nouns, as *bollore*, *malore*, *rancore*, *tristore*[2], *sentore*, *verdore*, Ital.; *frescor*, *rencor*, *verdor*, Span.; *frescor* or *fraichor*, *verdor*, Prov.; *fraicheur*, *lueur*, *lenteur*, *rancueur*, *pesanteur*, *profondeur*, *verdeur*, French. The chief part of the new substantives formed with this termination belong, however, to the other class of nouns signifying persons, as *miratore*, *servitore*, Ital., *mirador*, *servidor*, Span. and Prov., *serviteur*, French. So likewise *ambasciatore*, *coniatore*, *conoscitore*, *confettatore*, Ital., *embaxador*, *matador*, *picador*, *sangrador*, Span.; *accapareur*, *accoucheur*, *agioteur*, *escamoteur*, *farceur*, *siffleur*, *vendangeur*, French.

It has been already remarked that the Provençal and French changed the gender of the nouns in *or* signifying qualities, and said *la dolor*, *la color*, *la frescor*, *la verdor*, etc., while the Italian and Spanish preserved the masculine gender not only in the words retained from the Latin,

---

[1] On the Italian and Spanish augmentatives of this form see Grimm, vol. iii. p. 705. [Diez, *Rom. Gr.* vol. ii. p. 318.]

[2] On *tristore*, see Perticari, *Dif. di Dante*, c. 26, vol. ii. p. 36.

as *amore, colore, amor, color*, but also in the words newly formed, as in *rancore, verdore*, Ital., *frescor, rencor, verdor*, Spanish[1].

TAS, *tatis*, TUS, *tutis*, as in *servitus, virtus, bonitas, libertas*. Since (as has been above shown) all the modern languages, in forming nouns from Latin substantives of the third declension, took the accusative case as their type, these terminations became in Ital. *tate* and *tute*; in Span. *tad* and *tud*, anciently *tat* and *tut*; in Prov. *tat* and *tut*; in French *tet* and *tut*. In Italian the terminations in *tate* and *tute* were formerly written at full length, as *cittate, veritate, virtute*, or *cittade, veritade, virtude*; for some time, however, they have, by the omission of the last consonant, been contracted into *tà* and *tù*, (i. e. *tae* and *tue*), so that these words have now become *città, verità, virtù*: this change, nevertheless, has only affected the termination *tute* or *tude*, as *salute* and *palude* have preserved their ancient form. *Cittate* or *cittade, virtute* or *virtude*, and other similar nouns were contracted into *città* and *virtù* in order to avoid the repetition of the double *t*, or of the *t* and *d*; but *salute* and *palude* were not contracted, because there was no such cacophony to avoid. The French having, as in many other instances, changed the *a* into *e*, made originally *libertet, citet, nativitet, volontet*: it has since suppressed the final *t*, and indicated its suppression by the acute accent, as *liberté, cité, nativité, volonté*[2]: in the termination *tut*, it has merely suppressed the

---

[1] See above, p. 114. [Diez, *Rom. Gr.* vol. ii. p. 325.]

[2] When the ancient termination was not *at* but *ata*, the French, following its two rules of changing the final *a* into *e muet*, and *at* in a termination into *é*, converted it into *ée*: thus, *amat* (from *amo*) became *aimé*, *amata, aimée*. So likewise *fumée*, French, corresponds to *fummata* Ital.; *armée* French, to *armata* Ital. and *armada* Span.; *fée*

final *t*, and from *vertut* made *vertu*. (*Gr. Comp.* p. xix. 37—42, 68, 69.) Many new substantives have been formed in the modern languages with this termination, as *beltate* or *beltà* Ital., *beldad* Span., *beltat* Prov., *beauté* French; *lealtà*, *sovranità* Ital., *lealtad*, *sovranidad* Span., *loyauté*, *souveraineté* French. So likewise *schiavitù* Ital., *esclavitud* Span., *debonnaireté*, *gaité*, *honnêteté*, *netteté*, *pisiveté*, *papauté* French[1].

ULUS, ELLUS, ILLUS. *Ulus*, or *olus*, in Latin, was originally a mere formative termination, as in *sedulus*, *garrulus*, *famulus*, *credulus*, *gerulus*, *ungula*, *regula*, *fabula*, *Græculus*, *Pœnulus*, *Romulus*, *Scævola:* afterwards it obtained a diminutive sense, as in *regulus*, *filiolus*, and in Hadrian's address to his soul, *animula vagula, blandula*[2]. The Italian in adopting this termination changed it into *olo*, or *uolo*, as *favola*, *tavola*, *figliuolo*, from *fabula*, *tabula*, *filiolus*; and has formed with it many new words, as *bussolo*, *nuvola*, *gocciolo*, *piccolo*, (from *putus*,) *legnaiuolo*, etc. The Spanish modified this termination into *uelo*, as *aguelo*, or *abuelo*, (corresponding to the Ital. *avolo*,) *cozuelo*, *ojuelo*[3]. The French has made it *eul*, but has rarely used it: thus *filleul* answers to the Ital. *figliuolo* and the Span. *hijuelo*. Sometimes the Latin lengthened the termination *ulus* by a syllable, making it *aculus* or *iculus*, as in *cœnaculum*, *obstaculum*, *miraculum*, *auricula*, *curriculus*,

French, to *fata* Ital., and *hada* Span.; *journée* French, to *giornata* Ital. *jornada* Span. (see Machiav. *Disc.* ii. 17, ad init.); *vallée* Fr., to *vallata* Ital., and not to *valle:* as is implied by M. Raynouard, who speaks of "Le mot *val* roman qui a produit en français *vallée*." *Journ. des Sav.* 1823, p. 111.

[1] [Diez, *Rom. Gr.* vol. ii. p. 836.]
[2] See Niebuhr's *Rome*, vol. i. p. 55. Grimm, vol. iii. p. 696. Scheller's *Latin Grammar*, vol. i. p. 39.
[3] See above, p. 67, note [4].

fasciculus, ridiculus, Æquiculus from *Æquus*[1]. These terminations were softened by the Ital. into *acchio* and *icchio*, as in *oculus, occhio, circulus, cerchio, macula, macchia, gracula, gracchia, auricula, orecchia, pariculus, parecchio, speculum, specchio*[2]. The change took place thus, *auricula, auricla, aurichia*[3], *cl* being softened into *chi*, as in *chiave* from *clavis, chiostro* from *claustrum*, etc. After these models were formed the Ital. *pistacchio, pecchia*, (i. e. *apicula*,) *lentecchia, ginocchio, birracchio*[4]; and by a change of *acchio* and *icchio* into *accio* and *iccio*, *fossaccia, mostaccio, cappriccio, pasticcio*[5], *fantoccio*. The termination *accio*, as is often the case with diminutives, has sometimes in Ital. a contemptuous sense, as *donnaccia, giovinaccio, pitturaccia, robaccia*. While the Ital. changed the Latin termination *iculus* or *icula* into *icchia* or *icchio*, the Span. changed it into *ejo* and *eja*, the Prov. into *el* and *elha*, the French into *eil* and *eille*; thus *auricula, apicula, oculus, pariculus* Lat., *orecchia, pecchia*,

---

[1] Niebuhr, vol. i. n. 410, speaking of the Poediculi, says that 'the simpler forms Poedi and Poedici have not been preserved in books.' There is no doubt that the termination in *iculus* originated in the manner here indicated, and was a double affix: nevertheless in many words the simpler derivative form probably never existed, and it is perhaps as unsafe to infer from *Poediculus* the existence of a form *Poedicus*, as to infer from *auricula, curriculus,* and *ridiculus,* the existence of such words as *aurica, curricus,* and *ridicus*.

[2] See Muratori in *parecchio,* and Menage in *abbacchiare,* which he derives from *baculus,* and in *conocchia*, which he makes equivalent to *colucula* from *colus.* Also Pasqualini, *Vocabolario Siciliano*, vol. ii. p. x. xi.

[3] Muratori in *cerchio.* [4] Muratori in v.

[5] The termination *iccio* sometimes comes from *itius* or *icius*, as *posticcio* from *posticius* (Murat. in v.), *fatticcio* from *facticius*: but in other cases *accio* and *iccio* seem to be slightly modified from *acchio* and *icchio*.

occhio, parrecchio Ital., *oreja, abeja, ojo, parejo,* Span., *aurelha, abelha, huels* Prov., *oreille, abeille, oeuil, pareil* French. The Latin sometimes augmented the termination *ulus* by prefixing to it *el* or *il;* so that from *novus* it formed *novelulus,* from *pusus pusilulus.* These three syllables were afterwards contracted into two, so as to make *ellus* or *illus,* and thus were formed the words *novellus, pusillus, miscellus, Sabellus, Terentilla, codicillus, furcillæ,* etc. The same termination was, however, sometimes produced in a different manner, viz. by the softening of *r* into *l:* thus *liberulus, miserulus, puerulus,* became *libellus, misellus, puellus*[1]. Of these two forms in *ellus* and *illus* the Ital. made *ello,* the Span. *ello* and *illo,* the Prov. and French *el* (*Gr. Comp.* p. 43.) The modern French has changed the termination *el* into *eau:* thus instead of the ancient *chastel, drapel, faiscel, tonnel,* etc., it now says *château, drapeau, faisceau, tonneau:* the trace of the ancient form is, however, preserved in the inflexions, as *cervelle* from *cervel* (*cerveau*), *nouvelle* from *nouvel* (*nouveau*); and in the derivatives, as *niveler* from *nivel* (*niveau*), *chapelier* from *chapel* (*chapeau*), *sceller* from *scel* (*sceau*), *morceler* from *morcel*[2] (*morceau*), *Bordelais* from *Bordel* (*Bordeau*). When the French language was introduced into England this change had not been made: hence the English *castle, flail, mackerel, morsel, muzzle, tressel tunnel, vessel,* etc., correspond to the modern French *château, fléau*[3], *macquereau, morceau, museau, tréteau, tonneau, vaisseau.*

[1] See Grimm, vol. iii. p. 608.
[2] That is *morsel,* a little bit (bits) from *mors,* an old French word from *morsus.* See Raynouard in *Journ. des Savans,* 1831, p. 516.
[3] The old French had *flagel,* and also *flael,* whence our word is taken. It had likewise the word *flaeler.* On the French termination in *el,* see Orell, p. 32. [Burguy in *flaël.*]

NEW ROMANCE NOUNS FORMED BY AFFIXES. 139

This termination has been much used by the modern languages for the formation of new nouns. Sometimes the several languages agree remarkably in forming corresponding derivatives from the same root, as *mantello* Ital., *mantel* Span. Prov. and French; *martello* Ital., *martillo* Span., *martel* Prov. and French; *vassel* Prov., *vaisseau* French, *vascello* Ital., which latter form, however, partakes of a variety which will be presently noticed; *batello*[1], *agnello, anello, coltello, capello* Ital., *batel, anillo, cuchillo, cabello* Span., *batel, agnel, annel, coutel, chapel* French. The Italian has substituted several of these derivatives for the ancient underived forms: thus *fratello* and *sorella* for *frate* and *sorore*[2]: it has likewise still the power of using *ello* as a diminutive termination, as *ragazzello* from *ragazzo*. Other derivatives of this simple form in Span. are *camarilla, corcillo, guerilla, ladrillo, lagrimilla, lamparilla, pecadillo*, etc.; in French *bercel, boissel, chalumel, faiscel, panel*[3], *tombel, troupel*. Sometimes the form of this termination became more complicated, as *fiumicello, donzello,* (*domicellus*[4],) *leoncello, madamigella, monticello, vermicello, violoncello*[5], *vecchierello, pazzarello* Ital.; *leoncello, manecilla* Span.; *lioncel* French. Of the same form as *leoncello* is *vascello*, noticed above; as also *augello* or *uccello*, Ital.[6], contracted from '*avicello*,

[1] From *bat, boat*. Murat. in v.
[2] *Sorella* comes from *sore*, contracted from *sorore*, as *fratello* comes from *frate*, contracted from *fratre*. The old Ital. writers likewise use *sirocchia* for *sister*, i. e. *sororcula*.
[3] On *paneau* see Murat. in *pania*. [4] See Manzoni's notes to Adelchis.
[5] *Leon-cello, violon-cello*, etc. do not fall under the same class as the Latin *hom-unculus, av-unculus*, etc. (Grimm, vol. ii. p. 347,) as the *n* belongs not to the termination but to the root.
[6] See Menage in *augello*, who quotes *aucellus*, στρουθίον, from an ancient gloss.

like the Span. *avecillo:* the French *oisel* arose in a like manner.

Sometimes the French added to the termination *el* the termination *et*, of which I shall speak presently: hence having formed *oisel* from *avis*, from *oisel* it formed *oiselet*; having formed *chapel* from *chap*, from *chapel* it formed *chapelet*[1]; having formed *roitel* from *roi*, from *roitel* it formed *roitelet*.

URA, as in *censura, junctura, cultura*. This termination remained the same in all the modern languages except the French, which as usual changed the final *a* into *e*. Several new words were formed with it, as *aventura, armadura, verdura* Ital., Span., and Prov., *aventure, armure, verdure*, French, *cosidura* or *cucitura* Ital., *costura* Span., *cosdura* Prov., *couture* French. (*Gr. Comp.* p. 28.) Other new words of this form are *altura, bruttura, cambiatura, caricatura, fatatura, lordura, magagnatura, pianura, paura, seccatura* Ital., *domadura, embarradura, echadura, enjalbegadura, rebosadura, pavura* Span., *blessure, coiffure, decoupure, doublure, ferrure, nourriture, ordure, souillure* French[3].

There are likewise some Romance terminations of nouns adjective derived from the Latin, of which the following may be here noticed.

ENSIS, as in *forensis*. The Italian has preserved the termination under the form *ese*, as *Veronese, Lucchese,*

---

[1] See above, p. 70, note [4]. *Schapel*, which occurs several times in the *Nibelungen Lied*, in the sense of an ornament or covering for the head, is borrowed from the French *chapel*, and not from *chapelet*, as is stated by V. Hagen in v.

[2] [Compare Diez, *Rom. Gr.* vol. ii. p. 200.]

[3] [Diez, *Rom. Gr.* vol. ii. p. 323.]

NEW ROMANCE NOUNS FORMED BY AFFIXES. 141

paese from *pagensis*[1], which in Span. is *pais*, in French *pays*. It occurs in the derivatives of German roots, as from *marke* and *burg*, *marchese* and *borghese* Ital., *marques* Span., *marquis* and *bourgeois* French: so likewise *cortese* Ital., *cortes* Span. and Prov., *courtois* French. From the old German *hardneskja, lorica*, (now *harnisch*,) were formed *arnese* Ital., *arnes* Span., *harnois* French[2].

IVUS, as in *æstivus, fugitivus, captivus, lascivus*. The modern languages have formed new adjectives with this termination, as *tardivo, distruttivo* Ital., *destructivo* Span., *craintif, naif, oisif, pensif, tardif* French[3].

OSUS, as in *generosus, formosus, numerosus*. The Ital. and Span. made this termination in *oso*, the Prov. in *os*, and the French in *os* or *ox*, which latter termination it changed first into *our*, and then into *eux*. Thus the Ital. and Span. have formed *amoroso, perilloso, maraviglioso, maravilloso*, the Prov. *amoros, perillos, enuios, saboros*, the French *amoros, perillos, enuios, merveillos, doutos, envios*, which were sometimes written with a final *x*, as in *amorox, perillox*, etc. (*Gr. Comp.* p. 122.) Afterwards the *o* was changed into *ou*, so that the termination be-

---

[1] Muratori in v.
[2] See Grimm, vol. ii. p. 373, n. [Diez, *Rom. Gr.* vol. ii. p. 354.]
[3] Landor in his *Imaginary Conversations*, vol. i. p. 212, speaking of the moral inferences to be drawn from the use of words in Italian, says 'Misfortune is criminal: the captive is a wicked man, *cattivo*.' The same remark applies to the French *chetif*, whence the English *caitiff*. Nor does it appear that there is any peculiarity in this transfer of meanings: a prisoner usually became a slave, and there are numerous instances in both Romance and Teutonic languages of a close association of the ideas of slavery and of meanness, cowardice, and moral abasement. Thus the word *thraell* or *thrall* meant both a slave and a bad man. See Grimm, *Deutsche Rechtsalterthümer*, p. 303, 306. Arndt in the *Rheinisches Museum*, vol. ii. p. 348—52. [Compare Diez, ib., p. 339.]

came *ous* or *ouz*[1]: which is still preserved in the word *jaloux*; and this is the form of the termination in question in modern Provençal, as *argentous, cendrillous, famous, pietous, ponderous*. Such also was its form when the French language was introduced into England, and hence our adjectives *generous, clamorous, callous, famous, vigorous, monstrous*, etc. Each language has new words of this form peculiar to itself, as *noioso, neghittoso*[2], *ritroso, pensieroso, schizzinoso* Ital., *guardoso, hastioso, presagioso, primoroso* Span., *chanceux, fâcheux, heureux, oiseux, nuageux* French[3].

There are some other terminations of nouns which do not appear to be derived from the Latin, but which are used in all or some of the Romance languages. They are three in number, and of these two evidently spring from a Teutonic source, and the third probably has the same origin.

ARD. This German[4] termination has been received into the Romance languages, and has served to form a great variety of new nouns, especially in the Ital. and French. Thus *bugiardo*, (probably from a German root[5],) *azardo, bastardo, bombarda, chiavardo, codardo*, (from *cauda*, a person who lingered at the rear of an army,) *gagliardo, infingardo, leardo, maliardo, moscardo, mostarda, saccardo, tabarro, testardo, vecchiardo*, Ital., *cobarde, gallardo*, Span.,

---

[1] See Rayn. *Obs. sur le Roman de Rou*, p. 11, 12. *Envieuse, glorieuse, delitouse*, and *amorouz*, occur in a poem of Raoul de Coucy, who was killed in 1240, published in Sismondi, *Litt. du Midi*, vol i. p. 329. Compare Orell, p. 30.
[2] From *negligere*, see Muratori in v.
[3] [Diez, *Rom. Gr.* vol. ii. p. 330.]
[4] See Grimm, vol. ii. p. 339, vol. iii. p. 707.
[5] See Murat. in v. [Diez in *bugia*.]

NEW ROMANCE NOUNS FORMED BY AFFIXES.   143

campagnard, bavard, babillard, couard, gagliard, billard, brancard, brouillard, fuyard, milliard, pendard, etc. French. Many nouns have likewise been formed with this termination in English, as *braggart, drunkard, wizard, haggard, pollard, steward*, (from *to stow,*) *custard* (from *cost*, food,) *mazzard, froward*, etc.[1]

ETTO, ITO, ETE, ET; OTTO, OTE, OT. These terminations occur in Ital. in the words *boschetto, cavalletto, giovanotto, merlotto, signorotto :* in Span. in *caballete, senorito, muleto, papeleta, capote :* in French in *ballet, bonnet, filet, billet, couplet, poulet, sommet, violet, ballot, cachot, chariot, matelot, mignot, poulot.* It has been already mentioned that in French *et* is sometimes added to the termination *el*, as in *agnelet, batelet, bracelet, correlet, châtelet, rondelet.* In *cailletel* and *louvetel* (*cailleteau* and *louveteau*) this process has been reversed.

In some words these terminations merely serve to form new nouns; in others they have a diminutive sense, as *merlotto*[2], *señorito, poulet:* in Span., however, *ote* has an augmentative force, as *hombrote, capote*. Their origin, though it is probably to be found in some Teutonic formative syllable[3], is quite obscure.

ASCO, ESCO, ISCO, ESC, ESQUE. In Italian *asinesco, Bergamasco, buffonesco, burasca*[4], *cagnesco, cavaleresco, Dantesco, duchesco, donnesco, gigantesco, giovanesco, marineresco, naveresco, pittoresco, soldatesco :* in Span. *borrasca,*

---

[1] [Diez, *Rom. Gr.* vol. ii. p. 358.]
[2] Grimm is mistaken, vol. iii. p. 705, in stating that *otto* in Ital. has an augmentative force: it is always a diminutive, according to Marrini on the *Lamento di Cecco*, p. 106, who gives numerous examples of it.
[3] Grimm, vol. iii. p. 702. [Diez, ib. p. 345.]
[4] See Muratori in v.

gatesco, gigantesco, marisco, Morisco, marinesco, pintoresco, soldadesco, etc.: in Prov. *Espanesc, Francesc, Grezesc, Serrazinesc,* and *joglaresc.* Probably the French words of this form, as *burlesque, grottesque, gigantesque, pittoresque,* are borrowed from the Italian: the two latter, if they had been formed in French, would have been *géantesque, peinteuresque;* and the roots of the two former, *burlo* and *grotto,* are wanting in the same language.

This termination is derived from the German termination in *isch*[1]; thus *Tedesco* in Ital. corresponds to *Theotiscus* or *Theotisch* (*Teutsch*), as *fresco* was formed from *frisch.* Thus *Arabesco, barbaresco, Turchesco* Ital., answer to *Arabisch, barbarisch, Türkisch.* National names were often formed with this termination in the Romance languages, as they are both in German and English.

Now it cannot be contended that the result of this summary examination of the Romance terminations of nouns by any means necessitates M. Raynouard's hypothesis with respect to the parentage of the living Latin dialects, or indeed is at all favourable to it. We see, indeed, that the different languages subjected the Latin terminations to similar modifications, and used them for similar purposes; but in this fact there is nothing which compels us to suppose that they had anything more in common than their derivation from the Latin. In their corresponding words there is just that degree of resemblance and of difference which might have been expected in languages formed under the same circumstances from the same original. Thus there are some new nouns not derived from the Latin, such as

---

[1] See Grimm, vol. ii. p. 379. [Diez, *Rom. Gr.* vol. ii. p. 301.]

those formed with *aggio* and *age* from *lingua* and *cor*, with *ezza*, *eza*, and *esse* from *largus* and *probus*, with *one* and *on* from *kampf*, with *tale* or *tal* from *bellus*, with *ura* from *viridis*, which occur in all the languages: sometimes the different languages formed the same root with different terminations, as *allegrezza* and *allegria* Ital., *alegria* Span., *alegrage* Prov., *allégresse* French; *vicinanza* Ital., *voisinage* French; *frescor* Prov., *freschezza* Ital., *frescura* Span.; *schiavitù* Ital., *esclavage* French: sometimes each language had words of the several forms peculiar to itself, of which many examples have been cited above; and sometimes the corresponding words are formed from the differently modified roots belonging to each language, as *maritaggio*, *maridage*, and *mariage*; *romitaggio* and *hermitage*; *credencia*, *creencia*, and *croyance*. As these latter words could not have been derived from the same source, but were formed by means of the same terminations from similar roots; it is fair to conclude that the agreement in others where the roots were the same was the effect of chance, and does not necessitate the hypothesis of a common language in which these nouns were formed. It is not to be wondered that having the same terminations to work *with*, and the same roots to work *upon*, the languages should have often coincided in the new forms. Nor can it be doubted that nations, whose territories lay so near together, which were governed by institutions so closely resembling, between which there was so constant an intercourse, and whose languages had so strict an affinity, should frequently have borrowed words from each other. Under these circumstances such words as *omaggio*, *vassallagio*, and other political terms, would naturally pass from one to another country. The influence of the Church had, moreover, the effect of binding all the Romance nations into a species of federal republic, by making all the clergy members of a community dependent on the See of Rome. And on the whole, such a communication existed between these countries, as rendered it impossible that their cognate languages could have been developed altogether independently of one another[1].

The similarity of effects produced on language by similar causes, may likewise be perceived in the foreign words introduced into the Romance tongues during the middle ages, such as the derivatives of *werra*, *herberge*, *wante*, *harnisch*, *reim*, *sclavus*, *spatha*, etc., which probably were in most cases adopted by each language independently of the others. The subject of the non-Latin part of the Romance languages is, however, of sufficient importance to require a separate investigation[2]; and in this essay I shall confine myself to that which concerns the grammar, without endeavouring to explain that which concerns the dictionary of the modern Latin dialects.

[1] On the influence of the Italian on the French see Muratori, *Ant. It.* vol. ii. p. 1112, B.
[2] See note (D) at the end. [Diez, *Rom. Gram.* vol. i. p. 56—72.]

CHAPTER III.

Degrees of Comparison, Pronouns, and Numerals in the Romance Languages.

§ 1. DEGREES OF COMPARISON.

THE Provençal formed its degrees of comparison by means of the adverb *plus:* which word prefixed singly to an adjective denoted the comparative, and together with the article, the superlative degree: as *bels, plus bels, el plus bels.* Sometimes it preserved the Latin inflexion in *or* for the comparative, as *majers, miclhers, gensers,* (from *gent, gentilis* Latin,) *ausers* (*altior*[1],) and rarely that in *issimus* for the superlative, as *altismes, altissimus.* The superlative might likewise be expressed by means of the article and the Latin comparative: thus '*la genser,*' was equivalent to '*la plus genta.*' 'Am *la plus bella* et *la meillor;*' 'I love the fairest and the best.'

After the comparative degree, the relation between the two things compared is signified by the particle *que,* (derived from the Latin *quam,*) as 'plus ricx qu'el senher de Marroc,' 'more powerful than the lord of Morocco.' Sometimes the *que* was omitted between verbs, as

---

[1] The manner in which the Latin termination in *or* became *er* in Provençal, and received a final *s*, has been explained above, p. 83.

'E am la mais no faz cozin ni oncle:' 'and I love her more (than) I do cousin or uncle.'

Or the preposition might be used before substantives and pronouns, as 'plus fresca de lei,' 'fresher than her;' 'mielhs de mi,' 'better than me;' 'mas de cen,' 'more than a hundred.' M. Raynouard says that this usage was imitated from the Greek, (*Gr. Rom.* p. 55,) but there seems no reason for supposing that it was borrowed from a language which could not have exercised any influence on the Provençal, or indeed on any of the Romance languages. When two objects are compared, it is natural to say that one is the better, the worse, the more beautiful, etc. *of* the two; and it is an easy transition to say that one is better *of* the other: though it is an idiom which our language does not admit, (*Gr. Rom.* p. 51—8.)

The other Romance languages have in like manner lost the Latin mode of forming the degrees of comparison by inflexion, with the exception of a few words retained from the Latin, as *maggiore, maggio, meno, peggiore, peggio, migliore, meglio* Ital., *mayor, peor, mejor, ménos* Span., *majeur, meilleur, mieux, pire, moins* French; and the Italian and French, like the Provençal, form the comparative with *più* and *plus*, the superlative with *il più* and *le plus:* while the Spanish uses *mas* (from *magis*) for the same purpose. M. Raynouard says that the Provençal alone possesses both *plus* and *mais* (*Gr. Comp.* p. 137,): but he forgets that the Latin equally possesses them both; and the Provençal does not prefix *mais*, like the Spanish, to adjectives, but uses it only as an adverb of comparison. The Latin termination of the superlative, as has been already remarked, rarely occurs in

Provençal, and M. Raynouard cites a few instances of it in old French, in which language, with the exception of a few relics of the ancient form, such as *illustrissime*, *révérendissime*, etc., it is now disused. The Italian and Spanish have, however, preserved the use of this termination, and can annex it to any adjective[1]: but it has lost its proper superlative meaning, and only has an intensive force: thus 'maximus omnium' would be in Italian 'il più grande di tutti,' while 'vir maximus' would be 'uomo grandissimo.' Wherever it is meant that none possess the quality in an equal degree, the article and the adverb must be used: where it is meant that the subject possesses the quality in a high degree, the termination is proper. The same rule also applies to the Spanish. It should be remarked that in the retention of the superlative termination, the latter languages have adhered more closely than the Provençal to the Latin.

The employment of *que* after comparatives, and of *de* before substantives and pronouns, occurs in all the Romance languages; and of the suppression of *che* before verbs M. Raynouard gives some instances from old Italian: as 'E più soave dorme in vile e picciol letto ... no face segnore en grande e caro suo:' *Guit. d' Arezzo*, Lett. I. p. 4[2]. (*Gr. Comp.* p. 137—42.)

---

[1] The Italian only preserved the Latin termination in *issimus*: it has, however, retained some Latin superlatives of a different formation, as *ottimo, pessimo, minimo, infimo, supremo, acerrimo, celeberrimo*. These are collected by Biagioli, *Gr. Ital.* p. 62, who, however, ought not to have called *benissimo* a Latin superlative.

[2] This construction resembles the vulgar English idiom, 'better *nor* me,' 'older *nor* him,' etc.

§ 2. PRONOUNS.

The Provençal personal pronouns have for the most part only two cases in the singular, and one in the plural number, distinguished by the termination: the others are formed by prepositions. They are as follows:

	SINGULAR.	PLURAL.
Nom.	eu, ieu, me, mi	nos
Acc.	me, mi	

Nom.	tu	
Acc.	tu, te, ti	

MASC.

	Singular	Plural
Nom.	il, el	il, els
Acc.	il, el, lo, li, lui	els, los, ll : lor only after *de* or *a*

FEM.

	SINGULAR.	PLURAL.
Nom.	ella, il, lei, leis	ellas
Acc.	la, lei, leis	las
	after *a* and *de* ella and not la was used.	after *a* and *de* ellas or lor and not las was used.

Se and *si* were used either in the singular or the plural, either in the nominative or accusative case, and with the prepositions *de* and *a*, (*Gr. Rom.* p. 59—86.)

In these forms the greatest confusion prevails: while *me* and *mi* are used in the nom. case, together with *eu* derived from *ego*, *tu* is used in the acc. case, together with *te* and *ti*: although *eu* is never the accusative, or *te* the nominative. *Il*, *el*, and *ella*, in the nom. singular come from *ille* and *illa*: *il*, *el*, *lo*, *ella*, and *la*, in the oblique case are formed from *illum* and *illam:* *li, lui, lei,* and *leis*[1] from *illi*. The two latter feminine forms are likewise used as nominatives. In the nom. plural, *il, els,* and *ellas,* come from *illi, illos,* and *illas;* while *lor,* common to both genders, is derived from *illorum*. *Li* from *illi* nom. was transferred to the oblique case plural, as *lei* from *illi* dat. was transferred to the nom. singular.

To the personal pronouns were sometimes joined in the Provençal other pronouns, which had the effect of giving additional force to the affirmation; such as *eis,* (from *ipse,*) *mezies,* (the origin of which word will be explained presently,) and *altres.* Thus 'elh eis dieus la fetz,' 'God himself made her,' 'ille ipse Deus;' 'ab qu'el mezeis se balaya,' 'with which he himself flogs himself;' 'de se mezeis nos fe do,' 'he made us a gift of himself;' 'son ves els mezeis trachor,' 'they are traitors towards themselves.' *Altre* is only joined to *nos* and *vos:* thus 'Et afermi que mays valh Mahomet que ton Xrist loqual vos autres adoratz;' 'and I affirm that Mahomet is worth more than thy Christ whom you adore.'

En and *ne* were used in Provençal to mean, *of him, her, it, them; i, y,* and *hi,* to mean, *to him, her, it, them.* Although (says M. Raynouard) *en* and *ne* derived from *inde,* and *i, y,* or *hi* derived from *ibi,* ought only to have been used for the pronoun when they signified inanimate things, yet the Provençal used them to signify persons, both in the singular and plural, and both masculine and feminine, (*Gr. Rom.* p. 86.)

The modifications of the Latin personal pronouns made by the Provençal reappear, for the most part, in

---

[1] On this final *s* see below, ch. v. § 1.

the other Romance languages. The old Italian *eo* and the modern *io*, the Spanish *yo*, and the old French *jeo*, have retained the *o* of the Latin *ego*, which has become *u* in the Provençal. The use of *mi* in the nominative appears likewise to have anciently existed in Italian and Portuguese[1]: but that of *tu* in the acc. is peculiar to the Provençal. The Italian, from its intolerance of final consonants, has changed *nos* and *vos* into *noi* and *voi*[2]: 'notwithstanding which (says M. Raynouard) the Romance (i. e. Provençal) *nos* and *vos* appear in Italian joined with the preposition *co*,' (*Gr. Comp.* p. 148,): a singular assertion; for in the first place, *nos* and *vos* are as much Latin as Provençal, and if they were the common forms in Italian would not prove any connexion with the Provençal, and secondly, *nosco* and *vosco* are evidently contracted from *nobiscum* and *vobiscum*, forms of which there is no trace in the Provençal or any other Romance language.

It is remarkable that the practice of adding *alter* to *nos* and *vos*, occurs in all the Romance languages, and in Spanish particularly it has become inseparably joined to those pronouns, so that *nosotros* and *vosotros* are the common forms for the nom. case, *nos* and *vos* being reserved for the accusative.

With regard to the derivatives of the pronoun *ille*, it

---

[1] On the tendency to substitute the accusative for the nominative, as being more emphatic, some remarks have been already made, above, pp. 90, 91, and the same explanation probably applies to such expressions as 'io mi sono,' 'io non so ch'io mi dica o ch'io mi faccia' (Boccaccio), 'io mi vivea' (Petrarch), which occur in old Italian: the *mi* was doubtless added in order to give force to the affirmation, and afterwards might be used merely from habit, (see *Gr. Comp.* p. 146.)

[2] *Vi*, the accusative, appears to be merely a contraction of *voi*.

is to be observed that from this word all the Romance languages have formed their definite article[1]; and it is curious to observe how each language has chosen different forms, originally synonymous, to distinguish the one sense from the other. The Provençal used *el* as an article, and both *el* and *il* as the pronoun: the Italian originally used both *el* and *il* as the article, and *el* as the pronoun: the latter has now substituted *egli*, apparently from *illi*, as the Prov. used *lei* also from *illi* in the feminine gender. The Provençal used both *el* and *lo* (from *illum*) as the nom. of the article, but *lo* as a pronoun was only acc. The old French used both *el* and *lo* as the article, and *lo* as the accusative of the pronoun: but it has since disused *el* as an article, for which it uses *le* (*lo*,) and has retained *il* only as the nom. of the pronoun. *Lei*, though derived from *illi* the Latin dative, was used in old Italian, as well as in the Provençal, as a nom.: thus Petrarch,

E ho sì avezza
La mente a contemplar sola costei
Ch' altro non vede, e ciò, che non è *lei*,
Già per antica usanza odia e disprezza.

(See other instances in *Gr. Comp.* p. 155.) The same idiom is still retained in Italian in the language of conversation. With regard to *li, los, ellas* in Italian and Spanish, the same observation applies as to *li, los,* and *las,* the plural of the article; and *lor,* which in the Italian *loro* retains one more letter of *illorum,* does not

---

[1] Except the Sardinian dialect, in which the definite article is *so, sa,* from *ipse*: Raynouard, vol. i. p. 41. For the definite article in the Romance languages, see above, p. 50.

appear as a personal pronoun in Spanish and Portuguese.

The Provençal use of *se* occurs in all the other languages, of *en* and *ne* in French, of *ne* in Italian, and of *i* or *y* in all, (*Gr. Comp.* p. 143—58.)

The Provençal moreover often omitted the vowels of its personal pronouns, and affixed the remaining consonant or consonants to the preceding word: thus *me, ti, se, nos, vos*, were represented by *m, t, s, ns, us:* thus we find 'No sai en qual guiza-m¹ fui natz,' 'I know not in what guise I was born.' 'Per aisso-t tem amors,' 'For this I fear thee, Love.' 'Mos coratges no-s pot partir de vos,' 'my heart cannot part itself from you.' 'Lo jorn que-ns ac amor amdos eletz,' 'the day that love had chosen us both.' 'Tolre no-m podetz que no-us am,' 'You cannot prevent me from loving you.' *N* is likewise used as an affix for *ne* or *en*, (*Gr. Rom.* p. 91—5.) In poetry the pronoun was necessarily affixed to the preceding word, and could not be used in its uncontracted form².

This remarkable system of affixed pronouns occurs in old French, and is still preserved in some of the French *patois*: it was likewise very prevalent in old Spanish: but there is no trace of its existence either in Portuguese or Italian, though it still prevails in many of the dialects of Upper Italy, (*Gr. Comp.* p. 158—61, 402.)

The declension of the possessive pronouns has been

---

[1] In the manuscripts the affixed pronouns are written as part of the word with which they are in pronunciation combined. I have separated them (after Schlegel and Diez) with a hyphen for the sake of clearness.

[2] See Raynouard in the *Journal des Savans*, 1831, p. 348.

already given[1], and it only remains to be remarked that *lor* Prov. as not being derived from a word declinable in Latin, is itself indeclinable. The Provençal having obtained an article, naturally employed it before possessive pronouns used substantively, as in Greek: thus ' E non es benestan qu'hom cys *los sieus* aucia,' ' and it is not good that man should kill even his own.' ' Vos o'*lhs vostres* foratz totz mortz,' ' You and yours would be all dead,' (*Gr. Rom.* p. 96—116.)

The Provençal demonstrative pronouns are *cel*, *aicel*, *aquel*, *est*, *cest*, *aquest*. The three first appear to be compounded of *hic* or *hicce*, and *ille*; *est*, from *iste*, compounded with the same word, likewise appears to have made *cest* and *aquest*. The following is the declension of these words:

SINGULAR.

	MASC.		FEM.
Nom.	cel, celul	*Nom.*	cella, cil
and	aicel		alcella, aicil
Acc.	aquel		aquella, aquil
		Acc.	cella, celleis
			alcela
			aquella, aquelleis
Nom.	est	*Nom.*	esta, ist
and	cest		cesta, cist
Acc.	aquest		aquesta, aquist
		Acc.	esta
			cesta
			aquesta

[1] See above, p. 78.

CHAPTER III.

	Masc.	PLURAL.		Fem.
Nom.	ell, cels		*Nom.*	cellas
	aicil, alcels		*and*	aicellas
	aquil, aquels		*Acc.*	aquellas
Acc.	cels			
	alcels			
	aquels			
Nom.	ist, est		*Nom.*	estas
	cist, cest		*and*	cestas
	aquist, aquest		*Acc.*	aquestas
Acc.	ests			
	cests			
	aquests			

The remarks above made on the personal pronoun *el* apply with little variation to these forms. It will be observed that *celui* masc. from *illi* dat. is used in all the cases; though *celleis* and *aquelleis* fem., derived from the same case, are never nominatives. Moreover *cil*, *aicil*, *aquil*, *ist*, *cist*, and *aquist*, are used as nom. feminines, though in the acc. the final *a* is never omitted: probably because the former are derived from *illa* and *ista*, the latter from *illam* and *istam*. Besides these masculine and feminine forms, *aisso*, *so*, and *aquo*, are the neuter forms: they appear to have retained their final *o* on account of the *u* in the neuter *ipsum* and *illud*, which does not appear in the other genders, (*Gr. Rom.* p. 117—131.) So likewise in Spanish *aquel* is masculine and *aquello* neuter, *Gr. Comp.* p. 175.)

Nearly all these pronouns with their variations occur in the different languages. The Italian uses only the abbreviated form *quello*, which M. Raynouard compares with *aicel* and *aquel*, but which seems rather to correspond with *cel*, while the Spanish has not the shorter form, but only uses *aquel*, (*Gr. Comp.* p. 171—6.)

Of the Provençal relative pronouns it is only necessary to mention *qui*, which is used in the nom. and acc., both as masc. and fem. *Que* (derived from *quod*) is used in all cases, and as both masc. and fem.: and it is alone used after neuter demonstrative pronouns. *Qui* and *cui* sometimes perform the function of genitives, datives, and ablatives: *cui*, however, is commonly preceded by a preposition, which *che* always requires.

Don, derived from *de unde*, and indeclinable, had the sense of *whence, whose, by* or *from whom*. *On*, from *unde*, meant *where, to whom, in whom*.

The Provençal used another pronoun relative formed by prefixing the article to *qualis*: viz. *lo qual, la qual, los quals*, etc.

In Provençal, as in Latin, the antecedent is often understood: thus 'no say que dire,' 'nescio quid dicam.' 'Trobat avem qu' anam queren.' 'Invenimus quod quærimus,' etc. 'Qui en gaug semena, plazer cuelh,' '(He) who sows in joy, reaps pleasure.' 'La premiera ley demostra a qui ha sen e raczon,' 'The first law proves to (him) who has sense and reason.' 'Ai cum par franch o de bon aire qui l'au parlar,' 'Ah, how frank and debonair she appears (to him) who hears her speak.' Sometimes, on the other hand, the antecedent being a substantive, and not a pronoun, the relative was suppressed, particularly in poetry: thus 'Car anc no vi dona tan mi plagues,' 'For never saw I lady (who) pleased me so much,' (*Gr. Rom.* p. 131—43.)

The corruptions of the Latin *qui* appear with little

difference in the other languages, which likewise sometimes suppress the antecedent, and rarely the relative. *Onde* in Ital. has retained the form of the Latin *unde* more faithfully than the Prov. *on*: it has, however, occasionally the sense of a relative pronoun, which it has obtained by the same process of abstraction which has rejected the notion of time in the prepositions *de* and *ad*, as used in the Romance languages to express the relation of the genitive and dative cases, and in the verb *venire*, when used as an auxiliary verb, equivalent to *essere*, in Italian. *Dont* likewise remains in French as a relative pronoun, and in old Italian and Spanish *donde* and *don* had the same sense, (*Gr. Comp.* 176—86.)

Of the Provençal indefinite pronouns, the first to be noticed is *hom*, or *om*, from the Latin *homo*, which, followed by the verb in the singular number, had a distributive sense, and signified mankind in general, or a large number of people. Thus 'Hom ditz che gaug non es senes amor,' 'Man says (i. e. it is said) that there is no joy without love.' This very convenient idiom (which our language unfortunately wants) seems to have been introduced into the Romance languages by the Germans, who used the substantive *man* in this manner. In French, as is well known, this use of *on* is very prevalent; which word in ancient times was spelt very variously, retaining sometimes evident traces of its original form, viz. *hom, hon, hum, om, um, on*. The Italian[1], Spanish, and Portuguese, formerly used *uomo, omne,* and *ome,* in the same manner: but in them this idiom has now become obsolete, (*Gr. Comp.* p. 187—9.)

[1] See Menage, *Etym. Ital.* in *uom dice*.

The Provençal had two pronouns *quecx*, and *usquecx*, signifying *whoever, every-one*, derived from *quisque* and *unusquisque*; but no other Romance language had any derivatives of these words.

Cadauns or *caduns, cac, cascuns*, meant everyone; *alcuns*, some one ; *nuls, neguns, deguns, nessuns*, no one. Of these words *cadauns* or *caduns* appears to have been formed from *quotus unus* or *quotunus, cac* and *cascuns*[1] from *quisque* and *quisque unus* (*unusquisque*): *alcuns* was formed from *aliquis unus*, like *alicubi* in Latin from *aliquo ubi*: *nuls* from *nullus, neguns* and perhaps *nessuns*[2] from *nec unus*. The origin of *deguns*, unless it was a corruption of *neguns*, does not appear. Being derived from Latin pronouns in *us*, they were declined according to the rules given above: thus nom. *cascuns* or *cascus, cascuna*; acc. *cascun, cascuna*. *Cada* or *cad* is sometimes used in the sense of *every*: thus 'A Carduel una pentecosta On cad an gran pobels s'ajosta,' 'At Carduel, an Easter, where *every year* many people assemble': in which passage *cad an* appears to answer to the Latin *quot annis*, both in form and meaning. *Cada* has the same sense both in Italian and Spanish[3]. The French has it not, but only *chasque*, which, like the Provençal *cac*, probably comes from *quisque*; and *chascun*, which, as well as *ciascuno* Ital., probably comes from *quisque unus*. The Italian likewise

---

[1] If *cac* came from *quisque*, it would be the same word as *quecx* mentioned above, without the final *x* or *s*.

[2] There are instances in Provençal of the confusion of the final *c* and *s*: see below, ch. v. § 1. Muratori in v. derives *nessuno* from *nescio unum*, without any probability.

[3] The Spanish *nada* and *nadie* appear to be allied to *cada*: but I am unable to offer even a conjecture as to their origin.

has *cadauno*, compounded of *cada*[1]. Every language has the derivatives of *aliquis-unus* and *nullus:* but the Italian and French have *neuno* and *neun* formed from *ne unus*, as well as *nessuno* and *nesun* from *nec unus:* the Spanish alone has from *nec unus* made *ninguno*, like the Provençal *neguns*[2]. The Portuguese had *nenhum*.

From *alter* the Prov. made *altres* or *altre* declined, *altrui* undeclined, (which appears to have been formed from the dative *alteri*, like *lui* from *illi*, *costui* Ital. from *isti ;*) and lastly by contraction *al*. The other languages likewise have these forms, and particularly *al*, which (sometimes changed into *el*) occurs in old French, is still used in Spanish and Portuguese, and appears in some Italian words, as *alsi*.

Eis, eissa, meteis, metissa, signifying *self* or *own,* were used after all persons: thus ' Eu eis mi son traire,' ' I am a traitor to myself,' (ego ipse mihi sum traditor.) 'En eysa la semana,' 'in the very week.' 'Per mo mezeis follatge,' 'through my own folly.' 'Altresi com la candela Que si meteissa destrui,' ' like the candle which destroys itself.'

Eis, es, or *eps,* (as it is sometimes written in the more ancient monuments of the Provençal,) is derived from *ipse*[3]. *Meteis* (sometimes written *medeis* or *medes, mezeis,*

---

[1] *Catauno* occurs in an ancient Italian letter published by Muratori. *Diss. It.* vol. ii. p. 1047, E. [See Diez in *cadauno*.]

[2] See Grimm, vol. iii. p. 70 note. It will be observed that all the Romance languages have lost the Latin *nemo*.

[3] *Ips* or *eps* (the corruptions of *ipse*) sometimes became *eis*, and sometimes *es*. From the latter of these forms came the compounds *des* and *ades*, from the former the compounds *neis* and *anceis*, (*Gr. Rom.* p. 251,) as will be shown below, ch. v. §. 2. On *isso* and *esso* in Italian derived from *ipse*, see Perticari, *Dif. di Dante*, c. 13, vol. i. p. 321. Muratori, *Diss.* 32, vol. ii. p. 991, D.

and *messeis*) is evidently formed by the composition of *eis* with the emphatic particle *met*, which is subjoined to the Latin personal pronouns: thus the latter example would be word for word in Latin, 'velut candela quæ *se met ipsam* destruit.' When the suffix had been detached from the pronoun to which it belongs, and permanently prefixed to the following word, it is no wonder that the compound thus formed should be used without a pronoun immediately before it, as when it occurs as an adverb in the sense of *even*. It is remarkable that all the other Romance languages should agree in this peculiar corruption, although they have taken for their type the Latin superlative of *ipse*, and from *met-ipsissimus* have formed *medesimo* Ital., *mismo* Span., *mesme* French[1].

From the Latin *totus* the Provençal made *tots* or *totz*, declined according to the rule given above: it was sometimes compounded with the adverb *tras*, or *tres*, *very*; making *trastotz*, which had a stronger sense than the simple word. *Tras* (as will be mentioned below[2]) appears to be derived from *extra* by the addition of *s* and the suppression of the first syllable. The old French likewise had the compound *trestoz* or *trestout*. It is remarkable that the Latin word *omnis* was abandoned in all the Romance languages (except the Italian, which has *ogni*) and *totus* substituted for it.

From the Latin *multus* are derived the Ital. *molto*, the Prov. *molts*, the French *molt*, *mult*, or *moult*, and the Port. *muito*. From the German *manch* are derived the Prov. *mantz* or *maintz*, the French *maint*, and the Ital.

[1] See Menage and Muratori in *medesimo*, Grimm, vol. iii. p. 19. [Burguy, *Gr. de la Langue d'Oïl*, vol. i. p. 179.]
[2] Ch. v. §. 2.

M

mento. The Span. instead of these words has mucho, which M. Raynouard derives from *multus*, but which appears to be of Teutonic origin, and to be derived from an ancient word preserved in the English *much*, (*mik-ils* Goth., *mik-il* old H. German[1].) *Plusor*, formed from *plus*, appears in the Ital., Prov., and French: in Span. and Port. it is wanting. On the derivatives of *talis* and *qualis*, *tantus* and *quantus*, it is unnecessary to make any remark, (*Gr. Rom.* p. 145—60. *Gr. Comp.* p. 186—96.)

§ 3. NUMERALS.

The cardinal numbers of the Provençal, which will furnish an easy means of comparison for the different languages, are as follows: *uns* or *us*, *dui*, *trei*, *quatre*, *cinq*, *sex* and *sei*, *set*, *och* and *ot*, *nov*, *deze* and *dez*, *unze*, *doze*, *treze*, *quatorze*, *quinze*, *setze*, *vint*, *trenta*, *quaranta*, *cent*, *mil*. The ordinal numbers are *premiers*, *segons*, *ters*, *quarts*, *quints*, *seizens*, *setens*, *ochens*, *novens*, *dzens*, *unzens*, *dotzens*, *trezens*, *quatorzens*, *quinzins*, *sezemes*, *vintesmes*, *trentesmes*, *quarantesmes*, *centes*, *milles*. Of these forms *uns* or *us* was declined like the adjectives *bons* or *bos*: *dui* was nom. masc., *dos* acc. masc., and *doas* was fem. of both cases. The Prov. likewise used *ams* masc. and *ambas* fem. from *ambo*: by combining which word with *dui* it formed likewise the compound *ambedui* or *amdui*, declined like *dui*. *Trei* is nom. masc., and *tres* acc. masc. and also fem. of both cases. In the other cardinal numbers, the Prov., like the Latin, made no distinction of

[1] See Grimm, vol. iii. p. 608, 610.

cases. The ordinal numbers were declined like adjectives of both genders in *s*, except *ters*, which (as being contracted from *tert-ius*) was invariable in the masc. gender, and in the fem. made *tersa*. It is to be observed, moreover, that *segons* made in the fem. *segonda; centes, centesma; milles, millesma*: the fem. retaining in the middle the letter which had dropped from the masc. where it was a final; as in the French *beau, belle*, etc[1]. This was also the case with the ordinals in *ens*, of which the masc. was commonly in *es*, the fem. in *ena*, as *seizes, seizena*. Several ordinals had the termination *esmes*, as well as *ens*, thus *sezesmes*, as well as *seizens*, (*Gr. Rom.* p. 161—6.)

On comparing the numerals in the other Romance languages with the Prov. forms, it will be observed that the Ital., in deriving *quattro* from *quattuor, otto* from *octo, undici, dodici*, etc. from *undecim, duodecim*, etc. kept nearer to the Latin than did the Prov., which made *quatre, ot, unze, doze*, etc. It is inconceivable, as has been already remarked in a similar case, that the Latin *quattuor, octo*, and *undecim*, should first have been contracted or attenuated into *quatre, ot*, and *unze*, and then restored to *quattro, otto*, and *undici*. The old French used the cases *dui* and *dos*, like the Prov., as also the compound *ambedui* or *embedui*: it likewise distinguished between *troi* and *tres* for the nom. and acc., (*Gr. Comp.* p. 198—9.)

The first of the ordinals the Prov. took not from the Latin *primus*, but from *primarius;* in which it has been imitated by the French: the Ital. and Span., though they have *primiero* and *primero* from *primarius*, never-

---

[1] See above, p. 188.

theless use *primo* from *primus* as their ordinal. In the derivatives of *secundus, tertius, quartus,* and *quintus,* (except that the Spanish makes *tercero* from *tertiarius,*) all the languages agree. At this point, however, a disagreement takes place: for whereas the Ital. and Span. use the derivatives of the common Latin forms *sextus, septimus, octavus, nonus, decimus, undecimus, duodecimus;* the Prov. used the termination perceptible in the less common Latin forms *septenus, octonus, novenus, denus,* etc. to form ordinals of its own, by which means it made *seizen, seten, ochen,* etc. from *sei, set, och,* etc.

It is a singular circumstance that all the Romance languages should agree in deviating from the Latin with regard to the formation of the three numerals before twenty. The Latin forms all its cardinal numbers from eleven to nineteen inclusive, by annexing *decem* to the unit number: thus *undecim, duodecim*[1], *tredecim,* etc. to *novendecim.* The modern languages follow the same rule till they come to seventeen, when instead of affixing the word ten to the unit number, they reverse the order of the words, and to correspond to *septendecim, octodecim, novendecim,* we have in Prov. *deze set, deze ot, deze nov*[2];

[1] There is this difference between the Greek and Latin with its dialects on the one hand, and the Teutonic languages on the other, that in the former the numerals *eleven* and *twelve* are *compounded* of *one* and *two* and the word *ten:* whereas in the latter they are *derivatives* of *one* and *two*, and the word *ten* does not enter into them. Thus ἕνδεκα and *undecim,* δώδεκα and *duodecim:* but *eilf* and *zwelf* or *zwölf* from *ein* and *zwei* or *two. Andlefen* Goth. and *einlef* or *endlef* old H. Germ. show the relation of *eilf* to *eleven.* See Meidinger's Dictionary, p. 507.

[2] At least I suppose that this is M. Raynouard's meaning, as he omits the numerals between sixteen and twenty, (*Gr. Rom.* p. 161.)

in Ital. *diciasette, diciotto, diciannove :* in Span. *diez y siete, diez y ocho, diez y neuve ;* in French *dix sept, dix huit, dix neuf.* The change is the same as if in English after saying *thirteen, fourteen, fifteen, sixteen,* we were to proceed *tenseven, teneight, tennine.*

CHAPTER IV.

Formation, Conjugation, and Syntax of Verbs in the Romance Languages.

§ 1. FORMATION AND CONJUGATION OF VERBS.

THE Provençal verbs are arranged by M. Raynouard in three conjugations, viz. those whose infinitive mood ends in *ar*, in *er* or *re*, and *ir* or *ire*. The Provençal has three auxiliary verbs, *aver* from the Latin *habere*, *esser* from the Latin *esse*, and *estar* from the Latin *stare*[1].

The Latin had itself degenerated from the more perfect type of conjugation preserved in the Greek verb, and had admitted the use of an auxiliary verb in some tenses of the passive voice: the use of the auxiliary verb was, however, much extended in the Romance languages by the influence of the Germans, who, accustomed to this method of conjugation in their own language, and misunderstanding or not knowing the force of the Latin terminations, employed the easier method of compounding a tense out of an auxiliary verb and the past participle. Nevertheless it is to be observed that in the active voice all, or nearly all, the Latin tenses were preserved, and the compound tenses of the Romance languages were *added to* those of the Latin verb, and not *substituted for* them.

[1] On the use of *stare* for *esse* in Latin see Menage, *Orig. Ital.* in v.

CONJUGATION OF VERBS.

I will now set down the conjugations of the three Provençal auxiliary verbs, omitting the compound tenses.

Infin.	essor	estar	aver
Pres. Part.	essens	estans	avens
Past Part.		estatz	agutz
Gerund	essen	estan	aven

INDICATIVE MOOD.
Present.

son, sol, sui	estai, au	ai
est, iest	as	as
es	a, ai	a
sem, em	am	avem
etz	atz	avetz
san, son	an, on	an

Imperfect.

era	estava	avia
eras	avas	ias
era, er	ava	ia
eram	avam	iam
eratz	avatz	iatz
eran, eron	avan, avon	ian, ien, ion

Perfect.

fui	estoi	aigui, aic
fust	est	aguist, aguest
fo, fon	et	aguet, ac
fom	em	aguem
fotz	etz	aguetz
foren, foron	erem, eron	agueren, agueron

Future.

er, serai	estarai	aurai
seras	aras	as
er, sera	ara	a
serem	arem	em
seretz	aretz	etz
seran	aran	an

CHAPTER IV.

Conditional.

seria	fora	estaria	auria	agra
as	as	as	as	as
a	a	a	a	a
am	am	am	am	am
atz	atz	atz	atz	atz
an, on	an, en, on	an, on	an, on	an, on

IMPERATIVE MOOD.

alas	estas	alas
a	a	a
am	em	am, em
atz	atz	atz
an, on	en, on	an, on

SUBJUNCTIVE MOOD.

Present.

sia	este	aia
as	es	as
a	e	a
am	em	am
atz	etz	atz
an, on	an, on	an, on

Imperfect.

fos	estes	agues
fosses	esses	esses
fos	es	es
fossem	essem	essem
fossetz	essetz	essetz
fossen, on	essen, esson	essen, esson

It will be time to speak generally of the relation which the Provençal system of conjugation bears to that of the Latin and the other Romance languages, when we come to the three regular conjugations: here I shall only mention those circumstances which are peculiar to the three auxiliary verbs.

The three auxiliary verbs occur in all the Romance languages: the French alone has not the infinitive formed from *esse*, (*essere* Ital., *esser* Prov., *ser* Span.;) *être* being the modern form of *ester*, from *estar*: so likewise *ested*, the ancient French participle from *estat*, became first *esté*, and then *été*. All the modern languages agree in changing the *b* of *habere* into *v*: but this change is so common as not to have anything remarkable. M. Raynouard goes regularly through every tense, comparing the Provençal forms with those of the other languages, and in many places he shows that the Italian and Spanish anciently used forms more resembling the Provençal than those now in use: for the most part, however, there is nothing worthy of notice in these coincidences: thus the Italian formerly said *avemo*, and not *abbiamo*, which is nearer to the Latin *habemus*; *eramo*, and not *eravamo*, which is nearer to the Latin *eramus*: so likewise instead of *fù* it said, like the Provençal, *fò*: but the vowels *u* and *o* are so frequently interchanged in Italian that this variation is of no importance.

It is to be observed that the Provençal, like the French, declines the verb *être* with the auxiliary *aver*, as *ai estatz*, *j'ai été*; while the Italian declines *stare* with the verb *essere*, as *sono stato*.

The conjugations of the regular verbs, which have been mentioned above, are as follows:

Infin.	amar	temer	sentir
Pres. Part.	amans	temens	sentens
Past. Part.	amatz	temutz, sutz	sentitz
Gerund	aman	tomen	senten

CHAPTER IV.

Indicative Mood.

Present.

am, ami	tem, temi	sent, sente
amas	temes	sentis
ama, am	tome, tem	senti, sent
amam	temem	sentem
amatz	temetz	sentitz
aman, on, en	temen, on	senten, on

Imperfect.

amava	temia	sentia
avas	ias	ias
ava	ia	ia
avam	iam	iam
avatz	iatz	iatz
avan, avon	ian	ian

Perfect.

amei, iei	temi, ei	senti
est, iest	ist, est	ist
et	i, et	i
em	em, im	im
etz	etz, itz	itz
eren, eron	eren, eron	iron, iron

Future.

amarai	temerai	sentirai
avas	eras	iras
ava	era	ira
arem	erem	iram
aretz	eretz	iratz
aran	eran	iran

Conditional.

amaria, era	temeria, era	sentiria
arias, eras	erias, oras	irias
aria, era	eria, era	iria
ariam, eram	eriam, eram	iriam
ariatz, eratz	eriatz, eratz	iriatz
arian, eran	erian, eran	irian

CONJUGATION OF VERBS.

IMPERATIVE MOOD.

ama, am	tema	senti, sent
a	e, tem	1
em	em	am
etz	etz	etz
en, on	en, on	an, on

SUBJUNCTIVE MOOD.
Present.

ame	tema	senta
es	as	as
e	a	a
em	am	am
etz	atz	atz
en, on	an	an

Imperfect.

ames	temes	sentis
esses	esses	esses
es	es	is
essem	essem	issem
essetz	essetz	issetz
essen, esson	essen	issen, on

On comparing with this scheme of the Provençal verbs the conjugations of the Italian and Spanish verbs, analogous remarks to those already made on the terminations of nouns naturally suggest themselves. In almost all instances the Provençal cut off or contracted the final syllable of the Latin word: thus from *amare* it made *amar*, from *amo* it made *am*, from *amamus* it made *amam*, from *amasti* it made *amest*, from *amando* it made *aman*: the Italian, however, where the Latin word ended with a vowel, retained it unchanged, as *amare*, *amo*, *amasti*, *amando*; where the Latin word ended in *us*, instead, like the Provençal, of omitting altogether the final syllable, it only rejected the *s*, and changed the *u* into *o*, as *amamus amiamo, amabamus amavamo*, like *littus lido, pondus pondo, subtus sotto*, etc. The Spanish in some respects adhered less closely than the Italian to the Latin: thus it made the infinit. *amar:* and in the second person sing. of the preterite it made *amaste*, and not *amasti:* it retained, however, the final *o* in the first person sing. of the present, as *amo*, and in the gerund, as *amando*, and in the first person plural it only changed *us* into *os*, as *amamos, amabamos*. Now it is inconceivable that this close adherence to the Latin should have been accidental, and that the Latin terminations should be preserved in the Italian and Spanish, if these languages had been derived from the Provençal, in which all the terminations in question had been cut off. Nobody can believe that *amare, amo, amasti*, and *amando*, were first contracted into *amar, am, amast,* and *amon*, and then restored, by accident, for the sake of euphony, to their original forms: that *amamus* was changed into *amam*, and then lengthened into *amiamo* and *amamos*. These differences between the Provençal and the Italian and Spanish, pervading every tense of every verb, make it evident that the latter languages did not pass through the alembic of the former language in the process of their transmutation from the Latin.

The only instances in which the Italian appears to have arbitrarily added to its verbs a final vowel for the sake of euphony, are the third persons plural, such as *amano, amavano, amarono*, lengthened from *aman, amavan, amaron*, (the contractions of *amant, amabant, amarunt,*) which are the only forms used in Spanish: and in the third persons singular of the preterite in *ette*, thus *stetit* and *dedit*, having been contracted into *stet* and *det*, were lengthened into *stette* and *dette*, (*Gr. Comp.* p. 252.) The Italian likewise having changed *sum* as well as *sunt* into *son*, added to it the euphonic *o*, both in the first and third person.

The most remarkable divergence from the Latin verb, and one in which all the Romance languages agree, is in the future tense, as may be seen from the following table.

Latin.	Ital.	Span.	Prov.	French.
amabo	amerò	amaré	amarai	aimerai
timebo	temerò	temeré	temerai	
sentiam	sentirò	sentiré	sentirai	sentirai

The Latin has two modes of forming its future active, one for the two first conjugations by adding *bo*, and another for the two last conjugations by adding *am* to the characteristic letter: thus *ama-bo, time-bo, reg-am, senti-am*. In its derivative languages, both these modes of formation have been lost, and in their place a single termination has been substituted, viz. *r* followed by a vowel or diphthong. There is no trace of the formation of the Latin future by this consonant, except in *ero*, the future of the verb *esse*.

M. Raynouard supposes that the modern futures have been formed by annexing the present tense of *avere, haber, aver,* or *avoir,* to the infinitive mood of each verb, and in proof of this assertion he cites several passages where the infinitive mood of the auxiliary verb is in the Provençal separated by the interposition of another word: thus 'Et quant cobrat l'avran, *tornar l'an* e so poder per se e senes engan,' where the French exactly renders this idiom:

'Et quand recouvré l'auront, *tourner l'ont* en son pouvoir par foi et sans tromperic.'

So likewise in poems of the Troubadours; 'E si li platz, *alberguar* m'a' 'and if it pleases him, he has to lodge me.'

> E pos mon cor non aus dir a rescos,
> *Pregar* vos ai, s' en aus, en ma chanson.

'And since I do not dare to express my wish in secret, I have to entreat you, if I dare, in my song.'

> Amarai? oc; si li platz ni l'es gens,
> E si nol platz, *amar* l'ai eissamen.

'Shall I love? Yes; if it pleases her and she is kind, and if it does not please her, I have to love her (i. e. I will love her) equally.'

In Provençal, too, the verbs *aver* and *esser*, with the preposition *a* before another verb, were used to express the future: as 'ab lieys ai a guerir,' 'with her I have to recover :' i.e. 'I shall recover.' 'A l'advencment del qual tuit an a ressuscitar,' ' at whose coming all have to rise again :' i.e. 'all will rise again.' 'Tem que m'er a morir,' 'I fear it will be to me to die,' i.e. 'I fear I shall die, (*Gr. Rom.* p. 221—2. comp. vol. i. p. 70, 81. *Gr. Comp.* p. 206.)

Of these idioms the latter occurs, though with a sense not so closely allied to the future, in all the Romance languages: of the former, examples are to be found only in the Spanish and Portuguese; in the Italian and French this usage does not appear ever to have prevailed. The following are examples from the Spanish : 'Non te diran Jacob, mas *decir* te *han* Israel.' '*Castigar* los *hé* como

avran é far.' ' *Haber* les *hemos* como alevosos perjurados,'
(*Gr. Comp.* p. 297—8[1].)

These examples appear to prove the truth of M. Raynouard's assertion with respect to the origin of the Romance future; as becomes more evident by comparing the future tense in each language with the modern present tense of *habere:* thus

Ital.	Span.	Prov.	French.
ho	he	ai	ai
amer ò	amar é	aimar ai	aimer ai
perder ò	perder é	perder ai	perdr ai
sentir ò	sentir é	sentir ai	sontir ai

In old Italian, moreover, *haggio* and *abbo* were used for *ho*, (i.e. *habeo*,) as the first person of the present tense of *havere:* and thus we likewise find futures in *aggio* and *abbo*, as *faraggio, veniraggio, diraggio, torrabbo*[2].

When this form had once been established in the active verb, it was transferred to the auxiliary verbs, so that the verb *habere* was inflected by itself, (*Gr. Comp.* p. 206[3].)

[1] This origin of the Romance future is doubted, upon insufficient grounds, by Ampère, *Hist. de la Litt. Fr.* p. 160.

[2] See this fully explained by Castelvetro on *Bembo*, vol. ii. p. 203—5: compare Perticari, vol. i. p. 302, note 7, to col. 2. Galvani, *Poesie dei Trovatori*, p. 30, n. 1. Lanzi, *Lingua Etrusca*, vol. i. p. 338.

[3] The story which M. Raynouard cites from Aimoin, *De Gestis Francorum*, ii. 5, about Dara taking its name from the Emperor Justinian saying *Daras*, (thou shalt give,) and which he calls 'a *fact* difficult to explain,' (vol. i. p. x.) is, as Schlegel has remarked, evidently an etymological fable, (p. 45, 102,) like those which the Greeks so often invented about the origin of their cities, and not more authentic than the derivation of the name of Britain from Brutus the grandson of Æneas. [This city of Mesopotamia is called *Doras* in *Pasch. Chron.* vol. i. p. 608, ed. Bonn. and Malalas, p. 399, ed. Bonn.

CHAPTER IV.

As the future tense was formed by means of the present tense, so the conditional was probably formed by means of the imperfect, of *habere*: in Spanish some instances occur where this tense is, as it were, analysed into its component parts; as '*dexar me ias con el sola*;' ' E mas *pechere* me *hia* en pia diez mil maravedis;' '*Pechar* nos ya toda aquella pena,' (*Gr. Comp.* p. 278.) All the languages except the French have a double form of this tense.

Ital.	Span.	Prov.	French.
amerei	amara	amera	aimerei
ameria	amaria	amaria	
perderei	perdiera	perdera	perdereie
perderia	perderia	perderia	
sentirei	sentiera	sentiria	sentireie
sentiria	sentiria		

The simple forms in *ara* and *era* appear to be corrupted from the Latin *amarem, perderem, sentirem*: the form in *ia* M. Raynouard considers as taken from *avia*, (*aveie* in French,) the imperfect of *avere*. Nor would there be any doubt about this derivation, if it were certain that *ia* ever had the force of *avia*, and that such is its meaning in the passages quoted above from the Spanish. The Italian form in *ei*, however, is evidently borrowed, not from the imperfect, but from the preterite, of *avere*, *ebbi*, anciently *ei*, as may be seen from the inflexion of the different

in which passages it is said to have received its name, from being the place where Alexander the Great conquered Darius with the *spear* (δόρυ). Aimoin, a French Benedictine monk, was born about 950, and died in 1008 A.D. His *History of the Franks* abounds in fables. The reign of Justinian terminated in 565 A.D. Concerning the town in question, see Dr. Smith's *Dict. of Anc. Geogr.* art. Daras.]

persons[1]. The Venetian dialect has *vorave, sarave*, for *vorrei, sarei*, etc., which more distinctly shows the Latin *habui*[2]. *Parrave* for *parrebbe* was used by Dante da Maiano[3].

With regard to the other tenses of the regular verbs in the Italian and Spanish, and their relation to the Latin and Provençal, there is nothing which calls for particular notice. The formation of the French verb, however, having undergone more changes, and having departed further from its original type, requires a more detailed explanation.

The final *s* now added to the first and third persons of the present, to the second person of the imperative, and to the first person plural, of the French verb, formerly did not exist: and those tenses which have now *ois* as the termination of the first and second persons singular, originally made *eie* or *oie* in the first, and *eies* or *oies* in the second person: thus *je mand, je voi, je regard, je bais, il aim, il chant, pren-tu, fui-t-en, nous avum, nous devum, nous parlum, nous prion, nous gardon, j'aveie, je fereie, je soie, j'estoie, tu saveies, tu consenteies, tu devoies, tu tenoies*. In these respects the French verb approached nearer to the Latin and Provençal forms (*Gr. Comp.* 225—38.)

The French imperfect has undergone remarkable changes: *amabam*, the Latin form of the first conjugation, first, by a slight modification, as in the other languages became *amava*: then the internal *a* was, as in other French words, changed into *o*, and the final *a* underwent the regular change into the *e* muet: by which means *amava*

---
[1] Castelvetro on *Bembo*, vol. ii. p. 224.
[2] Denina, in the *Mém. de l'Acad. de Berlin*, 1797, p. 76.
[3] Castelvetro, ibid.

CHAPTER IV.

became *amoue*[1]. M. Raynouard cites many examples of this form; as *je crioue, je parlowe, je quidoue, tu parloes, il cuveitoue, ils alouent, ils contrariowent, ils errouent*; afterwards *u* was changed into *i*, so that *amoue* became *amoie*: the final *e* was then suppressed, when the imperative was written *j'estoy, j'escoutoy*, and lastly, a final *s* was added, which brought it to its present form. The other forms of the Latin imperfect, *ebam* and *ibam*, appear to have been changed in French, as in Provençal, into *ia*, then *ie*, *eie*, or *oie*, then *oi*, and lastly into *ois*: by which means the termination of the imperfect became uniform in all the conjugations, (*Gr. Comp.* p. 244—8, 271.)

In the preterite of the first conjugation the French has adhered more closely than the Provençal to the Latin original, as from *amavi, amavit*, it makes *j'aimai, il aima*, (anciently *aimat*,) whereas the Prov. has *amei* and *amet*. The Prov., however, sometimes, though rarely, used the termination *ai* in the first person (*Gr. Rom.* p. 217); and the terminations in *ei* and *et* or *eit* sometimes occur in old French: thus *je trouvey, je saluey, it chanteit, il desarmeit*, etc. (*Gr. Comp.* p. 248ᶜ). The first and third persons of the perfect, in the two other French conjugations, anciently were not as now terminated in *s* and *t*, but wanted those consonants, as *je perdi, je vi, il nasqui, il rendi, je converti, j'establi, il se departi, il failli*, (*Gr.*

---

[1] An intermediate form of the French imperfect between *amaea* and *amoue*, viz. *ameve*, omitted by M. Raynouard, is pointed out by Orell, p. 100—3: thus 'Certes li paiz ne *cessevet*,' (Si quidem non cessabat pax,) St. Bernard. 'Iu *jueyve* par defors en la place,' (ludebam ego foris in platea,) St. Bernard. 'Alsi com eles en après *raconterent*,' (ut post ipsam referebant,) St. Gregory. [See also Burguy, vol. i. p. 218.]

[2] On the third person of the French preterite, see Orell, p. 107.

Comp. p. 271, 281.) The addition of *s* to the first person of the preterite is an arbitrary change, which likewise sometimes occurred in the Provençal (*Gr. Rom.* p. 217): the final *t* of the third person appears, however, to have been retained from the Latin.

On the passive voice of the Provençal and the other languages there is little to be said, as it is formed in all by means of the past participle and the verb substantive. The destruction of the more perfect form of conjugation which is shown in the Greek verb, had already been begun by the change which compounded the Latin language of a Hellenic and a foreign element: so that some of the Latin passive tenses are formed by inflexion, as *amor, amabor,* others by means of the verb substantive, *amatus sum, eram, ero, forem,* etc. All these remains of inflexion were destroyed by the influence of the Germans, and the Romance languages form their passive tenses without exception by an auxiliary verb, (*Gr. Rom.* p. 192. *Comp.* p. 285.)

All these languages likewise agree in giving a passive sense to the third person of the verb active together with the pronoun *se*; as in Provençal, 'czo que *se conten* en aquesta leiczon,' 'that which is contained in that lesson,' (*Gr. Comp.* p. 287.) By this use of *se*, as well as of the other pronouns, a verb obtains a reflective sense, which at length becomes merely passive. The Italian makes great use of this mode of expression, and employs it as a substitute for the French *on*, which the Italian had originally copied from the German, but which never came into general use, and for some centuries has fallen into complete desuetude, (see above, p. 158.)

The Provençal infinitive has preserved the Latin termination, rejecting the final vowel, as *amar* from *amare*, *sentir* from *sentire*, *far* from *facere*, etc. Sometimes, however, there are two forms of the infinitive, one retaining the final vowel, which the other form rejected, and sometimes suppressing an internal vowel, which the other form preserved; thus *far* and *faire* from *facere*, *querer* and *querre* from *quærere*, *seguir* and *segre* from *sequi*, (modified into *sequire*, according to a principle which will be presently explained,) (*Gr. Rom.* p. 194—7.)

Of the other Romance languages the Italian has preserved unchanged the Latin terminations of the active infinitive: the Spanish, like the Provençal, has suppressed the final vowel. The French, suppressing the final *e*, has retained unchanged the termination in *ir*, as *sentir*; that in *ar* it has, as usual[1], changed into *er*, as *mander* from *mandar*, *aimer* from *amar*. The Latin infinitives of the second and third conjugations it subjected to greater modifications: in some it suppressed the penultimate vowel of the termination, as *defendre* from *defendere*, *fondre* from *fundere*, *rompre* from *rumpere*, *connoistre* from *cognoscere*[2]; in others it suppressed the final vowel, and then changed the last syllable into *eir*, and lastly into *oir*: thus *habere*, *aver*, *aveir*, *avoir*; *movere*, *mover*, *moveir*, *mouvoir*; *sedere*, *seer*, *seeir*, *seoir*; *videre*, *veer*, *veeir* or *veir*, *voir*. It will be observed that for the most part the French suppressed the *penult* vowel when it was *short*,

[1] See above, p. 123, on the termination in *arius*, which the French sometimes changed into *aire*, but more frequently into *er*.

[2] Anciently, however, these terminations were sometimes written with *er*: thus *aprender*, *committer*, *deffender*, *discender*, *mitter*, *prender*, etc. M. Raynouard by an oversight cites *ester*, from Littleton, s. 276, as an instance of this form, which, as he himself has explained, is for *estar* from *stare*.

that is, in verbs of the third conjugation, as in *rendre, vendre, fendre, perdre, croire, naître,* etc. ; and suppressed the *final* vowel when the penult was *long,* as in *avoir, chaloir, douloir, mouvoir, souloir, valoir, voir,* etc. This distinction, however, is by no means invariably observed, as on the one hand there are *taire* from *tacēre, rire* from *ridēre;* on the other there are *decevoir, falloir, percevoir, pleuvoir, savoir, cheoir*[1], from *decipĕre, fallĕre, percipĕre, pluĕre, sapĕre, cadĕre: pouvoir* and *vouloir* are derived from *potere* and *volere,* barbarous forms for *posse* and *velle*[2], which may perhaps have had the penult long from the beginning, as they are now pronounced by the Italians, who (it may be remarked) likewise lengthen the penult of *sapere,* (*Gr. Comp.* p. 239, 257—63.)

The Latin termination in *ere* has often become *ire* in the Romance languages: thus in the Provençal *delir* and *florir* from *delere* and *florere* Lat. The following table exhibits some verbs in the three principal Romance languages, which have respectively undergone this change.

From *ēre* of the second Latin conjugation:

Latin.	Ital.	Span.	French.
abolere	abolire	abolir	abolir
implere	empiere and empire		emplir
florere	florire		fleurir

[1] On the verb *cheoir,* see Orell, p. 213, Burguy, vol. ii. p. 18.
[2] Other instances of the reduction of anomalous Latin infinitives to the regular terminations in the Romance languages are afforded by the word *esse,* which became *essere* or *esser:* and by *ferre,* which, though lost in its simple form, has been variously modified in its compound forms into *deferire, profferire, riferire, sofferire, trasferire* Ital., *deferir, proferir, referir, sufrir, transferir* Span., *souffrir* French.

Latin	Ital.	Span.	French.
languere	languire		languir
pœnitere	ripentere and ripentire	arrepentir	repentir
tenere	tenere	tenir	tenir

From *ĕre* of the third Latin conjugation:

Latin	Ital.	Span.	French.
adquirere		adquirir	acquérir
agere	agire		agir
applaudere	applaudere and applaudire	aplaudir	applaudir
advertere	avvertire	advertir	avertir
capere	capire		
currere	correre	currer	courir
concurrere	concorrere	concurrir	concourir
convertere	convertere and convertire	convertir	convertir
fallere	fallire	fallir	faillir
fremere	fremere and fremire		frémir
fugere	fuggire	huir	fuir
gemere	gemere and gemire	gemir	gémir
includere	inchiudere	incluir	
incidere	incidere	incidir	
regere	reggere	regir	régir
reprimere	reprimere	reprimir	réprimer
tradere	tradire		trahir
traducere	tradurre	traducir	traduire
vomere			vomir[1]

The Romance languages substituted for the inflected form of the passive infinitive mood, the past participle and the verb substantive: as for *amari, essere amato* Ital., *ser amado* Span., *esser amatz* Prov., *être aimé* French.

[1] [Compare Diez, *Rom. Gr.* vol. ii. p. 126.]

In the deponent verbs this expedient would not suffice: therefore the infinitive was by different means reduced to an active form. The following are instances of this change.

Latin.	Ital.	Span.	Prov.	French.
exhortari	esortare	exhortar		exhorter
irasci			irascer	
luctari	lottare	luchar	luchar	lutter
mori	morire	morir	morir	mourir
mentiri	mentire	mentir	mentir	mentir
nasci	nascere	nacer	nascer	naître[1]
pati	patir	padecer		
progredi	progredire			
recordari	ricordare	recordar		
sequi	seguire	seguir	seguir and segre	suivir and suivre[2]
sortiri	sortire		sortir	sortir

The principle of declension for present and past participles in the Provençal has been already stated in connexion with that of nouns, (above, p. 79, 80): it now only remains to ascertain the manner of their formation.

The present participle was in all the Romance languages preserved from the Latin without change, except that those of the second and third conjugation were the same, as *temens* from *temer*, *sentens* from *sentir*, Prov.

The past participles in the Prov. followed the track of the Latin, except that the penult vowel of the participle of the second conjugation was slightly altered, as is shown in the following scheme.

---

[1] *Naistre* (*naître*) from *nascere*, like *paistre* (*paître*) from *pascere*, and *croitre* from *crescere*.
[2] *Suivir* was used in old French, Orell, p. 257. Roquefort in v. *suir*. [Burguy, vol. ii. p. 210.]

CHAPTER IV.

	First Conj.	Second Conj.	Third Conj.
Lat.	amatus	placitus, perditus	anditus
Prov.	amatz	plazutz, perdutz	auzitz

This is the regular mode of formation; and new participles were thus created independently of the Latin, and in cases where the Latin verb had no participles, or where they were different; as in the subjoined examples.

Lat. infin.	Lat. part.	Prov. infin.	Prov. part.
florere[1]		florir	floritz
lucere		luzer	luzitz[2]
timere		temer	temutz
cadere	casus	cazer	cazutz
recipere	receptus	recebre	recebutz
mordere	morsus	mordre	mordutz
vivere	victus	vivre	viscutz

In other cases, however, the Provençal verb did not form its participle according to the rule, but retained only the anomalous Latin form.

Lat. infin.	Lat. part.	Prov. infin.	Prov. part.
aperire	apertus	ubrir	ubertz
claudere	clausus	olorre	claus
coquere	coctus	cozer	colz
frangere	fractus	franher	frach
mori	mortuus	morir	morts
nasci	natus	nascer	natz
occidere	occisus	occir	occis

Gr. Rom. p. 197—204. *Comp.* p. 289, 90.

In other instances, however, the Prov. verb had two

---

[1] M. Raynouard gives *florescere*, not *florere*, as the original of the Prov. *florir*: but see the explanation above, p. 181—2.

[2] These words are perhaps not the participles of *florir* and *luzer*, but adjectives from *floridus* and *lucidus*.

participles, one anomalous retained from the Latin, and
one regular formed according to the Prov. analogy.

Lat. part.	Irreg. Prov. part.	reg. Prov. part.
absconsus	rescons	rescondutz
corruptus	corrotz	corromputz
electus	eleitz	eligitz, eliguiz
defensus	defos	defendutz
iratus	iratz	irascutz
redemptus	rezomtz	rezemutz
ruptus	rotz	romputz

Gr. Rom. p. 202, 205.   *Comp.* p. 290, 91[1].

The formation of the past participles of the first and
third conjugations in the other Romance languages offers

[1] M. Raynouard, *Gr. Rom.* p. 204, makes an anomalous class of
'past participles in *at*, which changing the Latin termination have
passed into the conjugation in *or*, although originally they belonged to
another Latin conjugation.' His examples are

Lat. infin.	Lat. part.	Prov. infin.	Prov. part.
1 cupere	cupitus	cobeitar	cobeitatz
2 oblivisci	oblitus	oblidar	oblidatz
3 uti	usus	usar	usatz
4 tremere		tremblar	tremblatz
5 calefacere	calefactus	calfar	calfatz
6 dulcescere	dulcitus	adolzar	adolzatz

In the first four of these instances the Prov. does not correspond to
the Latin verb: in the three first it is a derivative formed from the
Latin participle or supine, viz., *cupitare* from *cupitum*, *oblitare* from
oblitum, *usitare* from *usum*, (like *ventitare* from *ventum*, *excitare* from
excitum, etc.): the fourth, which in Latin would be *tremulare*, appears
to be formed from *tremulus:* the Ital. and Span. have *tremolare* and
tremolar, (see above, p. 71, note [1].) *Calfar* is contracted from *calfacere*,
as *far* from *facere : calfatz* is likewise contracted from *calefactus;* where
the final *a* belongs not to the termination, but to the body of the word.
Adolzar is likewise a new verb formed from *dulcis* or *dulcor*, and has no
reference to *dulcescere*. These words, therefore, ought not to be arranged, with M. Raynouard, under the head of anomalous participles.

no difficulty or anomaly: from *atus* and *itus* the Ital. and Span., according to the rule already explained, make *ato* and *ito*, and the French, so long as it observed the distinction of cases, made *ets* or *ez*, *its* or *iz* in the nom., *et* and *it* in the acc.: which latter forms it now retains in use, having rejected the final *t*, as *aimet*, *aimé*, *sentit*, *senti*: the former, like *libertat*, *libertet*, *liberté*, (above, p. 135. *Gr. Comp.* p. 239—41, 277—9.) It is curious to observe the number of changes to which the past participle of the first conjugation has been subjected in different Romance languages: thus from *amatus*, *amatz* Prov., from *amatum*, *amat* Prov., (whence *aimet*, *aimé* French,) *amato* Ital., *amado* Span., *amao*, *umà*, and *amò*, in different Italian dialects[1].

In the second conjugation the Prov., as we have already seen, constantly changed the *i* in the penult of the Latin participle into *u*, and formed new participles according to that analogy, making, for example, *perdutz* from *perder*, and *irascutz* from *irascer*. The Italian likewise makes the same change, and says *perduto*, *temuto*, *tenuto*, etc. The Span. now makes these participles in *ido*, as *temido*, *perdido*, *tenido*: anciently, however, their termination was sometimes *udo*, as *connosudo*, *contenudo*, *perdudo*, *tenudo*, *vendudo*, etc. The regular termination of the French participles of this conjugation was likewise *uz* or *ut*, now simply *u*, as *venditus*, *venduts*, *vendus*, *vendut*, *vendu*, like *virtutem*, *vertut*, *vertu*, (*Gr. Comp.* p. 239—41, 263—8.)

M. Raynouard appears to lay great stress on the coincidence of terminations just stated, and he thinks

[1] See Gamba, *Serie di Scrittori Veneziani*, p. 28, 74.

that such an agreement is a decisive proof that some of the Romance languages were derived from a language intermediate between them and the Latin. 'I will remark,' he says, 'that the participles in *udo* which occur in ancient Spanish cannot have been borrowed directly from the Latin, as the corresponding Latin participles were not in *utus*.' (p. 265.) If the change had been very considerable, for instance, if for the Latin termination in *itus*, all the Romance languages had substituted the Greek termination ομενος, and had made *perdomeno, temomeno,* etc., then every one would agree with M. Raynouard that it would be necessary to look for a common cause independent of the Latin usage. But when the change is so inconsiderable as that in question, when it is a mere modification of a vowel sound, it does not appear to warrant any such hypothesis as that attempted to be raised upon it. The *i* in the penult of the Latin participle became *u* in the Ital., Prov., and French: in ancient Span. it was sometimes one and sometimes the other: but usage has now given universal currency to the Latin vowel. In Span. moreover, the Latin *t* has become *d*: a change of perpetual occurrence, and which likewise appears to have taken place in the Provençal, as the feminines of the past participles all exhibit that letter; thus *amatz, amada, amadas: temutz, temuda, temudas; sentitz, sentida, sentidas,* (*Gr. Rom.* p. 206—7[1].) In these variations from the

[1] The modern Provençal makes the same change in past participles, as well as in adjectives formed from ancient participles, though it has lost the final *t* of the masc. gender: thus, masc. sing. *bouliga* moved, fem. sing. *bouligado,* fem. pl. *bouligados: bandi,* banished, fem. sing. *bandido,* fem. pl. *bandidas: cousi,* heard, fem. sing. *cousido,* fem. pl.

Latin there seems to me to be nothing which each language may not reasonably be conceived to have effected for itself, independently of any foreign influence: in the Span., moreover, the Latin termination has been universally restored, which would scarcely have happened if it had not been retained by an uninterrupted tradition, and if the modern language had been entirely derived from the Prov. It is to be remarked that the change of *i* into *u* has only taken place in participles where, like *tacitus, perditus, venditus,* it was short, and where probably it had a thick indistinct sound, which might easily pass into *u*: in participles of the last conjugation, as *sentitus, auditus, feritus,* where the *i* was long, that vowel is in all the modern forms preserved unchanged.

As in the Provençal, so in the other Romance languages, many participles of the second and third conjugations were not formed according to the rules just explained, but were derived immediately from the Latin: thus in Italian *rompere* makes not *romputo* but *rotto, cuocere* not *cociuto* but *cotto, morire* not *morito* but *morto*: in Span. *poner* not *ponido* but *puesto*: *abrir* not *abrido* but *aperto*: in French the participles *né, clos, mis, ouvert,* are borrowed directly from the Latin participles *natus, clausus, missus, apertus,* and not formed regularly from *naître, clorre, mettre, ouvrir,* etc. M. Raynouard describes the derivation in question, by saying that 'the irregular Latin participles, having become Romance, passed into

---

cousidos ? pouli, beautiful, from *politus; fortuna,* fortunate, from *fortunatus,* fem. sing. *pouldo, fortunado,* fem. pl. *poulidos, fortunados.* See *Grammaire Française expliquée au moyen de la Langue Provençale,* (Marseille, 1826,) p. 32, 73, 78, 86.

CONJUGATION OF VERBS. 189

the other Latin languages¹:' a supposition perfectly gratuitous, as there is no reason why these forms should not have passed directly from the Latin into each modern language without any foreign assistance.

The Ital. and Span., moreover, like the Prov., have in many instances not only preserved the Latin participle, but have also formed another according to their own analogy. In this manner many verbs have two past participles, one irregular, the other regular, one ancient and the other modern.

Lat. part.	Ital. irreg. part.	Ital. reg. part.
natus	nato	nasciuto (nascere)
occisus	ucciso	ucciduto (uccidere)
pronsus	preso	prenduto (prendere)
quæsitus	chiesto	chieduto (chiedere)
rasus	raso	raduto (radere)
tonsus	tonso	tonduto (tondere)

Lat. part.	Span. irreg. part.	Span. reg. part.
conversus	converso	convertido (convertir)
extinctus	extincto	extinguido (extinguir)
natus	nado	nacido (nacer)
prensus	preso	prendido (prender)
ruptus	rotto	rompido (romper)
scriptus	escrito	escribido (escribir)²

Gr. Comp. p. 289—97.

¹ 'Ces participes, devenus romans, passèrent dans les autres langues de l'Europe latine.' Gr. Comp. p. 290. By Romance, it is to be observed, M. Raynouard means Provençal.

² These double forms, it will be observed, properly belong to the same verb, like ἔτυψα and ἔτυπον; and they are altogether different from those cases in which a more recently formed verb has not only its own regular participle, but also a participle of an obsolete form, which is assigned to it as having no owner, and being a sort of waif or

CHAPTER IV.

A system of double forms, exactly analogous to those pointed out in the participles of some of the Romance languages, prevails in the preterites and participles of many English verbs, which have preserved their ancient Saxon form, and at the same time coined a new one according to the more prevailing analogy. Thus the common participle of *acquaint* is *acquainted*, in Scotch it is *acquent*: on the other hand the common preterites of *wind* and *grind* are *wound* and *ground*, in Scotch they are *winded* and *grinded*: in many other cases the original form has become antiquated and the modern form is alone in use, as *clomb* and *climbed*, *spat* and *spit*, *clave* and *cleft*, *puck* and *picked*, *squoze* and *squeezed*: although these ancient preterites still retain their currency as provincialisms[1]. Some English nouns likewise have a double plural, as *brethren* and *brothers*, one formed according to the ancient, one according to the more recent practice; like the Ital. nouns mentioned above, such as *corpo*, pl. *corpora* and *corpi*; *prato* pl. *prata* and *prati*, which have the Latin as well as the Ital. form of the plural[2]. The double genitive case in English, one formed by synthesis, the other by analysis, (as *Shakspeare's plays, an edition of Shakspeare*,) is another example of an ancient and a modern form running parallel in a language, without the one supplanting the other.

estray. Thus in Spanish *juntar* and *soltar* (*solutare*) have their regular passive participles *juntado* and *soltado*: but, besides these, they likewise lay claim to *junto* and *suelto*, from *junctus* and *solutus*, the participles of the obsolete Latin verbs *jungere* and *solvere*. See *Gr. Comp.* p. 203.

[1] See *Philol. Museum*, vol. ii. p. 106 and 214, and other parts of the same article, where this subject is treated at length and fully explained.

[2] Above, p. 117.

§ 2. SYNTAX OF VERBS.

Having thus examined the structure of the Provençal and the other Romance verbs, I will now transcribe from M. Raynouard a few remarks on their syntax, and their relations with other parts of speech.

The Prov. sometimes uses its gerund like the Latin, as 'aman viv o aman morrai,' 'I live in loving and I shall die in loving:' sometimes it prefixed the preposition *en* or *a*, as 'en ploran serai chantaire,' 'in weeping I shall be a singer.' 'Al pareissen de las flors,' 'at the appearing of the flowers,' (*Gr. Rom.* p. 230.)

All the Romance languages, like the Greek and sometimes the Latin, used the infinitive mood as a substantive, (which indeed it must in strictness be considered,) and prefixed prepositions to it, as in Prov. 'En agradar et en voler Es l'amors de dos fis amans,' 'In pleasing and in wishing is the love of two pure lovers.' In the other languages this idiom is too well known to require the repetition of examples, (*Gr. Rom.* p. 231. *Comp.* p. 300[1].)

In Latin, as is well known, pronouns when the subjects of verbs were rarely expressed. In all the Romance languages this usage was retained, both when the suppressed pronoun signified a person, and when it signified a thing, in which case a verb is said to be employed impersonally. In French the ellipsis of the pronoun has now become obsolete: but it was anciently universal, and used in all styles whether lofty or familiar; nor was it to the jocular poetry of Marot, or to the style known in France by the name of *Marotique*, that this idiom was

---

[1] [See Diez, *Rom. Gr.* vol. iii. p. 208.]

confined, as some writers have supposed, (*Gr. Rom.* p. 233—7. *Comp.* p. 301.)

The infinitive preceded by a negation was in Prov. sometimes used with an imperative force[1]: as 'Non temer, Maria,' 'Fear not, Mary.' ' Ai amors, no m'aucire,' 'ah, love, do not kill me.' This idiom is still used in Italian[2], and it existed in old French; but M. Raynouard states that he has not been able to find any instance of it in Spanish or Portuguese, (*Gr. Rom.* p. 237. *Comp.* p. 302.)

All the Romance languages have used the custom of addressing a person in the plural number of the verb, any adjective which refers to the subject nevertheless remaining in the singular, (*Gr. Comp.* p. 238. *Comp.* p. 303.) The Provençal, moreover, like the Latin, often put the verb in the sing. number after several nouns: as

> Dieus sal vos, en cui *es assis*
> Mos joys, mos desportz e mos ris.

'God save you, in whom *is* placed my joy, my happiness, and my laughter.'

The Prov. likewise used the plural after a noun of multitude, as

> Amor *blasmon* per non saber
> Fola gens, mais lei non es dans.

'Foolish people blame love from ignorance, but it does not suffer.'

---

[1] The infinitive is never thus used except in a negative address: see Raynouard, *Journ. des Sav.* 1825, p. 184.

[2] See Perticari, *Dif. di Dante*, c. 18. vol. i. p. 375. [Diez, *Rom. Gr.* vol. iii. p. 204.]

M. Raynouard says that 'the following form is remarkable: *ab*, with, is considered as a conjunction.'

> E pueis lo reis, ab sos baros,
> Pueion e lor spazas ceinzon.

'And then the king with his barons get up and gird their swords.'

This is one of those forms which are called ungrammatical; that is, the sentence is formed according to the sense, and not according to the structure of the words. Instances of this peculiar idiom occur in Latin, and it is of frequent occurrence in English, (*Gr. Rom.* p. 239—40[1].)

M. Raynouard closes his remarks by an explanation of the use of *que* in connexion with verbs. *Que*, as a pronoun, is derived, as has been already mentioned (p. 157,) from *quod*: as a conjunction it is taken from *quia*[2], to which word the lower Latinity attributed the senses both of *that*

---

[1] The following are Latin examples of this construction. Livy, xxi. 60. Ipse dux cum aliquot principibus capiuntur; where see Ruperti. Sallust. *Jug.* c. 38. Cohors una Ligurum cum duabus turmis Thracum...transiere ad regem. c. 101. Bocchus cum peditibus... postremam Romanorum aciem invadunt.

[2] *Ca* for *that*, used by the early Ital. poets, shows its original more plainly than *che*: thus in some verses of Ruggerone of Palermo, written about 1230 A.D. 'E la mi priega per la sua bontate *Ca* mi deggia tenere lealtate:' see Perticari, *Dif. di Dante*, c. 22, vol. ii. p. 5. *Cha* occurs in the *Lamento di Cecco*, st. 9.

> E si da un ago il cor m'ñ sentii punto,
> Cha'n vederti restai magio e balordo.

Ca (for *quia*) occurs frequently in old Spanish: see for example Milagros de N. Señora, v. 37, 47, 71, 77, 84, 87, etc. Sanchez, vol. ii.

O

and *because*[1]. The Prov. conjunction *que* thus obtained two senses: 1. where it either replaced the use of the Latin accusative before a second verb in the infinitive mood, according to the German construction, as 'E conosc bo *que* ai dic gran follatge,' 'I know well that I have said a great absurdity,' where the classical Latin would say 'scio me dixisse:' or where the Latin would use *ut, quod*, or some other particle, as 'vos preo que m' entendatz,' 'I pray you that you will hear me.' 'Guart si que res no mi cambi,' 'Let him take care that nothing changes me.' And 2dly where it replaces *quia*, in the ordinary classical sense of *because*, as 'Alberguem lo tot plan e gen, Que ben es mutz,' 'Let us lodge him plainly and well, since he is dumb.' 'Ni contra mi malvat conselh non creia, Qu'eu sui sos hom liges,' 'And let him not believe evil counsel against me, since I am his liegeman.' M. Raynouard mentions that the manuscripts often have the various reading *quar* or *car* (from *quare*) for *que* in this sense, (*Gr. Rom.* p. 241—4.)

All the other Romance languages have this double use

[1] Matth. xxvi. 21, is in the Vulgate translated 'Amen dico vobis *quia* unus vestrum me traditurus est.' Διότι in Greek also properly and originally meant *because*: but it obtained the sense of *that* at a comparatively early period of the language, and is used for ὅτι by good writers, as Herodotus and Plato: see Welcker's *Rheinisches Museum*, vol. ii. p. 205. Dobrie, *Adversaria*, vol. i. p. 403. *Perchè* in Ital. has also a similar ambiguity; and like *quia* and διότι its original sense is *because*.

The well known assertion, 'credo quia impossibile est,' is commonly taken as a declaration of passive belief: but the truth is, that no man in his senses ever believed a thing *because* it is impossible, though he might believe a thing *in spite of* its apparent impossibility: this sentence merely means, as has been remarked by others, 'I believe *that* it is impossible.'

of the particle *que* (in Ital. *che*) in the sense both of *that* and *because*, and employ it with verbs in the same manner. The French alone has disused the causal sense of *que*, which, however, occurs in old writers, as in Amyot's translation of Plutarch,

> Il faut qu'il soit assisté d'un des dieux,
> Qu'il est si fort au combat furieux.
> *Gr. Comp.* p. 304—8.

The Prov. and the other languages sometimes suppressed the particle *that* between two verbs, as in Prov. 'Ben sapchatz ... s'icu tan non l'ames, Ja no saupra far vers ni sos.' 'Know well, if I did not love her so, I should never know how to make verses or sounds.' So in Ital. 'Dubitava ... non fosse alcuna dea :' in Span. 'temo ... seré culpado :' in old French, 'Ne nous ne pourrions nier ... Ne nous aiez par armes pris,' (*Gr. Rom.* p. 245. *Comp.* p. 308—11.)

M. Raynouard concludes his chapter on the comparison of the Romance verbs, with a brief enumeration of some of their most important points of resemblance: and he then enquires whether any one who sees such conformities can believe that these different languages could have presented them, if they had not been derived from a common origin[1]. There is no doubt or difference of opinion about the answer to be given to this question: every one admits that the Romance languages had a common origin; that common origin has generally been supposed to be the Latin, and the Latin alone: M.

---

[1] 'Quand on voit de telles conformités, peut-on croire que ces diverses langues auraient pu les offrir, si elles n'avaient en primitivement une origine commune.' p. 811.

Raynouard undertakes to show that it was the ancient Provençal: but his argument is not assisted by proofs which, however consistent with the truth of his own hypothesis, are equally consistent with the truth of that which he is attempting to overthrow.

CHAPTER V.

Prepositions, Adverbs, and Conjunctions in the Romance Languages.

§ 1. PREPOSITIONS.

IN examining the indeclinable parts of speech in the Romance languages, viz. prepositions, adverbs, and conjunctions or particles, it will be convenient to begin with the prepositions, as many are used adverbially, and need not be repeated under the head of adverbs.

AB, A. This Latin preposition was preserved in the Provençal, but its meaning was entirely changed, as it received the sense of *with* instead of *from* or *by*. This wide departure from the original meaning of prepositions will be pointed out below in other instances.

Thus in the oath of 842: '*Ab Ludher* nul plai nunquam prindrai,' 'I will never make any treaty *with* Lothaire;' in the poem on Boethius, 'Ella *ab Boeci* parla ta dolzament,' 'She spoke so sweetly *with Boethius*.' Or the *b* was omitted, as '*Es a dreit* jugatz,' 'he is judged *with justice*.' The Ital., Span., and French likewise sometimes used the preposition *a* in the sense of *with*, as 'Furo ricevuti tutti a grandissimo honore,' (*Giov. Villani.*) 'La cinta fué obrada a muy grant maestria,' (*Poema de Alexandro.*) 'Et furent reçu a grant feste et a grant joie,'

(Villehardouin.)[1] These languages, however, had other prepositions which they commonly employed in that sense[2].

The Provençal subjected this word to a change of which there are examples in other languages[3], by inserting *m* before *b*, when it became *amb*; as 'Et aqui atrobero lor fraire Thomas et l'arcevesque Turpi *amb elhs*,' 'And there they found their brother Thomas and the archbishop Turpin *with them*.' Afterwards the final *b* after *m* was rejected, as was also the case with the final *d* or *t* after *n*[4], and the preposition became *am*, as 'Am l'ajutori de Dieu,' 'With the help of God.'— From the completest of these forms the modern Provençal has derived its preposition *embe*, which is in common use in the sense of *with*.

The French on the other hand has formed its preposition *avec*[5] from *ab*, by the addition of a suffix, to which I am not aware of any parallel, (*Gr. Rom.* p. 249—51. *Comp.* p. 318—20[6].)

---

[1] Galvani, *Osservazioni sulla Poesia dei Trovatori*, p. 131, quotes some instances of the use of *ab* for *cum* in Latin authors, as 'Et tenerum molli torquet ab arte latus,' Ovid. *Amor.* ii. 4, 30. 'Ne possent tacto stringere ab axe latus,' Propert. iii. 11, 24.

[2] Some instances of *d* being used in ancient French with the sense of the Latin *ab*, as 'aprenciz à moi,' 'discite a me,' in St. Bernard, are cited by Orell, *Alt-französische Grammatik*, p. 317, (Zurich, 1830.)

[3] Thus ὄβριμος and ὄμβριμος, ἀπλακίω and ἀμπλακίω, Σηλυβρία and Σηλυμβρία, Τύφρηστος and Τύμφρηστος, θιβρός and θιμβρός, Θίβρων and Θίμβρων (see Meineke, *Euphor. Fragm.* p. 140, 157,) in Greek: *Robert* is Ρόμπερτος in the Byzantine writers. See above, p. 71, note [1].

[4] See above, p. 80.

[5] See Orell, ibid. p. 318.

[6] [See Diez, *Rom. Gr.* vol. ii. p. 453, vol. iii. p. 167, and Burguy, *Gr. de la Langue d'Oil*, vol. ii. p. 345, who, relying upon the ancient

AD, A. This preposition was preserved in the Provençal, the final consonant being always suppressed before a consonant, and sometimes before a vowel. M. Raynouard says that 'sometimes the *d* is for the sake of euphony changed into *z*: thus in the *Roman de Jaufre*, of which there are two manuscripts, one has 'El pres eran ad anar,' the other 'az anar,' (*Gr. Rom.* p. 66.) *Az* in the latter instance is *ads*, (like *Thiebauz* for *Thiebauds*,) and is obtained by the addition of *s*, many other examples of which will be noticed.

All the other Romance languages have retained *a* from the Latin *ad*, and use it prefixed to a noun as a substitute for the Latin dative[1], (*Gr. Rom.* p. 251.)

ANTE. This preposition underwent the following changes in Provençal, *ant, an, ans* or *anz;* of which form the first only occurs as an adverb, the last is formed by the addition of a final *s*. The second only occurs in composition, as *enan, denan, adenant, abans, davan* or *devan*, which resolved into their elements are *in ante, de in ante, ad in ante, ab ante, de ab ante; antan,* 'formerly,' comes from *ante annum; derenan* and *deserenan*, 'henceforth,' M. Raynouard derives from 'de hora in antea,' and 'de ipsa hora in antea.'

forms *avoc* and *avuec*, derive the word from *ab hoc*. Ampère, p. 202, thinks that *ove* was the original form of *avec*, and derives it from *ubi*.]

[1] Cinonio in his Treatise on the Italian particles, c. 1, does not distinguish between *a* derived from *ab*, and *a* derived from *ad*: which, although they have the same sound, are, like *che* from *quod* and *che* from *quia*, etymologically different words. The same observation likewise applies to the preposition *da*, which in such expressions as 'da sera a mane,' 'fatto da me,' comes from *de ab*; in such expressions as 'verrò da voi,' 'I will come to your house,' 'ginje da donne,' 'età da marito,' 'carta da scrivere,' 'da dieci mesi,' 'about ten months,' it comes from *de ad*. [Compare Diez, *Rom. Gr.* vol. iii. p. 150.]

The other Romance languages had also various derivatives of this preposition. The Italian once used *ante* unchanged: its common forms are, however, *avanti* and *davanti* (anciently *avante* and *davante*[1]) from *ab ante* and *de ab ante*; also *dianzi* and *dinanzi* from *de antius* and *de in antius*. The Span. has retained *ante* as a preposition unchanged; as an adverb it used *antes*, with a final *s*. *Ant* for *ante*, and *avant* for *avante*, occur in ancient writers. It has likewise *antaño* in the same sense and with the same origin as the Prov. *antan*. The French has *avant* and *devant*, like the Prov. and Ital. and *dorénavant* from *de hora in ab ante*, which does not precisely agree with the Prov. *derenan* or *deserenan*, and moreover adheres more closely to the Latin, (*Gr. Rom.* p. 258—61. *Comp.* p. 344.)

From *antius* the neuter comparative of *ante*, like *propius* from *prope*, Menage derives *anzi* Ital., *antes* Span., and *ainsi*, anciently *ans* and *ains*, French. The Prov. has *ans* or *aintz*, in the sense of *rather*, which confirms this etymology. The Ital. uses *anzi* not only in the sense of *rather*, but also as a preposition equivalent to *ante*[2].

APUD. From this preposition the Ital. has made *appo*, like *capo* from *caput*; none of the other Romance languages appear to have preserved it.

CIRCA. Preserved unchanged in Italian: the Spanish makes it *cerca*. M. Raynouard does not mention any Provençal derivative of this preposition, nor is it preserved in French[3].

---

[1] Cinonio, *Trattato delle Particelle*, c. 36, 76, 82, 89.
[2] Cinonio, c. 27. [Diez, *Rom. Gr.* vol. iii. p. 176. Burguy, vol. ii. p. 271.]
[3] [Diez, ib. p. 176.]

CONTRA. The Ital., Span., and Prov., have this preposition unchanged: the French has softened the final *a* into *e*. The Ital. likewise has the form *contro*, whence it has formed *incontro*: the Span. also has the adverb *al encuentro*. The Prov. has *encontra*, (*Gr. Rom.* p. 264[1].)

CUM. In Ital. and Span. this preposition has been preserved under the form *con*[2]; in Prov. and French its place has been supplied (as already stated) by *ab* and *avec*. Nevertheless the Prov. used it as an adverb or conjunction in the sense of *as* or *how*, sometimes in its Latin form, sometimes making it *con* or *co*: thus ' no sai com,' ' I know not how ;' ' Fresca *cum* rosa en mai,' ' fresh as rose in May;' 'Si *com* in isto pergamen es scrit,' ' as it is written in that parchment;' ' Aissi *col* peis an en l'aigua lor vida,' ' Like as the fishes have their life in the water.'

The Ital. and Span. have from *cum* formed *come* and *como*, which they use in the same manner as the Prov. *com*[3]: the French has made *comme* (anciently *com*) and *comment*, which latter is a lengthened form corresponding to the Ital. *comente* employed by ancient writers. The Ital. likewise sometimes used *chente* for *che*, and *finente* for *fino*: which Perticari compares with *Moisente* for *Mose*, which occurs in the *Nobla Leycon*[4]: it will be shown hereafter that *niente* is probably a paragogic form of this kind, from the acc. of the Latin *res*, (*Gr. Rom.* p. 265 —7. *Comp.* p. 342[5].)

[1] [Diez, *Rom. Gr.* p. 178. Burguy, vol. ii. p. 346.]
[2] See above, p. 66.
[3] *Com* occurs without the euphonic vowel in both Italian and Spanish.
[4] *Difesa di Dante*, c. 12, n. 12 to the text.
[5] [Diez, ib. p. 167. Burguy, vol. ii. p. 281.]

DE. All the languages derived from the Latin have retained this preposition unchanged, (except the Ital. which now, except in certain cases, uses *di*;) and employ it before a noun to express the meaning conveyed in Latin by the genitive and sometimes by the ablative case, (*Gr. Rom.* p. 267. *Comp.* p. 321[1].)

EXTRA. From this word the Prov. made *estra*, *ester*, and *esters*, used both as prepositions and adverbs. The latter forms appear to have arisen thus: *estra*, *estre*, *ester*, and with the final *s*, *esters*, (*Gr. Rom.* p. 272.) The Span. has preserved this preposition unchanged: it likewise occurs as *estre* in old French[c].

From *extra*, by the suppression of the first syllable and the addition of a final *s*, appears to be derived the Prov. adverb *tras*, as well as the French *très*: in Ital. *stra* and *tra* occur sometimes in the same sense, which show their origin more distinctly, as '*straricco*,' '*strabbondanza*,' '*strabuono*,' 'travalente e tranobile imperadore,' etc.[3]

IN. The Prov. changed this preposition into *en*, and before a consonant sometimes suppressed the *n*: the Span. and French likewise use *en*, but never omit the *n*: the Ital. alone has preserved *in* unchanged, though *en* sometimes occurs in ancient writers, (*Gr. Rom.* p. 267. *Comp.* p. 322[4].)

INFRA. The Ital. alone (as it appears) has retained this preposition, which it has changed into *fra*, giving it the sense of *among* and *in*. There appears to be no way of accounting for so great a change of signification as

---

[1] [Diez, *Rom. Gr.* p. 166.]
[2] Orell, p. 324. [Diez, ib. p. 161. Burguy, vol. ii. p. 853.]
[3] Annot. 59 to Cinonio, c. 191. [Burguy, vol. ii. p. 353.]
[4] [Diez, ib. p. 163.]

this word has undergone, except by supposing that *fra*
and *tra* have been confounded, (see Cinonio, c. 112, 134.)

INTER or INTRA. Hence the Span., Prov., and French
formed their preposition *entre*; the Ital. sometimes preserves the Latin form without change, sometimes it omits
the first syllable, and makes *tra* from *intra*, like *fra* from
infra. Probably in both these words the first syllable
was omitted, as being taken for the preposition *in*, and a
separate word; in the same way that *super* lost its last
syllable, which was mistaken for the preposition *per*[1].

Entre in Prov. was sometimes used as a conjunction
with *que* in the sense of *whilst*, as 'entre qu'es tos,'
'while he is young:' which particle at other times took
the form of *mentre* with the same sense. This latter
word, which likewise occurs in Ital., in Span. under the
form of *mientras*, (anciently sometimes written *mientre*,)
and in French as *endementres* or *endementiers*, appears to
be compounded of *dum intra*: for in old Ital. *domentre*
sometimes occurs[2], which evidently betrays its origin.
Domentre was doubtless corrupted into *di mentre* or *dementre*, and the first syllable being taken for the preposition
de was rejected as superfluous.

From *intro* the Prov. made a preposition *entro*, which
had the sense of *until*, as 'entro a la fin del mont,' 'until
the end of the world.' Sometimes the first syllable was
omitted, and it became *tro*, as the Ital. made *tra* from
intra, as 'del cap tro al talo,' 'from the head to the heel.'

---

[1] See below in *super*, p. 207. [Diez, *Rom. Gr.* p. 180.]

[2] See Cinonio, c. 171, who gives examples both of *domentre* and *di
mentre*, and Muratori in v. who derives *domentre* from *dum interea*, or
dum interim. *Dementre* occurs in Provençal, see Galvani, p. 262.
See also Orell, p. 334. [Burguy, vol. ii. p. 380.]

In both these forms it could be used as a conjunction. From *intro* the Ital. has made *entro*, and by prefixing *de*, *dentro*, in the sense of *within*. The Span. likewise made *dentro*, and likewise *adentro* by prefixing *a* as well as *de*, (*Gr. Rom.* p. 268—71. *Comp.* p. 323, 343.)

JUXTA. The Prov. changed this preposition into *justa*, *josta*, and, prefixing *de*, *dejosta*. The Ital. has *giusta* and *giusto*, the old French *jouxte*[1], (*Gr. Rom.* p. 283—4.)

PER. The Prov. and Ital. made no change in this preposition: the Span. made it *por* and *para*, the French *pour* and *par*, but the original form occurs in old writers of both these languages. The Prov. as well as the Ital. has the particle *pero* from *per hoc*, (*Gr. Rom.* p. 300—2. *Comp.* p. 322[2].)

POST. This word the Prov. changed into the forms *pos*, *pois*, *puois*, *poisas*, *pus*, and *pueis*: using it, however, as an adverb and conjunction, and not as a preposition. It likewise, as in many other instances, prefixed the preposition *de* and thus made *de pois*. From *post* the Ital. made *poi*, which once was sometimes used as a preposition[3]; but now is only used as an adverb or conjunction. *Dopo*, which appears to be compounded of *de* and *post*, (*dopoi* from *depoi*, like *domani* from *demane*, and *domandare* from *demandare*,) has taken the place of the Latin preposition. The Span. made anciently *pos* and *pois*, and, by a composition with *de*, *depos*[4]. Afterwards, as in other instances[5], it changed *pos* into *pues*, and by adding a final *s* after *de*,

---

[1] Orell, p. 826. [Diez, *Rom. Gr.* p. 174.]
[2] [Diez, ib. p. 169.]
[3] Cinonio, c. 201, § 4.
[4] *Poema de Alexandro*, 1842. Sanchez, vol. ii. p. 261.
[5] See above, p. 67, n. 1.

made *depos* into *despues*, the modern form. So the French made *puis* and *depuis*; the former of which was formerly, the latter is now, used as a preposition. It may be remarked that the Ital. has *poscia* from *postea*, a form which all the other Romance languages have lost, (*Gr. Rom.* p. 303. *Comp.* p. 326[1].)

PROPE. From this word the Prov. formed as adverbs and prepositions *prop* and *pres*, and by composition *aprop*, *apres*, *en apres*, *de prop*. *Pres* appears to have been formed from *prope* as follows: *prop, pro, pre, pres*: all which changes, viz. the rejection of a final consonant, the change of *o* into *e*, and the addition of a final *s*, may be paralleled by many instances in the Romance languages. The corresponding forms are *presso* and *appresso* in Ital. *apres* in old Span. *près, après*, (anciently *aprop*,) and *auprès* in French.

In Prov. as in French, *apres* or *aprop* signified *after*: thus

Cal prezatz mais e respondetz premiers;
Et *aprop vos* respond En Perdigos.

'which prize you most and answer first, and *after you*, let Lord Perdigon answer.'

This change of meaning took place on account of the facility of transition from the notion of place to that of time. As *prope* meant *near*, from signifying next in the order of place, it came to mean next in order of time: after which it was easy to pass to the notion of more posteriority. This transition in Ital. may be distinctly traced in the uses of the word *appresso*: thus 'La giovane

---

[1] [Diez, *Rom. Gr.* p. 177. Burguy, vol. ii. p. 363.]
[2] See Orell, p. 318.

CHAPTER V.

subitamente si levò in piò e cominciò a fuggire verso il mare, o i cani appresso di lei:' (Boccaccio, Giorn. 5, nov. 8,) where *appresso di lei* means 'close upon her.' Again, 'Venuta era Elisa alla fine della sua novella, quando la reina ad Emilia voltatasi le mostrò voler che ella appresso d'Elisa la sua raccontasse,' (ibid, Giorn. 4, nov. 1,) where *appresso d'Elisa* means 'next after Elisa in order of time:' as in Dante,

> Però non lagrimai nè rispos'lo
> Tutto quel giorno nè la notte appresso.
> *Inferno*, c. 33[1].

Appresso, however, in Ital. never obtained the general sense which belonged to *après* in French, but was (as it appears) only used to signify immediate succession, without anything intervening. The confusion between succession of place and time may be observed in many words, as in *interval* from *intervallum*[2], and in *after*, which has both significations, (*Gr. Rom.* p. 304—6. *Comp.* p. 323[3].)

SECUNDUM. From this preposition the Prov. made *segont*, and by a change most frequent in that language *segon*. The Ital. adhering closely to the Latin made *secondo*, the Span. *segun*, anciently *segund* and *segunt*, the French originally *segont*, which has now become *selon*, (*Gr. Rom.* p. 308. *Comp.* p. 325.)

SINE. From this preposition the Prov. by adding *s* made *senes*, modified into *sens*, *ses*, and *sans*. The Ital. *senza* or *sanza* has been formed from *sens* or *sans*, by the addition of an euphonic vowel, which the French *sans*

---

[1] Cinonio, o. 31.
[2] See D. Stewart's Essay 1, on *the Beautiful*, c. 1.
[3] [Burguy, vol. ii. p. 302.]

has not taken: the old Ital., however, used both *son* and *sen*[1]. The Span. alone has remained faithful to the Latin, and says *sin:* anciently, however, it used *sen* and *senes*, like the Prov., (*Gr. Rom.* p. 308. *Comp.* p. 324².)

SUPER. This word was used by the Italian without change, but each syllable was written separately, so that the latter part was taken for the preposition *per*, and the first syllable became an independent preposition in the sense of *on*: thus 'Tutto ... su per la nave quasi morto giacevano,' (Bocc. Giorn. 2, nov. 7.) 'E lei segnendo su per l'erbe verdi, Udì dir alta voce di lontano,' (Petr. p. 1, mad. 2.) *Su* was then used by itself, as 'Siedo la terra dove nata fui Su la marina dove il Po discende Per aver pace, etc.' (Dante³.) The form *sur*, however, contracted from *super*, also occurs in Italian⁴.

It should be observed that *su* the preposition in Ital. has quite a different origin from *su* the adverb: see below in *jusum*.

SUPRA. Changed by the Prov. into *sobre*, and compounded with *de* into *desobre*, which latter was also used adverbially. The Ital. slightly modified it into *sopra* or *sovra:* the Span. has *sobre:* the French changed *sovre* or *soure* into *sore* by omitting the *v*, into *seure* by modifying the *o* into *e:* whence came the modern form *sur:* unless indeed it was formed more compendiously from *super*, (*Gr. Rom.* p. 313. *Comp.* p. 324⁵.)

---

[1] *Vocab. della Crusca* in *san.* *Cento Osservazioni al Dizionario Dantesco di Viviani* (Turin, 1830), p. 56.
[2] [Diez, *Rom. Gr.* p. 161. Burguy, vol. ii. p. 364.]
[3] Cinonio, c. 233, § 1—4.
[4] Annot. 74, to Cinonio, c. 231. [Diez, ib. p. 179.]
[5] [Burguy, vol. ii. p. 366.]

SUBTUS. As from *supra* the Prov. made *sobre* and *desobre*, so from *subtus* it made *sotz* and *desotz*. The Ital. and Span. following their own mode of formation changed *subtus* into *sotto* and *soto*: the French has contracted it into *sous*, anciently *soubs*, (*Gr. Rom.* p. 213[1].)

TRANS. This word the Prov. changed into *tras*, and by composition made *atras* and *detras*, adverbs. The identical forms recur in Span. and they bear in both languages the sense of *behind*. The old French likewise used *tres* and *tries* in the sense of *behind*[2]. The transition from the ancient to the modern sense is easily explained: thus in a passage of the *Roman de Jaufre* cited by M. Raynouard, 'Et abaitant us nas issi Qui estava tras un boisson,' 'and at the instant a dwarf came out who was behind a bush:' it comes to the same thing whether he is said to be *on the other side of* the bush or *behind* it. From this particular to the more general sense of *behind*, the distance is not great. The Ital. has not, as far as I am aware, any derivative of *trans*, (*Gr. Rom.* p. 261.)

VERSUS. The Prov. modified this word into *vers*, *ves*, *vais*, and *vas*, and by composition made *deves*, *envers*, *envas*, *enves*. The Ital. has *verso* and *inverso*: the French *vers*, *envers*, and *devers*. The Span. has lost this preposition, (*Gr. Rom.* p. 319[3].)

ULTRA. The Prov. has *ultra*, *oltra*, and *outra*; the Ital. *oltra* and *oltre*; the Span. *ultra*; the French *ultre*, now *outre*, (*Gr. Rom.* p. 271, *Comp.* p. 328[4].)

[1] [Burguy, vol. ii. p. 365.]
[2] [Burguy, ib. p. 369.]
[3] [Diez, *Rom. Gr.* vol. iii. p. 178.]
[4] It is possible that the Prov. adverb *tras* (see above, p. 208,) and the French adverb *très* have been derived from *ultra* by the addition of the final *s*: thus the Ital. has *oltracotanza* and *tracotanza*, different

USQUE. By combining with this word the particles *dum* and *tro* (the latter of which has been explained above, p. 203,) the Prov. made the prepositions *duesca* and *troesca*, which had the sense of *until*. M. Raynouard considers the former word as compounded of *de* and *usque*; but the composition just suggested seems more probable, (*Gr. Rom.* p. 318.). To *duesca* the French *jusque* appears to correspond, the final *a* being softened into *e*.

In Ital. the word *usque* has been lost and its place is supplied by *infino* and *fino*, derived from *finis*, and often corrupted into *sino* and *insino*. Muratori (in v.) cites a passage from an Italian charter belonging to the year 899, 'Qui habet fines de capu fine via publica antiqua, de alio latu finem flumen Calore, de alia parte fine flumen Cottia¹.'

The Span. has substituted for *usque* the word *hasta*, of the origin of which I am ignorant.

§ 2. ADVERBS.

The most common and at the same time the most remarkable class of adverbs in the Romance languages is that formed by the union of an adjective with the ablative case of the Latin word *mens*, so that instead of retaining the classical forms *alte*, *large*, *dure*, they said

---

forms of the same word, (*outrecuidance* French.) The derivation from *extra* suggested above, seems, however, preferable. *Trapassare* Ital. and *trespasser* French appear evidently to be compounded of *ultra* not *extra*. [Diez, *Rom. Gr.* p. 197.]

¹ For an explanation of these accusative cases, see above, pp. 59, 60, sqq. [Compare Diez, vol. iii. p. 155.]

alta-mente, larga-mente, dura-mente[1]. The Ital. and Span. have preserved these forms unchanged; though the Span. often omitted the final vowel[2]. The Prov. and French, as usual, did the same: and the French likewise, according to its custom, softened the *a* into *e*, and made *altement (hautement,) largement, durement*. This mode of forming adverbs was naturally resorted to, when the ancient inflexions had been lost, and when in some of the Romance languages, as the Prov. and French, the vowel terminations had been altogether suppressed, so that all distinction between the adjective and the adverb formed from it was obliterated[3].

Sometimes when two or more of these adverbs were used in succession, the termination *mente*, as if it were still a separate word, was only placed at the end of *one* of the adjectives: thus in Provençal:

> Dona non deu parlar mas gen
> E *suau* e *causidament* . . .
> Amatz *suau* e *bellament*.
> Mostret lur grans reliquias
> Qu' avia lonc temps guardat
> *Sanctament* e *devota*.
>
> E Guarentz respondet
> *Follament* et *irada*.

M. Raynouard gives examples of the same construction

---

[1] Maffei, *Verona Illustrata*, part i. col. 318, finds some traces of this formation of adverbs in Latin, as 'Insistam forti mente,' in Ovid, *Am.* iii. 2. 10, and 'jucunda mente respondit,' in Apuleius.
[2] On the ancient Spanish adverbs of this form see Raynouard, *Journ. des Sav.* 1818, p. 480.
[3] See Grimm, vol. iii. p. 123.

in Italian: 'Quanto *prudente* e *giudiziosamente* m' ammaestrò Aristotile,' (Varchi, Ercolano:) in Span. 'Los trata *cortes* y *amigablemente*,' (Cervantes:) in Portuguese 'ondo *sotil* é *artificiosamente* estava lavrada e esculpida toda a maniera de sua vida,' (*Palmeirim de Inglaterra*:) and in French 'Son chef trecie moult richement, Bien, et *bel* et *estroitement*,' (*Rom. de la Rose*.) Some parallel idioms occur in English and German[1], where of two consecutive compounds having the first part different and the last part the same, the part which agrees is only expressed once. Thus as the Germans say *ein-und ausgehen*, as the English say *a wine and spirit merchant*, so the Romance languages said *suau e bellament, sanctament e devota, cortes y amigablemente*, etc. It will be observed, however, that the Romance languages sometimes used *mente* after the first word, which is intelligible when it is remembered that these adverbs are not proper compounds, but two words, with their grammatical structure, which have as it were coalesced together: hence if the sentence is resolved into its elements, it is as easy to say 'sancta mente et devota,' as 'sancta et devota mente:' whereas such expressions as 'a wine merchant and spirit,' 'a teadealer and coffee,' do not make sense, as these are proper compounds, the elements of which reassume their original meaning when disjoined from their composition, (*Gr. Rom.* p. 322—3. *Comp.* p. 312—6.)

In adverbs of this kind the Ital., Span., and Prov. omitted the final vowel of the adjective when it was not *a*; thus *generalmente* Ital. and Span., *humilmen, soptilmen*

---

[1] See *Philol. Museum*, vol. ii. p. 257.

Prov.: the French now inserts *e* after the final consonant of the adjective, as *fortement, généralement :* anciently, however, it followed the same orthography as the others, and wrote *imperialment, loyalment, cruelment, vilment, (Gr. Comp.* p. 316—7[1].)

The adverbs which do not belong to any general class distinguished by the termination may be conveniently considered under two heads, 1. Those derived directly with slight modifications from corresponding Latin adverbs, and 2. Those formed anew in the modern languages.

The following are the principal adverbs derived from the Latin.

ALIORSUM. From this word the Prov. made *alhors* and *ailhors*, the French *ailleurs*. The Ital. and Span. have not retained it.

ALIQUOTIES. In Prov. *alques*, which language alone (as it appears) has a derivative of this adverb.

FORAS. In Prov. this adverb has various forms, viz. *foras, fors, fora, for :* and compounded, as *deforas, defor*. The Ital. has both *fuori* from *foris*, and *fuora* from *foras*. The Span. now has only *fuera*, formerly it used *foras* and *fueras :* the French has *fors, (Gr. Rom.* p. 272. *Comp.* p. 327.)

HODIE, HERI. The first of these adverbs became in Prov. *hoi, oi, ui, uoi, huei :* in Ital. *hoggi* or *oggi :* in Span. *hoy* or *oi :* in French *oi* and *huy*. In Prov. this word was sometimes compounded with *mais*, as *hueimai* or *oimai*, when it signified 'henceforth:' sometimes *desser hueimais* was used, which resolved into its Latin ele-

[1] [See Diez, vol. ii. p. 432. Burguy, vol. ii. p. 263. Ampère, p. 266.]

ments is, 'de ipsa hora hodie magis,' like the French *désormais*.

The modern languages, forgetting the composition of *hodie* (*hoc die*), sometimes compounded it again with the same words: thus the Prov. had *enchoy* or *encoi*, i.e. 'in hoc hodie ;' which occurs in Ital. under the form *ancoi*: in like manner the French and Ital. compound it with *jour* and *di*, saying *aujourd'hui* and *oggidì*[1].

From *heri* the Ital. made *hieri* or *ieri*, the Prov. *her*, the French *hier*, the Span. *ayer*.

JAM. *Ja*, and with the final *s jasse*, (that is, *ja, jas, jasse*, like *anc* from *unquam, ancs, ancse*: see below;) and compounded with *mais* (from *magis*) *jamais* in Prov., which exactly corresponds to the English *evermore*, and the German *immermehr*. Hence *jamais* is always used with reference to future times, whereas *anc* from *unquam* always has reference to past times. *Ja*, like the Latin *jam* and the English *ever*, may refer both to the past and the future. *Jasse* means *always*, as 'vos am e us amarai jasse,' 'I love you, and shall ever love you.' Sometimes *ja* and *mais* are separated, as 'E *ja* non volria *mais* esser residatz,' 'I would not wish ever to be awakened.' The Ital. has *già*, and compounded with *mai, giammai*, which words are used both of past and future times[2]: the Span. has *jamas*: the French had formerly *ja*, whence are formed *déja* (i.e. *desja*) and *jadis*, and it now uses *jamais*, (*Gr. Rom.* p. 280. *Comp.* p. 332[3].)

IBI. The Prov. contracted this adverb into *i, y*, and *hi*, which combined with *aisso* and *aquo* neuter demon-

---
[1] [Burguy, vol. ii. p. 296.]
[2] Cinonio, c. 114.
[3] See Grimm, vol. iii. p. 223. [Burguy, vol. ii. p. 800.]

strative pronouns, made *aissi*, *aqui;* with *ipse* (*sa*) and *ille* (*la*) *sai* and *lai*, sometimes written *sa* and *la*.

The Ital. has preserved the Latin word in its integrity under the form of *ivi*, which it sometimes contracts into *vi:* formerly it sometimes used *i*, as in Dante, *Inf.* c. 8, v. 4, 'Per due fiammette che i vedremmo porre.' It likewise has the double forms *la* and *li*, *qua* and *qui:* which doubtless were respectively contracted from *lai* and *qui*, as from πρόατος came the double forms πρῶτος and πρᾶτος.

The French has *y* from *ibi;* it formerly used *lai*, and doubtless also *çai*, now *la* and *ça*. *Ci* from *çai* is preserved in the word *voici*.

The Span. has lost *ibi*, but has the compound forms *aquí*, *allé*, and *allá*, (*Gr. Rom.* p. 276—8. *Comp.* p. 340—1[1].)

INDE. Changed by the Prov. into *ent*, *enz*, (i. e. *ents*,) *en*, and *ne*, as 'Veder enz pot l'om per quaranta ciptaz,' 'One can see from thence over forty cities.' 'Ieu m'en anarai en cyssilh,' 'I will go hence in exile.' The use of *ne* or *en* as a pronoun has been explained above, p. 151.

The Ital. and French have the same double sense of the derivatives of *inde;* in Ital. *ne*, (that is, *ine*, *ne*,) in French *en* (that is, *ind*, *end*, *en:*) thus *andarsene*, *s'en aller; averne bisogno*, *en avoir besoin*, (*Gr. Rom.* p. 268.)

INSIMUL. In Prov. *ensems* and *essems*, by the rejection of the last syllable and the addition of *s:* in Ital. *insieme*, in French *ensemble*[2], (*Gr. Rom.* p. 270.)

---

[1] [Diez, *Rom. Gr.* vol. iii. p. 53.]

[2] There seems to be no reason for suspecting with Muratori in v. that *insieme* comes from the German *sammen:* though doubtless *simul*

ADVERBS. 215

INTUS, DEINTUS. From these two words the Prov. made *ins* and *dins*, by composition *dedins:* the former word compounded with *ipsa* and *illa* made *lainz* and *sainz*. Parallel forms in French are *dans, dedans*, and the old words *léans* and *céans*, (*Gr. Rom*. p. 278—9.)

JOSUM, SUSUM. Of these two words which occur in Low Latin writers, the latter appears evidently to come from *sursum*, the former according to Muratori (*Diss*. 32,) is a different word from *deorsum*. The Prov. changed them into *jos* and *sus:* the Ital. into *giuso* and *giù, suso* and *su*[1]*:* the old Span. had *juso* and *jus*, and *suso, desuso*, and *desus:* the old French had *jus* and *sus*, whence the compound *dessus*, (*Gr. Rom*. p. 282. *Comp*. p. 338.)

MAGIS. Changed by the Prov. into *mais, mas*, and *mai*, and used sometimes as an adverb in its primitive sense of *more;* sometimes as a conjunction in the sense of *but*, which it acquired through the intermediate sense of *rather*. In Ital. *maggio* from *majus* bore the adverbial sense of *magis:* it uses, however, *mai* from *magis* as a conjunction[2]: as also *mai*, in the expressions *mai si* and *mai no*. The French formerly had *mais* both as an adverb and conjunction: it now only retains this word in the sense of *but*[3]*:* the Span. has *mas* (formerly *mais*,)

---

and *sammen* are cognate words. The same writer thinks that *assembrare* Ital., and *assembrer* (or *assembler*) and *ensemble* French, come from *sammelen*. *Ensemble* is probably from *insimul*, i.e. *ensemi, ensemble*, like *cumulo, comle, comble; marmor, marmer, marmre, marmbre, marbre*.

[1] The forms *gioso, giu*, and *soso* likewise occur: Perticari, *Dif. di Dante*, c. 16, vol. i. p. 317. Compare Facciolati in *susum*. [Burguy, vol. ii. p. 301.]
[2] See Muratori in v.
[3] [Burguy, vol. ii. p. 303.]

in both acceptations: whence by composition with *a* and *de*, *ademas*, 'besides,' (*Gr. Rom.* p. 285. *Comp.* p. 335.)

MANE. The modern languages having all lost the Latin adverb *cras*[1], supply its place by means of this word: the Ital., Prov., and French, by compounding it with *de*, have *dimane, dimani,* or *domani*[2], *deman,* and *demain;* the Span. has formed from it the substantive *mañana,* which it uses adverbially, (*Gr. Rom.* p. 274.)

MEDIUM. *Mezzo* or *mezo* as an adverb in Ital. and frequently used as an adjective, like the Latin *medius:* as 'in mezza strada,' 'a mezza state,' 'per mezzo il sangue.' Sometimes it became indeclinable, as 'per mezzo questa oscura valle,' Petrarch (Cinonio, c. 173.) The Prov. changed this word into *miei, mieg,* and *mest;* and used it without declination, sometimes with a preposition, as 'per mici lo cors,' 'per mieg la giardina,' 'en mieg la via,' 'per mest las bonas gens.' The French made this word into *mi;* whence *le mi lieu,* 'the middle place,' and *par mi,* 'through the middle,' used without declination, like the Ital. *per mezzo,* and the Prov. *per miei.* *Mezzo* Ital. is formed from *medius,* like *aguzzo* from *acutus, prezzo* from *pretium, pozzo* from *puteus, Arezzo* from *Arretium, Abruzzi* from *Bruttii.* It still, however, preserves the trace of the Latin, as it is pronounced *medso* from *medius,* as *prezzo* from *pretium* is pronounced *pretso.* The Prov. *mest* appears to have originated in a

---

[1] *Cras* was, however, preserved in old Spanish: thus, *Poema del Cid,* v. 545. 'Cras á la mañana pensemos de cavalzar;' and *Poerias de Arcipreste de Hita,* v. 1433. 'Quando á U sacaren á judgar hoy ó cras.'

[2] Muratori in v.

like manner, with a transposition of letters, i.e. *mest* for *mets* (*mez*), (*Gr. Rom.* p. 290.)

MINUS, PEJUS, PLUS. *Meno, peggio, più* (*plù*) in Ital., *mens* and *meins, pietz* and *piegz, plus* and *pus* in Prov., *moins* and *plus* in French. The Span. and French have no derivative of *pejus*, but have *peor* and *pire* from *pejor*, (*Gr. Rom.* p. 289, 302. *Comp.* p. 334, 336.)

QUANDO. *Quant* and *quan* in Prov., which had also the compound word *lanquan*, i.e. *l'an quan*, 'the year (or the time) when.' The French has *quand*: the Ital. and Span. have retained the Latin form unchanged: the ancient Span., however, sometimes used *quand* and *quant*, (*Gr. Rom.* p. 306. *Comp.* p. 343.)

QUARE. *Quar* and *car* in Prov. properly signifying *for*, but sometimes having the sense of *that*: like *quia* in Latin and *perchè* in Ital. The Ital. and Span. have lost this word, which is preserved in the French *car*, with the single sense of *for*, (*Gr. Rom.* p. 307[1].)

RETRO. This adverb, compounded with *a* and *de*, became *areire* and *dereer* or *derer* in Prov., *arrière* and *derrière* in French, and *diretro* or *dietro* in Ital. (*Gr. Rom.* p. 261[2].)

SATIS. Compounded with *a* became *asatz* or *assatz* in Prov., *assaz* in Span., *assez* in French, *assai* in Ital., (*Gr. Rom.* p. 262.)

M. Raynouard remarks (*Gr. Comp.* p. 336,) that, 'l'*assai* italien prouve que cette langue a souvent fait des modifications très importantes aux désinences des mots pour les accommoder à l'euphonie locale:' but the Ital. has made

---

[1] [Burguy, vol. ii. p. 377.]
[2] [Burguy, ib. p. 277.]

no greater change than the Prov.: it has only made a different change. The Prov. always contracting, and not objecting to final consonants, changed *satis* into *sats;* the Ital., not so fond of contractions, but always avoiding final consonants, changed *satis* into *sai.*

SEMPER. *Sempre* Ital. and Prov., *siempre* Span., *sempres* in old Span. (*Gr. R.* 308. *Comp.* 332.)

SIC. *Si* in Prov. and compounded *aissi* and *cossi:* the latter of which words is *com si*, i.e. *ut sic* instead of *sicut:* the former is perhaps *ac sic.* It had also *altresi* or *atresi*, from *alterum sic.* The Ital. has *si* and *cosi* (the same as *siccome*, the elements of composition being only reversed), and *altresì.* The Span. has *sí*, *assí*, and *otrosí:* the French, *si*, *aussi*, and anciently *altresi* or *autresi*[1].

On the use of *si* as an affirmative particle I shall speak lower down. (*Gr. R.* p. 309—12. *Comp.* p. 337.)

SUBINDE. *Sovente* Ital., *sovent* and *soven* Prov. *souvent* French. M. Raynouard (*Gr. Rom.* p. 314,) derives *sovent* from *sæpe:* but Menage's etymology (in *sovente*) appears evidently true[2].

TUNC. In Prov. *donc*, which by different modifications became *adonc, doncas, doncx, adoncas, adonx; ad tunc*, which occurs in Low Latin, is, as M. Raynouard remarks, borrowed from the Romance *adonc.* In Ital. *dunque* and *adunque*, anciently likewise *dunqua, donqua* and *adonqua*[3]: in old Span. *doncas:* in French, *donc*,

---

[1] [Diez, vol. iii. p. 367.]

[2] [The etymology of Menage is followed by Diez, *Rom. Gram.* vol. ii. p. 444. It is confirmed by the use of *soventre* for *after*, in old French, which approaches closely to the Latin sense of *subinde.* Burguy, vol. ii. p. 368.]

[3] See Annotat. 6, to Cinonio, Part. c. 8.

formerly *dunc* and *adunc*, *donkes* and *adonkes*. The Span. has moreover the form *entonces*, compounded with the preposition *en*. (*Gr. R.* p. 254—6. *Comp.* 331.)

UBI. *Ou* and *o* in Prov., *ove* in Ital., in which the forms *u*[1] and *o* likewise occur: *ó* in old Span., *ou* in French. (*Gr. R.* p. 298. *Comp.* 340².)

UNDE. *Ont*, *on*, and by comparison with *de*, *dunt* or *don* in Prov. *onde* and *donde* in Ital. *donde* in Span. which anciently had the forms *ond*, *ont*, and *don: dont* and formerly *unt* or *ont* in French. (*Gr. R.* p. 296. *Comp.* 339³.)

UNQUAM, NUNQUAM. In Prov. *ongan*, *oan*, *unca*, *anc*, and by the addition of a final *s*, *oncas*, and *ancse* from *ancs*, like *jasse* from *jas* (above p. 213.) From *nunquam* there is only the form *nonca*. The Ital. has *unqua* and also *uguanno*, used by Boccaccio[4]: the Span. has *nunca*: the French *onc* and *oncques* are now obsolete. (*Gr. R.* p. 291⁵.)

I will now set down the most remarkable Provençal adverbs, not derived from corresponding Latin adverbs, nor formed from them by a simple composition; and compare them with similar forms in the other Romance languages.

AMON, AVAL. These adverbs, sometimes *damon* and *daval*, are derived from *mons* and *vallis*, in French *à mont* and *à val*, in Ital. *a monte* and *a valle*[6], formed after the

---

[1] Cinonio, Part. c. 193, § 11, 12.
[2] [Diez, vol. iii. p. 354.]
[3] [Diez, ib. p. 353.]
[4] See Perticari, *Dif. di Dante*, c. 15, vol. i. p. 339.
[5] [Burguy, vol. ii. p. 311.]
[6] *A monte* occurs in the *Tesoro* of Brunetti, (*Voc. della Crusca* in v.): *a valle* is used by many writers (ibid. in v.), for instance by

model of the German *zetal* and *zeberge*[1]. From *aval* the French has made *avaler*, to swallow (i.e to put down the throat,) and the Span. *avalar*, to tremble like the earth (i.e. to sink down.) *Gr. R.* p. 257.

ADES, *now;* ADESSE or DES, *since:* formed with *ad* and *de,* and *es,* from *ipse* (above p. 160,) The Ital. has *adesso:* the French, *dès.* *Neis* 'even,' and *anceis* 'on the contrary,' Prov. were formed by compounding the same pronoun with *in* and *ante.* (*Gr. R.* p. 251—9.)

ENTORN, ENVIRON, from *tornare* and *girare.* The Ital. has *intorno, d'intorno, a torno* or *attorno,* and *dattorno:* the French, *à l'entour,* and *autour* without the preposition *en*[2]. It has likewise *environ.* (*Gr. R.* p. 271.)

Dante, *Inferno,* xii. 46. *Da valle* and *da monte* are still in use among all the inhabitants of the Apennines, according to Perticari, *Dif. di Dante,* c. 10, vol. i. p. 340.

[1] See V. Hagen, Glossary to *Nibelungen Lied,* in tal. Grimm, vol. iii. pp. 148, 163. [Burguy, vol. ii. p. 271.]

[2] *Tour* comes from *torn,* or *turn,* as *jour* from *jorn, chair* from *carn, enfer* from *enfern, cor* from *corn, four* from *furn:* see *Gr. Comp.* p. 63—4. [See Diez, vol. iii. p. 176.]

Giorno and *jour* come from *diurnum,* as *inverno* and *hiver* come from *hibernum (tempus* being understood,) which I should have thought it unnecessary to mention if a modern Italian critic had not derived *giorno* from *horn* German, because the Alemans and Franks announced the day by the sound of the horn! (Benci on *Malispini,* vol. ii. p. 433, ed. Leghorn, 1830.)

It may be observed that the Spanish has alone retained the derivative of the Latin *dies, dia,* in common use: the Ital. has the word *dì* but commonly uses *giorno:* the French has only *jour.* The substitution of the periphrasis *diurnum (tempus)* for *dies* is paralleled by *hybernum (tempus)* for *hyems,* (*inverno* Ital., *invierno* Span., *hiver,* anciently *hyvern* French; *æstivum (tempus)* for *æstas (estío* Span., the Ital. and French have *estate* and *esté,*) and. *matutinum (tempus)* for *mane (mattino* Ital., *matin* French, the Span. has *mañana,* i.e. *hora matutina.*) *Autumnus* is retained in all three languages; *ver* is lost in French, which has *printemps,* but is retained by the Ital. and Span. in the compound *primavera.*

LEV, from *leve*, which had the double sense of the English word *lightly*, viz. *quickly* and (joined with *ben*) *easily*, whence it came to signify *perhaps;* as

    D'amor non dei dire mas be,
    Quar non ai ni petit ni re,
    Quar ben leu plus no m'en cove.

'Of love I ought not to speak well more, as I have not any, either small or great, for perhaps more does not beseem me.'

It is probable that this adverb, which appears to be peculiar to the Provençal, was imitated from the German. (*Gr. R.* p. 284.)

MALGRAT. This word is used in all the Romance languages, with a personal pronoun often inserted immediately before *grat:* thus *malgrat vostre, mal mon grat, mal lui grat* Prov., *mau gré sien, mau gré lor* French, *mal su grado* Span., *mal mio grado, mal grado suo* Ital. These expressions may be rendered, 'with my ill pleasure,' 'with his ill pleasure,' etc. If a possessive pronoun is not used, the phrase takes a different turn, as 'malgrat de Karle' 'with the ill pleasure of Charles.' *Grat* (from *gratum*) is here used substantively as *grato* or *grado* in Ital., (*Voc. della Crusca* in v.), *agrado* in Span., and *gré* in French, in the expressions *savoir gré, à mon gré,* etc. (*Gr. R.* p. 286. *Comp.* 359—61[1].)

MANTENEN, sometimes *de mantenen*, from *manu tenens; mantenente, immantenente* Ital.[2], *maintenant* French, *á man teniente* in Span., has a different meaning. *De manes,* another Prov. adverb, signifying *suddenly,* appears evi-

---
[1] [Burguy, vol. ii. p. 337.]
[2] Perticari, *Dif. di Dante,* c. 16, vol. i. p. 349.

dently to come from *manus*, corresponding to 'offhand' English, 'aus der Hand' German; and not from *mane* in the sense of *early*, as M. Raynouard supposes. (*Gr. R.* p. 28¹.)

HORA. This Latin word was first used in Provençal adverbially, with the preposition *a*, as *ora*, in the sense of *now*: afterwards the preposition was omitted, and it became *ara, ar, era, er*, and with a final *s, oras, eras*. From *in hanc horam* was derived *encar* or *encara*, with the final *s, encarns* or *enqueras*, 'hitherto:' from *des l'ora* (i.e. *de ipsa illa hora*) *deslor*, 'henceforth;' from *qua hora, quora*, 'when;' *derenan* has been already mentioned (p. 200.) *Ora* occurs as an adverb with the same sense in Ital., which also has *ancora*. *Ore, or, ores* were formerly used in French, which now uses *encor* and *déslors*. M. Raynouard cites a passage from an ancient French chronicle, which well illustrates this application of *hora:* 'Barcinone est une cité qui siet en la marche d'Espaigne : *une heure* estoit des Sarrazins, et *une heure* estoit des Crestiens.' (*Comp. R.* p. 293—6. *Comp.* 330².)

PRON or PRO. This word occurs in Prov. with the sense of *Satis* :

Dol papa sai che dara largamen
Pron del pardon o pauc de son argen.

'Of the pope I know that he will give liberally plenty of indulgences and little of his money.'

The old French had *prou* in the same sense. M. Raynouard offers no suggestion on the derivation of these words. (*Gr. R.* p. 263³.)

---

¹ [Burguy, vol. ii. p. 304.] ² [Burguy, ib. p. 311.]
³ [Diez, *Rom. Gr.* vol. iii. p. 148. *Rom. Wörterbuch*, p. 273. Burguy, ib. p. 320.]

Tost. This enigmatic word occurs in all the Romance languages: *tosto* Ital., *tost* old Span. and Prov., *toste* old Portug., *tost* now *tôt* French. No probable explanation of its origin has hitherto been given. (See Muratori in v. *Gr. R.* p. 316. Comp. 333[1].)

Trop. In Prov. this word meant *very*, and *too much*: thus 'Sap trop ben violar' 'he knew very well how to play on the viol.' 'Per qu'om no-s deu per gaug trop esjuazir, Ni per ira trop esser anguoyssos.' 'Wherefore one ought not for joy to exult too much, Nor for sadness to be too much cast down.' *Troppo* in Ital., has both these senses (Cinonio, c. 243) *trop* French, only the last. As *troppus* is used in the Latin of the middle ages with the sense of a herd or flock, Muratori (in v.) thinks that it is derived from some German word, whence the French *troupe* and *troupeau*, (also *truppa* Ital.) *Troppo*, a substantive, is preserved in Ital. (*Gr. R.* p. 317[2].)

Veti, i.e. 'See thou,' or in the plural *vecvos* (softened into *veus*) 'see ye,' used adverbially like the French *voici* and *voilà*, which are compounded with the particles *ci* here, and *là* there. The Ital. alone has preserved *ecco*, from the Latin *eccum*. (*Gr. Rom.* p. 320[3].)

---

[1] [Diez, *Gr. Rom.* vol. ii. p. 442, derives the word from *tot cito;* Burguy, vol. ii. p. 320, from *tostus*.]

[2] It might be thought that the French adverb *très* is formed from *trop*, like *près* from *prop;* but the Prov. form *tras*, shows that it had not this origin, and that one of the two derivations above suggested is correct: see p. 208. [Concerning *trop*, see Burguy, vol. ii. p. 330.]

[3] So *sih-tir* was used in old German, Grimm, vol. iii. p. 247.

§ 3. CONJUNCTIONS.

I shall next proceed to the conjunctions and the affirmative and negative particles, which may be conveniently treated apart, as they are marked with some peculiar features in the Romance languages.

AUT. In Prov. and old French this word became *o* or *ou*; in modern French the latter form alone is used; in the Span. it is *ó*. The Ital. alone has retained the consonant changed into *d*, and has made the word *od*; before a consonant, however, the *d* is dropped, as in English the *n* of *an* is only used before a vowel, (*Gr. Rom.* p. 336. *Comp.* p. 346.)

ET. Preserved unchanged in Prov., but. the *t* was generally dropped before consonants: in Ital. *et* or *ed*, subject to the same rule. The French now only has *et*, but the *t* is not pronounced: *e* is sometimes written in old French: the Spanish formerly used both *et* and *é*, now it has only *y*, (*Gr. Rom.* p. 328. *Comp.* p. 345.)

All the modern derivatives of *aut* and *et* have retained their ancient sense unchanged.

GAIRE or GUAIRE in Prov., *guari* in Ital., *guère* or *guères* French. These adverbs are evidently derived from the German *gar* or *wahr*, (*very* Eng.)[1]: the force of which (*much*) has been retained in each language, though in French *guère* is generally supposed to have a contrary meaning. The confusion has arisen from this particle being almost constantly used in negative propositions: thus in Prov. 'Que sciensa *no* pretz *gaire* S'al ops no la vey valer,' ' As I do not value knowledge much, If I do

---
[1] See Muratori in *guari*.

not see it avail in time of need.' 'Non istette *guari* che trapassò,' 'he was not long before he died,' Boccaccio (Cinonio, c. 121.) 'Et n'eut pas *gueres* demeuré a Sparte, qu'il fut incontinent soupçonné,' etc., Amyot Plut. *Vie d'Agesilas.* 'La plupart des œuvres d'Aristote et de Théophraste qui n'estoient *pas gueres* encore cogneus, etc.' Id. *Vie de Sylla.* Being constantly used in this manner, it appeared to acquire a negative force, independently of the proper negation; and thus while *guari* in Ital. is explained to mean *much*, *guère* in French is explained to mean *little*. Nevertheless *guère* is never used by itself with a negative force, like *pas, point, personne,* and other words which originally being affirmatives in a negative sentence, at first like *guère* were used constantly with a negative particle, from which they seemed to catch a negative force by contact; and then were employed by themselves as negatives, (*Gr. Rom.* p. 274, 333. *Journ. des Sav.* 1824, p. 180[1].)

GENS. The Prov. used *gens* or *ges* as an expletive particle of affirmation: thus, 'Ella-s fen sorda: *gens* a lui *non* atend,' 'She feigns herself deaf: she does not attend to him at all.' 'No-m mogui ges,' 'I did not move at all.' M. Raynouard derives this particle from the Latin *gens*; in which case it would probably be *gent* or *gen* (from *gentem*;) the meanings of the Latin and Prov. words moreover do not at all correspond: the suggestion of Schlegel[2], who derives it from the Teutonic *ganz* (like *gaire* from *gar*) is far more probable[3], (*Gr. Rom.* p. 333. Galvani, *Poesie dei Trovat.* p. 39, n. 1. Orell, p. 303.)

[1] See Orell, p. 303. [Burguy, vol. ii. p. 394.]
[2] *Observations*, p. 115.
[3] Grimm, vol. iii. p. 749, says that M. Raynouard's explanation is

CHAPTER V.

MICA. Sometimes used unchanged, sometimes modified into *miga*, *minga*, and *mia* in Prov.[1], *mica* and *minga* in Ital., *mie* in French. In Prov. it is always used in negative sentences, to give force to the negation, as 'Pero no desesper mia,' 'wherefore do not despair at all.' In Ital. this is generally the case, as 'Fosse nascosto un dio? Non mica un dio Selvaggio, o della plebe degli dei.' Tasso, *Aminta*. 'Signor mio, non sogno mica.' Bocc. Giorn. 7, n. 9[2].

In the following passage, however, of a poem written in the language of the Tuscan peasants, it does not add force to a negative:

> Gli è rigoglioso, come un berlingaccio,
> Talchè non par, che morir voglia mica[3].

In French it has a similar force: 'Mais comme un harenc ne faut mie Que tousjours le bec aye en l'eau,' Basselin[4].

In Italian it is sometimes used familiarly by itself, with a negative sense, like other particles, which will be presently noticed[5].

---

probably incorrect, as a notion of a *thing*, not a *person*, is required. He then adds, '*gee* must signify something small: in Italian *ghezzo* is a mushroom, *ghiozzo* is a little bit.' Schlegel's etymology is, however, confirmed by *gaire*.

[1] *Gr. Rom.* p. 3:14.
[2] See Annot. 50, to Clnonio, c. 58. Marrini on the *Lamento di Cecco da Varlungo*, p. 185.
[3] Marrini, ibid, p. 103.
[4] Cited by M. Raynouard, *Journ. des Sav.* 1823, p. 118. See Orell, p. 307. *Mie* is still used in some familiar phrases: see *Dict. de l'Acad.* in v. which defines it to be a 'particule négative, qui signifie, *Pas, point*.' Properly speaking, neither *mie*, *pas*, nor *point*, are negative particles.
[5] [Concerning this class of negative particles, formed from affirm-

CONJUNCTIONS. 227

NEC. *Ne* and *ni* in Prov. and French, *ne* in Ital., *ni* in Span. In Prov. *ne* or *ni* sometimes retained its Latin sense of a negative disjunction, as ' Davans son vis nulz om no-s pot celar; Ne eps li omne qui sun ultra la mar,' ' Before his face man can conceal himself, nor even the men who are beyond the sea.' ' Non avent macula ni ruga,' ' not having stain nor wrinkle.' Now where a negative precedes a disjunctive negative particle, the repetition of the negation is unnecessary to the sense, though it may add force to the expression: thus it is the same thing to say ' he has *neither* wife *nor* children,' or ' he has *not* wife *and* children.' Hence as *nec* is composed of *et non*, in such cases as that just described it was indifferent whether it was understood to have an affirmative or a negative sense, and thus it vacillated between the two, in Prov. generally having the former, and being synonymous with *et:* thus St. John, viii. 14 is translated ' Quar iou sai don vonc ni on vauc.' This use never became common in any other Romance language except the Provençal: instances of it, however, occur both in old French and Ital., as ' Dès que Diex fit Adan ne Eve.' ' Se gli occhi suoi ti fur dolci ne cari,' Petrarch[1]. This use of *ne* still prevails in the Piedmontese and Lombard dialects, (*Gr. Rom.* p. 829—30. *Comp.* p. 347.)

NON. Preserved without change of meaning in all the Romance languages. The Prov. used both *non* and *no* in the same manner as the Latin *non*. The Ital. has both forms: but it uses the former in connection with

ative substantives, see Diez, *Rom. Gr.* vol. ii. p. 447, vol. iii. p. 412. Ampère, p. 273—6. Burguy, vol. ii. p. 352.]

[1] See Cinonio, c. 178, s. 2, 4, 7. Particari, *Dif. di Dante*, c. 18, vol. ii. p. 878.

other words, as 'non è là;' 'non lungo tempo dopo;' the latter as an answer, as 'Sta dentro? No¹.' The Span. now only uses *no*: it formerly had the full Latin form. The French has *non*: but the other form *no* has been attenuated into *ne*, like *lo* into *le*, (above, p. 56².)

A very peculiar use of the particles *si non* 'except' occurs in all the Romance languages: not only are they used together, as in Latin, but they are often separated by several words interposed: thus

> Tant es mortals lo danz, che no i a sospeisson
> Que jamais si revenha, s'en aital guisa *non*
> Qu'om li traga lo cor.

'The loss is so great that there is no suspicion that ever it can be repaired, except, in such guise, that they take his heart, etc.'

So in Ital. 'Nullo è buono s'ello è buon no,' and in Span. 'De al no li membraba si de esto solo non.' In old French it is of frequent occurrence: thus 'Maintes gens dient que en songes N'a se fables non et mensonges³.'

---

[1] See this difference explained in the *Philol. Museum*, vol. ii. p. 322.
[2] See Grimm, vol. iii. p. 746.
[3] These two verses are taken from the beginning of the *Roman de la Rose*, which were modernized as follows by Marot, in an edition of that poem published by him in the sixteenth century:

> Maintes gens vont disant que songes
> Ne sont que fables et mensonges.

By which means (says M. Raynouard, *Gr. Comp.* p. 364,) he changed *fables* and *mensonges* from the singular to the plural number. This appears to be an oversight: *fable*, from *fabula*, had not the final *s* in the singular number, but took it in the plural, which was modified from *fabulas*.

'Il ne parle se de toi non,' (*Gr. Rom.* p. 332. Comp. p. 348—50.)

PASSUS. The Prov. used *pas* as an expletive particle, but always with a negation, as '*non pas* dos jorns ni tres,' 'not two days nor three.' The French, as is well known, has the same use of this particle. In both languages it appears to have obtained this sense from being originally used with verbs of motion, as 'ne bougez un pas,' or 'ne bougez pas,' 'do not stir a step;' and this being equivalent to 'do not stir *at all*,' by a process of abstraction of perpetual occurrence in the use of words, it was transferred to other verbs in the more general sense: and thus it was said, 'je ne l'aime pas,' 'je ne veux pas,' 'I do not love him at all,' 'I do not wish it at all,' 'non pas,' 'not at all.' Being constantly used in negative propositions, *pas* thus seemed to have itself a negative sense, and by degrees came to be used independently as a negative particle: thus 'pas un,' 'pas mal,' 'pas souvent,' 'not one,' 'not ill,' 'not often,' for 'non pas un,' 'non pas mal,' 'non pas souvent,' 'not even one,' 'not at all ill,' 'not at all often,' (*Gr. Rom.* p. 335. Orell, p. 313.)

PERSONA. Both Ital. and French use this substantive for *alcuno* and *aucun* in both affirmative and negative phrases, as 'Guatiam per l'orto, se persona ci è, e s'egli non c'è persona, che abbiamo noi a fare, etc.' Boccaccio, Nov. xxi. 14. So in French, 'Si jamais personne est assez hardi pour l'entreprendre, il réussira,' 'Personne ne sera assez hardi,' i. e. '*any person* will *not* be bold enough,' in other words '*No* person *will* be bold enough.' From being used frequently in negative propositions, *personne* has sometimes a negative senso: thus 'Y a-t-il

230   CHAPTER V.

quelqu'un ici?   Personne,' i. e. 'Personne n'est ici,' 'a person is *not* here.'

PUNCTUM. This was adopted as an expletive affirmatory particle, as signifying a very small quantity, like *mica* or *mie* a grain of salt, *goutte* a drop, *brin* a small leaf[1], and in English 'not a jot,' 'not a bit,' 'not a morsel,' etc. In Ital. it is sometimes used in affirmative, sometimes in negative propositions, as ' Qual di questa greggia S'arresta punto giace poi cent' anni.' Dante, *Inf.* xv. 37. 'Who ever stops *an instant.*' 'A cui il pelegrin disse: Madonna, Tebaldo non è punto morto.' Bocc. G. 3 nov. 7. Hence it sometimes denies without a negative particle, as 'V'è egli piaciuto quello stile? Punto,' i. e. 'not at all[2].' In French from being used in

[1] These words are used familiarly in the very same manner as *pas, point, mica, punto,* and other expletives, as in the phrases, 'ne voir goutte,' 'n'entendre goutte,' 'il n'y en a brin.' See *Dict. de l'Acad.* in v. The Bolognese has likewise an expletive of this kind, as is explained in the following extract from a dictionary of that dialect:

'*Brisa*. Voce rimarcata da' forestieri, per cui in vece di nomar Bologna *la citta del sipa*, la direi piuttosto *la cittd del brisa*. Equivale al *point o pas* de' franzesi, e s'usa da noi in tutti i casi, in cui da essi si adopera. Corrisponde al *punto* de' Toscani. Detto assolutamente vale la negativa, e sempre in rispondendo ad altri, p. e. *Sei stato nel tal luogo? Brisa. No* (Point du tout.) Nel discorso poi serve di riempitivo come il *point* de' Francesi. An'i n'è brisa. *Non re n' pa punto* (il n'y en a point.)—An'i n'è brisa brisa. *Non ve n' ha punto punto* (il n'y en a point du tout.)—An'i sòn brisa stà. *Non ci sono stato* (je n'y ai pas été.) An' ho brisa séid. *Non ho sete* (je n'ai point de soif.)—*Brisa* si volge molte volte in Toscano col *mica* nello stesso modo che noi diciam *mega*. Al n'è brisa vèira, al n'è mega vèira. *Non é mica vero.*—*Brisa* sembra aver origine da *brisla*, che vale *briciola*; siccome *briciola* significa *quasi* niente.' Ferrari, *Vocabolario Bolognese*, p. 45, (Bologna, 1820.)

[2] See Tommaseo, *Nuovo Diz. dei Sinonimi della Ling. Ital.* in *mica*. And Cinonio, c. 205.

order to give force to negative propositions, as 'il n'est point mort,' 'il ne s'arrête point,' 'he is not by any means dead,' 'he does not stop at all,' it contracted, like other words already mentioned, a negative sense, and was used by itself as a negation, as 'point du tout,' '*not* at all.' 'Lisez vous ces vers? Point.' 'Are you reading those verses.' By *no* means.'

REN. This substantive was retained unchanged in the Prov., making *res* in the nominative, and *ren* or *re* in the accusative case. Thus 'Qu'ieu non soi alegres per al, Ni al res no-m fai viure,' 'For I am not joyful for another, and another thing does not make me live,' i.e. 'no other thing makes me live.' (*Gr. Rom.* p. 152.) 'Ieu am la plus debonaire Del mon mais que nulla re,' 'I love the fairest woman in the world more than anything. (Ib. p. 76.) 'Nuls homs ses amor ren non vau,' 'No man without love is (not) worth anything.' 'Ja ren non dirai,' 'Never will I say anything.' (Ib. p. 333.) 'Res mas merces no i es a dire,' 'Anything except mercy is not wanting,' i.e. 'nothing except mercy is wanting.' (Ib. p. 337.)

The Ital. used the accusative case of *res*, doubtless first changed into *ren* and *rien*[1], in the same manner; but subjected it to farther alterations, by adding a paragogic syllable, as in *come, comente, che, chente*, already observed[2], by which means it became *riente;* and by changing *r* into *n*, (as in the Span. *hombre, nombre, lumbre,*

[1] Perticari, *Dif. di Dante*, c. 15, p. 334, n. 4, says that the Italians used *rien*, referring to the *Cento Novelle Antiche*, No. 61. In c. 21, however, p. 419, n. 0, he shows that *rien* in that place is a Provençal, not an Italian word, which occurs in a Provençal song introduced by the novelist, and he blames Lombardi for introducing it into the *Vocab. della Crusca* on the authority of that passage.

[2] Above, p. 201.

from *hominem, nomen, lumen*[1],) which made it *niente*[2]. *Niente* sometimes retains its ancient affirmative sense, as 'Rispose che egli non ne voleva far niente.' Bocc. Giorn. x. nov. 2. 'Et in questa maniera fece due notti, senza che la donna di niente s'accorgesse.' Bocc. Giorn. 2, nov. 9. Sometimes it has a negative sense, acquired in the manner already explained with respect to other words, as 'Ma fin a qui niente mi rileva Pianto o sospiro o lagrimar ch'io faccio.' Petrarch, P. 1, canz. 1. 'El fuggir val niente Dinanzi a l'ali, che'l segnor nostro usa.' Petrarch, (Cinonio, c. 181.) The rule at present established in Ital. with respect to the use of *niente* is, that where it precedes the verb, it has a negative, where it follows, it has an affirmative, sense: as 'niente ho,' 'I have nothing,' 'non ho niente,' 'I have not anything.' In answer to a question, moreover, *niente* has a negative sense: as 'cosa fate? Niente.' 'What are you doing? Nothing.'

The old Span. likewise used the accusative *ren* from *res:* thus Milagros de N. Señora, v. 195.

> Vidien que de ladrones non era degollado,
> Ca nol tollieron nada nil avien *ren* robado.

Also v. 293.

> Cata non alas miedo, por *ren* non te demuden,
> Piensa como me fables ò como me pescudes[3].

[1] See above, p. 71, note [1].
[2] *Rien* and *niente* from *rem* are like *miei* from *mei, Dieu* from *Deus,* etc. Muratori in v. rejects the absurd derivation of *niente* from *ne ens; ens* was a scholastic, not a popular term. The French *néant* appears to come from *negans:* 'a *negative* quantity.' See Orell, p. 809.
[3] Sanchez, vol. ii. p. 311—324.

CONJUNCTIONS. 233

The use of *rien* in French is precisely analogous to that of *niente* in Italian[1]. Sometimes it retains its original affirmative sense, as 'Y a-t-il rien de si beau que cela.' 'Il ne sait rien de rien,' i.e. 'he knows nothing of *anything*.' But from being used after *ne*, it has itself acquired a negative force, and sometimes means *nothing* instead of *anything*, as 'Dieu a créé le monde de rien.' 'On ne fait rien de rien,' i.e. 'Ex nihilo nil fit.' 'Qu' avez vous trouvé? Rien.'

Sic. This word, changed into si^e, became the affirmative particle of the Ital. and Span.: in French it is still often employed in familiar style[2], and it also occurs in the old Prov.: thus in the *Nobla Leyçon*:

> La ley velha deffent solament perjurar,
> E plus de si o de no non sia en ton parlar.

The last line being a translation of St. Matthew, 'and let thy conversation be yea, yea, nay, nay.' (*Gr. Rom.* p. 312. *Comp.* p. 346.)

It is known that the difference of the affirmative particle was used to distinguish the three Romance languages, of Italy, northern and southern France: the former being called the language of *si*, the latter of *oil* and *oc*. The agreement of all these languages in the use of *si* may therefore seem a proof of their derivation from a language posterior to the Latin, in which this particle had a

---

[1] Schlegel's *Kritische Schriften*, vol. i. p. 358. On *rien*, used in old French as a feminine substantive for *chose*, see Orell, p. 70.

[2] Grimm, *Deutsche Rechtsalterthümer*, p. 600, cites a formula from the Lombard laws: 'Spondes ita? Sic facio,' comparing the French *si fais* and the Italian *si*.

[3] [See Burguy, vol. ii. p. 301.]

different sense. It is, however, easy to conceive that the use of the Latin *sic* for *yes* should have been introduced by the Germans, with whom *so* had a familiar sense; or that *sic* should have been used without reference to the German practice, as the Latin formerly employed *ita*, a nearly synonymous particle. But although the languages of *oil* and *oc* sometimes used *si* in the same sense as the Italian, yet they had other particles which they commonly used in that sense. The characteristic of the Italian, as opposed to the languages of France, was not that it used *si*, but that it used *si* alone; the characteristic of the languages of France, as opposed to that of Italy, was not that they did not use *si*, but that they commonly used *oil* and *oc*, particles of which no trace is to be found in any Italian dialect.

The Bolognese dialect has been characterized by its use of *sipa*:

> E non pur lo qui plango Bolognese:
> Anzi n'è questo luogo tanto pieno,
> Che tante lingue non son ora apprese
> A *dicer sipa* tra Savena e'l Reno.
> Dante, *Inf.* xviii. 58.

Sipa or *sepa*, however, now no longer in use, is a peculiar form of *sia*, and is not connected with *si*[1]: though it appears evidently to have been used as equivalent to *si*, since Dante elsewhere takes this affirmative particle as the distinguishing mark of a language.

With regard to the affirmative particles *oil* and *oc*, it cannot be doubted that they are both derived from the form *o*, which was used in old French. *Oil* is doubtless

[1] See Monage, *Orig. Ital.* in *sipa*. Ferrari, *Vocab. Bologn.* in *sepa*.

formed by the addition of the pronoun *il*, like *nenil* from *non* or *nen*. *Oc* is considered by Grimm as equivalent to *já ich:* an etymology of which the probability is much increased, if, as Grimm suggests, and as appears likely, the Romance *o* is borrowed from the German *já*[1]. Should this explanation be received, the adoption of a German affirmative particle in France, while in Italy and Spain a Latin word was used for this purpose, must be considered as a proof of the greater amount of German influence in the former than in the latter countries.

The modern French *oui* appears to be formed from *oil* by dropping the final *l*, as *nenni* from *nennil*, the *o* before *i* being pronounced like *ou*, as *Louis*, anciently *Loys*[2]. The final *l* has in French commonly passed into *u*, as *acel*, *sceau*, *morcel*, *morceau*[3]: but if *oil* had suffered a change of this kind, it would have become *oiu*, and not *oui*.

Among the particles which have been just enumerated it will be observed that several having originally had an affirmative sense, and having been introduced into negative propositions for the sake of strengthening the negation, in process of time themselves contracted a negative force. Negation may, as Grimm states, be strengthened in two ways: either by a repetition of the proper negative

---

[1] Grimm, vol. iii. p. 768. See *Philol. Museum*, vol. ii. p. 324. Some instances of the change of the broad *a* into *o* are mentioned there, p. 326. [Burguy, vol. ii. p. 309, 407—9, approves of the derivation of *oil* from *o* and *il*. He rejects the derivation of *oc* from the Latin *hoc*, and thinks that the origin of the word is quite uncertain.]

[2] This is satisfactorily proved by Diester on *oc* and *oyl*, *Philol. Museum*, vol. ii. p. 843, cf. ib. 324.

[3] See above, p. 138.

particles, or by the addition of a positive word. With regard to the latter of these he remarks: 'A positive expression may sometimes expel and replace the simple negation: the proper negative force of the lost negative particle then falls upon it, and it denies by means of it, as the moon shines with borrowed light. Such words, however, though not properly negative, must yet originally have some natural fitness for expressing negation. Words of this kind commonly convey a notion of *smallness*, and as it were of *nullity*. At first they appear to have suggested a sensible image, which afterwards was lost, and a mere grammatical abstraction remained[1].' The introduction of words signifying small, insignificant, worthless and mean objects, prevailed to a great extent in the old German, and numerous examples of this usage are cited by Grimm from poets of the thirteenth century. Among these are *blat*, a leaf, *bast* bark, *ber* a berry, *strô* a straw, *bône* a bone, *nuz* a nut, *ei* an egg, *brôt* a loaf of bread, *drof* a drop, *hâr* a hair, *fuoz* a foot, *twint* a twinkle, *wiht* a thing, etc.[2] For the most part these words were used after a negation: as 'daz hulfe niht ein blat;' 'wan ez half niht ein bast;' 'ich wære niht einer bône wërt.' Sometimes, however, the same word occurs both with and without the negative particle, as 'dat halp allent nicht ein stôf, (i.e. *stoup*, an atom,) *with* the negative particle; but 'ez was in allez ein stoup,' *without* it. It appears probable, as Schlegel[3] had remarked before Grimm, that

---

[1] Grimm, vol. iii. p. 726—8.
[2] Grimm, vol. iii. p. 728—40. [Similar expressions are cited from the classical Latin writers by Diez, *Rom. Gr.* vol. iii. p. 412.]
[3] *Observ. sur la Litt. Prov.* p. 34. Schlegel's remark is, however, limited to the French language.

the system of explotive particles in negative phrases was formed in the Romance languages on the model of the German idiom; as in the Latin there are no traces of any idiom to which the usage in question can be referred[1]. The Italian has some, but not many, particles of this kind, viz. *mica, niente, persona, punto*, derived from Latin words, and *guari* from a German word. The Provençal has *pas, ren, mica,* from the Latin, *gaire* and *gens* from the German. The Spanish does not appear to have any particles belonging to this class. The French, on the other hand, formerly luxuriated in the use of this idiom: among the instances cited by Grimm, are *gant, ail, feuille, oef, pome, poire, bouton,* etc.[2] *Mie, goutte,* and *brin,* still retain a certain currency in the same manner: but *pas, point, guère, personne,* and *rien,* are in constant use, and show in the clearest manner the transition from the affirmative to the negative sense.

The Romance and Teutonic words of this kind often correspond in their meaning, as *pas* and *fuoz, drof* and

---

[1] However, it is possible that in the case of this idiom, as of others which have been incorrectly derived from the influence of the German, (above, p. 25,) the change may have developed itself in the spontaneous working of the language: for analogous changes have taken place in several Greek words, as I am informed by a friend who is well acquainted with modern Greek. Thus καθόλου and ποτέ have, as answers to a question, a negative sense, (precisely analogous to *point du tout* and *jamais*:) for example, σᾶς ἀρίσει ἐκεῖνο; καθόλου. 'Does that please you? Not at all.' Σταθήκατε ποτέ εἰς τὰς 'Αθήνας; ποτέ. 'Have you ever been at Athens? Never.' So in other words: μᾶς φέρετε τίποτε νέον; Ἴνα ρίπετα. 'Do you bring us any news? None,' (i.e. *un rien,* a mere nothing.) Τινὸς is used for 'no one:' also κανίνας, μὶ κανένα τρόπον, 'in no wise:' παντελῶς, 'by no means:' ὁλότελα, 'in no way.' (sometimes used affirmatively:) ἀκόμη means both 'again,' and 'not yet.'

[2] Grimm, vol. iii. p. 750.

goutte, oef and *ei, blat* and *feuille*, though this cannot be considered as a proof that the one is derived from the other. It will be observed that *nihil* has not been retained in any of the Romance languages, three of which have agreed in substituting for it a derivative of *res*, preceded by a negative particle, in the same manner that the German *nichts* or *nicht* was formed from *nivaihts* or *niowiht*, nothing[1].

The other mode of strengthening a negation, viz. a repetition of the negative particles, likewise occurs in the Teutonic languages[2]: whence it was probably derived to those formed from the Latin, as will appear from the following examples.

Nullo, niuno, and *nessuno* in Ital., *neguns* and *nuls* in Prov., are equivalent to *nullus* and *nemo* in Latin, and thus they are often used: nevertheless a negative particle is often added to the proposition, the sense remaining the same, contrary to the rule that two negatives make an affirmative. Thus in Ital., 'non dico nulla,' 'non v'è niuno,' 'non è neuna cosa sì bella che ella non rincresca altrui,' Bocc. 'Che Annibale non fusse maestro di guerra, nessuno mai non lo dirà,' Machiavelli, *Disc.* iii. 10. In Provençal, 'Negus vezers mon bel pensar no-m val,' 'No sight is (not) worth to me my thoughts.' 'Nuls hom non pot ben chantar sens amar,' 'No man can (not) sing well without loving[3].' All of which are affirmative, not negative propositions. Now in Latin the use was in this respect completely reversed: *non-nullus* meant *some*, *non-nemo* meant *somebody;* and whereas 'non c'è nessuno' is

---

[1] Grimm, vol. iii. p. 748.
[2] Grimm, vol. iii. p. 727.
[3] Cinonio, c. 180, 188. Rayn. *Gr. Rom.* p. 149.

CONJUNCTIONS. 239

in Italian a negative, 'non nulli adfuerunt' is in Latin an affirmative proposition. The confusion has indeed gone a step further, and as affirmative particles, such as *mica, niente, rien, pas, point*, etc. by being continually used in negative sentences acquired a negative sense; so the negative pronouns by being used after a negation which absorbed their own meaning, retained only an affirmative force. Thus Machiavel says in the preface to his History: 'Se *niuna cosa* diletta o insegna nella istoria, è quella che particolarmente si descrive,' that is, if *anything*.

On the other hand, affirmative terms sometimes contract a negative meaning, and make a proposition negative which in its form is affirmative. Of this we have seen many examples in the words, *niente, rien, personne*, etc.: but these are not the only instances of such a change. Thus *mai* in Ital., which properly signifies *ever*, from being used in negative sentences, came to signify *never*: thus 'Ti priego che *mai* ad alcuna persona dichi d'avermi veduta,' Bocc. G. 2. n. 7, i.e. '*non* mai,' *never*[1]. So in French, 'Avez vous jamais été là ? Jamais.' 'Have you *ever* been there? *Never*.' *Veruno* in Italian is another word of this kind, which, though properly synonymous with *aliquis*, sometimes has a negative sense: thus 'I peccati veniali in verun modo si perdonano sanza i mortali,' i.e. 'in no way[2].' Whether *alcuno* in Italian ever had a negative meaning seems doubtful[3]: in French,

[1] See other instances in Cinonio, c. 164, s. 2.
[2] Cinonio, c. 250. *Veruno* appears to be derived from *vel unus*, in the same manner that *medesmo* came from *met ipsissimus*, and *dimentre* from *dum interea*. Thus, for example, such a sentence as 'ut non vel unus sciret,' might be rendered in Italian by 'che non veruno sapesse.'
[3] See Cinonio, c. 13, s. 6.

however, *aucun* frequently denies; as, Ce livre mérite-t-il aucune confiance? Aucune,' i.e. None[1].

The use of expletive particles in negative propositions, their subsequent assumption of a negative sense, the repetition of negative particles, and the confusion of affirmation and negation which prevail in the Romance languages, have all been introduced since the Latin, in which none of these idioms are to be observed. Nevertheless the comparison just made proves that there is only an analogy, and not an identity in the words which have undergone these changes, and that the conformity is to be accounted for, not by deriving one idiom from the other, but by referring them all partly to the disposition (which appears to be general to all men) to strengthen negation by additional words, and to confound affirmative and negative meanings: partly to the existence of the idioms in question among the nations who mixed their languages with the Latin.

It is moreover to be remarked that in the Spanish language (as far as I am aware) expletive particles of affirmation are not used in negative propositions, that consequently these particles have never acquired a negative sense, and in general that there are fewer examples

---

[1] The present rule with respect to *aucun* is that its negative sense is limited to the singular number, with certain narrow exceptions. Racine, in the *Phèdre*, has the following couplet:

Qu' *aucuns* monstres par moi domtés jusqu' aujourd'hui
Ne m'ont acquis le droit de faillir comme lui.
(Act i. sc. 1.)

Where the commentator says: ' *aucun* signifiant *nul*, *pas un*, ne peut s'employer au pluriel, si ce n'est avant les mots qui n'ont pas de singulier, ou qui dans certain sens doivent nécessairement être au pluriel.'

of the confusion of negation so common in its sister tongues. Thus the Spanish does not use a negative between the comparative and the verb, like the Provençal, Italian, and French; and the words *nada* and *nadie*, though their derivation is not very obvious, appear at any rate to be allied to the negative particle *no*, and not like *niente*, *rien*, and *personne*, to have a negative force, having originally been affirmative terms.

In reviewing the various prepositions, adverbs, and particles, compared in this chapter, it appears that although the several languages sometimes agree in remarkable deviations from the Latin, as in making *pres* and *presso* from *prope*, *sens* and *senza* from *sine*, and in introducing new words not found in the Latin, as the adverbs *malgrat* and *malgrado*, *tost* and *tosto*, *trop* and *troppo*: yet the Italian, the Spanish, and the French, and especially the two former, exhibit peculiarities which could not have been borrowed from the Provençal, and could not have been derived from any other source than the Latin itself. Thus the Ital. has preserved *apud*, *circa*, *infra*, and *eccum*, which the Prov. has lost: so likewise the Ital. and Prov. in modifying the Latin forms followed the different analogies respectively observed by them in other parts of speech: thus from *subtus*, *versus*, *minus*, *pejus*, *secundum*, *jusum*, *susum*, *medium*, the Ital. made *sotto*, *verso*, *meno*, *peggio*, *secondo*, *giuso*, *suso*, *mezzo*, like *petto* and *mostro* from *pectus* and *monstrum*: whereas the Prov. made *sotz* from *subtus*, *ves* from *versus*, *mens* from *minus*, *pietz* from *pejus*, like *amatz* from *amatus*: and *segont* from *secundum*, *miei* or *mieg* from *medium*, *jos* and *sos* from *jusum* and *susum*, like *amic* from *amicum*. It will be observed, moreover, that the Ital. retained in many words the final Latin vowel unchanged, which the Prov. either modified or cut off: thus *intra* and *sopra* Ital., *intre* and *sobre* Prov.; *sovente, onde* Ital., *sovent, ont* Prov.; *fuori, hieri, assai* Ital., *fors, hier, assatz* Prov. Sometimes also a Latin consonant which had disappeared in the Prov. was preserved in the Ital.: as from *hodie* and *ibi, hoggi* and *ivi* Ital., *oi* and *i* Prov. The Prov. likewise has several peculiar words, such as the derivatives of *aliquoties* and *aliorsum*, and the use of *gens* as an expletive in the sense of 'something:' the adverbs *pron*, moreover, and *pas* employed as an affirmative (or negative) particle, are common only to the French with the Prov., and are wanting in Ital. and Span. If, however, the Provençal had been the mother tongue of the Italian and Spanish, it is inconceivable that they should have preserved traces of the Latin, which the other had not: and it is very improbable that there should be any words peculiar to the original language, and not retained in any of the various dialects which, according to the supposition, sprung from it. It would be easy to carry this analysis further, and to point out other peculiarities in the latter languages, which could not have been derived from the Provençal: but enough has been said to illustrate the differences now in question, and to indicate the numerous difficulties to which M. Raynouard's theory is liable. I will only in conclusion remark, that with respect to the indeclinable parts of speech last examined, the Spanish departs widely from its sister languages, and bears strong marks of an independent origin.

§ 4. CONCLUDING REMARKS ON M. RAYNOUARD'S HYPOTHESIS.

M. Raynouard concludes his proofs of the derivation of the Italian, Spanish, and French, from the Provençal, by collecting several peculiar idioms not traceable to the Latin, in which these languages agree, as the use of *avere* instead of *essere*, of *lasciare stare*, *far la fica*, *aver nome*[1], etc. This kind of proof has been much insisted on by Perticari, who has collected a long series of corresponding idioms and expressions in Italian and the language of the Troubadours[2], which is interesting as

---

[1] *Gr. Comp.* p. 351—61. The expression *nomen habere* is, however, Latin, as M. Raynouard himself shows:

> Est via sublimis, coelo manifesta sereno,
> Lactea *nomen habet*, candore notabilis ipso.
> Ovid. *Met.* 1, 168–9.

[2] *Dif. di Dante*, c. 13–19. The reader must, however, be on his guard against an artifice practised by Perticari, in order to render the resemblances which he points out more striking, by assimilating the inflexions and terminations, as well as the syntax. In almost all the passages which he quotes, he obliterates the more salient peculiarities of the Provençal, and brings the forms nearer to the Italian, without informing his readers that the words are not faithfully transcribed, and then he calls on them to observe how close the Provençal is to the Italian. Thus in his very first example, c. 13, taken from the poem on Boethius, he says: 'questi sono versi citati dal dottissimo Renuardo:

> D'avant son vis null' om non te pot celar,
> Nè ess li omen chi sun ultra la mar.'

Which by adding the final vowels becomes, as he says, Italian:

> D' avanti 'l suo viso null' omo non si pote celare,
> Nè essi li omini che son oltra 'l mare.
> Vol. I. p. 318.

throwing light on both those languages, and as showing the close affinity which subsisted between them, but which cannot be considered as proving the derivation of one from the other, more than a table of parallel idioms in German, Dutch, and English, would prove the mutual dependence of those three sister languages. The close analogy between many of the idioms, no less than between the words and forms of the Romance languages, for the most part arises not from their propagation from one language into another, but from the similarity of effects produced by similar causes. Not only were the circumstances attending the mixture of the conquering and conquered populations similar all over western Europe, (as has been before explained,) but all the kingdoms

Now in M. Raynouard's *Gr. Rom.* p. 330, these verses are cited thus:

Davan son vis nuls om no s pot celar,
Ne eps li omne qui son ultra la mar.

There is no wonder that these verses should pass so easily into Italian, when they had been prepared for their reduction by taking away all that characterizes the language in which they were written ; and even after Perticari had restored the Provençal contractions to their fuller form by writing *d'avant* for *davan*, and *non se* for *no-s*, after he had introduced the Italian variations *ess* for *eps*, *omen* for *omne*, *chi* for *qui*, and after he had suppressed the final *s* retained from the Latin, the distinctive mark of the Provençal nominatives, by writing *null'* (meaning *nullo*) for *nuls*, he was unable to get rid of *son* instead of *suo* and *la mar* instead of *il mare*, with the gender changed, as in Spanish and French. (See above, p. 113–14.) Numerous other instances of changes of this kind in passages cited by Perticari (which I fear could not have been unintentional) are collected by Galvani, in his collection of Troubadour poetry, p. 504–20. M. Raynouard, whose good faith and accuracy in citation cannot be exceeded, probably did not perceive that Perticari had garbled the passages which he quoted, when he referred to that writer as an authority, without cautioning the reader against his misrepresentations.

created by the invaders had nearly the same form of government, the same system of laws, the same religion, the same manners; they existed in the same age; and a frequent communication both in peace and war, was reciprocally kept up between them, especially among the class of writers, whether chroniclers, theologians, or poets. In this state of things similar phrases would not unnaturally be suggested by similar wants, and by similar ideas: and some expressions likewise would doubtless pass from one language to the other (as we see at the present day,) though their number would probably be inconsiderable as compared with those of native growth, and would chiefly be confined to poets and other writers in an exotic style[1]. Any resemblance, therefore, whether of words, forms, or idioms, in the Romance languages, is quite compatible with the supposition that they were derived immediately from the Latin: whereas any marked dissimilarity between the Provençal and any other modern language is incompatible with the supposition that the latter is derived from the former. Thus it may be remarkable that the futures of all the modern verbs should be formed by adding the future tense of *habeo* to the infinitive mood of the verb: nevertheless it is conceivable that this mode of formation should have been adopted independently by different languages: but it is inconceivable that the Ital. *hebbi* or *hebbero*, the Span. *hube* and *hubiéron* should have been formed from *agui* or *aic*, *agueron* or *agueren*, the first person singular and the third

[1] See above, page 146, on the introduction of Italian words into French. Some likewise appear to have been borrowed from the Spanish, as *salade*, *limonade*, *esplanade*, *estrade*, etc. *Salade* if formed according to the French analogy would be *salée*.

person plural of the perfect of *aver*, whereas they might all three be independent corruptions of the Latin *habui* and *habuerunt*. A comparison of the Romance languages with the Latin will probably convince any person who examines the relations with an unbiased mind, that the Italian is in every respect nearer to the Latin than any of its cognate tongues; that it has retained the most Latin words, and subjected them to the fewest and least considerable alterations of form[1]. Next to the Italian,

[1] Passages which are at once Italian and Latin serve to show the close affinity of the two languages. The following couplet is well known:

> In mare irato, in subita procella
> Invoco te, nostra benigna stella.

Matthews, *Diary of an Invalid*, c. 10, adds these verses:

> Vivo in acerba pena, in mesto orrore,
> Quando te non imploro, in te non spero
> Purissima Maria, et in sincero
> Te non adoro et in divino ardore.

The following address to Venice is a still longer composition:

> Te saluto, alma Dea, Dea generosa,
> O gloria nostra, o Veneta regina!
> In procelloso turbine funesto
> Tu regnasti secura; mille membra
> Intrepida prostrasti in pugna acerba.
> Per te miser non fui, per te non gemo;
> Vivo in pace per te. Regna, o beata,
> Regna in prospera sorte, in alta pompa,
> In augusto splendore, in aurea sede.
> Tu serena, tu placida, tu pia,
> Tu benigna; tu salva, ama, conserva.

(Cited in the *Journ. of Education*, vol. vi. p. 260.)

Although these passages were doubtless composed in order to show the coincidence of the two languages, I question whether it would be possible to do as much in any other modern language derived from the Latin.

The Latin language probably remained longer in current use in Italy, especially in the central and southern parts, than in any other

though after a long interval, comes the Spanish, which has not so much changed the Latin form, as it has lost numerous Latin words preserved in Italian. After the Spanish is the language of *oc*, which has clipped the Latin standard much more closely than the two former languages, especially the Italian, and has not only rejected many vowel terminations which the others have preserved, but has introduced various contractions in the body of words which the others have not admitted. Last of all comes the language of *oïl*[1], which had at a very early period undergone the considerable modifications which may be seen in the modern French, and which caused it to be opposed as a distinct Romance dialect to the language of *oc*. Nevertheless in tracing the French language to its present form, it appears evidently to have passed

part of western Europe. Of this we have a proof in the two Latin songs composed in 871 and 924 A.D. referred to by M. Raynouard, (*Gram. Comp.* p. L.) which must have been understood by a large number of persons. (See above, pp. 58, 59.) Dante likewise introduces Cacciaguida in the *Paradise* as addressing his descendant in Latin (xv. 28–30,) and afterwards he says that Cacciaguida spoke to him 'con voce più dolce e suave, Ma non con questa moderna favella,' xvi. 32, which Daniello explains to mean 'that Cacciaguida spoke not in Italian but in Latin, as was the custom of persons of some education in his time.' It was this practice which made it so difficult to eradicate the use of Latin from the modern literature of Italy, and which even to a great degree banished the Italian from books after the age of Dante, Petrarch, and Boccaccio: it would, however, be absurd to suppose that in Cacciaguida's time the *lingua volgare* was not as much the language of the *volgo* of Florence as it is at the present day. The practice of preaching in Latin to mixed audiences prevailed in Italy so late as the sixteenth century: M'Crie's *History of the Reformation in Italy*, p. 51. Compare Wachsmuth in the *Athenæum*, vol. i. p. 287 note.

[1] 'Parmi les langues modernes, la langue française est celle qui a éprouvée le plus de variations.' Raynouard in *Journal des Sav.* 1818, p. 282.

through a stage little different from the language of *oc*, as preserved in the poems of the Troubadours: thus these two languages agreed in marking, in nouns and participles not ending in *a*, the nom. sing. and the acc. plural by the presence of *s*, the acc. sing. and nom. plural by the absence of *s*; and in forming the plural of feminine nouns

---

[1] M. Raynouard, at the end of his *Gram. Comp.* p. 380–04, considers what would have been the effect on the literature of France, if the French court had been established in a town south of the Loire, and the *langue d'oc* had become the language of government; and he appears to regret that the fates of the two languages of *oc* and *oil* had not been reversed, and the former had become the subordinate instead of the superior dialect. If one is to judge from the modern Provençal what would have been the present form of the French language under the circumstances supposed, it is difficult to assent to M. Raynouard's opinion. The language would doubtless have taken a more perfect form than it now bears in the southern *patois*, if it had been cultivated by the chief writers of France: but it would unquestionably have lost many of the advantages which M. Raynouard ascribes to it, and which induce him to give it the preference over the language of *oil*. Thus he says that it would have had the power of distinguishing the subject and regimen in both numbers, by the absence or presence of a final *s*; and he instances a verse of Thomas Corneille:

Le crime fait la honte et non pas l'échafaud,

which by means of this distinction would have lost its ambiguity, being written,

Le crimes fait la honte et non pas l'échafauds.

I will say nothing of M. Raynouard's inconsistency in extolling the superiority of the modern Romance languages over the Latin as being free 'from the slavery of declensions,' (above, p. 57,) and yet preferring the ancient Provençal to the modern French on the very ground of its possessing declensions: but I would remark that M. Raynouard appears to forget that the distinction of cases which he points out existed equally in ancient French, in which it has been lost, as it has likewise been lost in all the dialects of the language of *oc*. This advantage, therefore, which he finds in the *langue d'oc* would doubtless have disappeared if that language had become predominant in France, and it also existed in the *langue d'oil*. The final *s*, moreover, in the

in *a* from the Latin accusative: in both which points the
Ital. and Span. differ, as well from these two languages
as from each other. Hence when M. Raynouard selects
passages from Ital., Span., and French writers, which
are at once Ital. and Prov., Span. and Prov., French and
Prov., he is forced in the former to confine himself to
sentences, such as 'la vista angelica serena per subita
partenza,' in Petrarch, where are only singular feminine
nouns in *a;* for passages containing masculine nouns
either singular or plural, (unless the terminations are cut
off,) and feminine nouns in the plural, would have immediately betrayed the characteristic differences of the
two languages. In Spanish he is less confined, for he
can there cite not only the singular but also the plural of
nouns in *a*, (as 'mas son que arenas in riba de la mar'
from Berceo,) since the Spanish, like the Provençal and
unlike the Italian, forms its feminine plural from the
Latin accusative. In old French, on the other hand, he
has a wider field; for there is a strong resemblance between the languages of northern and southern France,
and it is easier to find passages where even in their later
form they agree, than to establish any characteristic distinction between them in their earlier form[1].

However singular the close concordance of the languages of *oc* and *oïl* may appear, as well of the Romance
languages in general, without the hypothesis of their
mutual dependence, or their common derivation from a
language already corrupted from the Latin; yet the

---

verse of Corneille would be a distinction only to the eye, and not to
the ear, like the *s* of the French plural: anciently the last letter of
Thiebaus, chascuns, etc. was doubtless pronounced as well as written,
like the modern *fils*.

[1] *Gr. Comp.* p. 376—84.

English and Scotch offer an analogy of languages between which there is the closest resemblance, but which were nevertheless formed independently of each other. Both in England and the Lowlands of Scotland the Norman invaders found an Anglo-Saxon population, and in both countries a new language was formed by mixing the language of the conquered with that of the conquerors. The further we go back the closer we find the relation between the Scotch and English, both in structure and in words, though each language has peculiarities of its own, which having been more strongly marked in the course of years, at last have created so considerable a difference between the two dialects, that a large part of a Scotch composition is unintelligible to a person acquainted only with modern English.

In reviewing the whole series of proofs collected by M. Raynouard, of the derivation of the Italian, Spanish, and French, from the ancient language of Provence as preserved in the poetry of the Troubadours, it appears to me that he has failed to establish his theory, and that he has shown nothing more than the close affinity which exists between these languages, as being derived from the Latin, their only common origin. Although, however, we may withhold our assent to the inference which he would draw from his premises, it is impossible to be blind to the light which he has thrown on the relations of the languages of which he treats, or to deny the service which he has rendered to the elucidation of the history of the modern dialects of the Latin: nor in the preceding essay do I aspire to any higher merit than of having reconstructed the materials furnished by M. Raynouard himself, into a more consistent theory than that which he formed from them.

APPENDIX.

Note (A.)

PERTICARI, in his account of the formation of the Italian language, and of the relation which its several dialects bear to one another, perpetually confounds *grammatical forms* and *style*. The question is not, whether in early times, writers in other parts of Italy besides Tuscany wrote in an elevated and noble style, avoiding low and plebeian terms, or whether they composed good poetry: but whether the forms of the Italian language, such as it is now, its terminations, contractions, and inflexions, existed in any other dialect except the Tuscan. There can be no doubt that in all the north of Italy the same character of language, which prevails now, has prevailed universally from a very early period, even if it has not existed since the Latin settled into its new form[1]. The dialects of Milan, Piedmont, Bologna, and other towns of northern Italy, are not confined to the lower and middle classes: they are to this day used by the upper classes in their familiar intercourse when no stranger from southern Italy is present. That these were not in the thirteenth and fourteenth centuries the languages of Milan, Piedmont, etc. is by no means proved by alleging a few verses written in the Tuscan Italian by the natives

---

[1] See above, p. 94—98, 104.

of those countries. It is remarkable to what an extent the power of composition in a foreign language may be acquired. We have abundant proofs of this fact in our public schools, where youths of sixteen or seventeen frequently compose even Latin poetry with a facility, elegance, and correctness, probably far beyond many native Romans who had not cultivated the art of versification. Many foreigners have written in modern languages with complete success, as Manzoni and Schlegel in French, Baretti in English, etc. A century and a half ago, when Latin was the language of Science, most mathematical and physical philosophers probably wrote in Latin with as much facility as in their own languages, although their thoughts were not turned to philological studies. To Newton it would doubtless have been a matter of perfect indifference, as far as the facility of composition was concerned, whether he wrote the *Principia* in Latin or in English. These instances are sufficient to show that there is not so much difficulty as would at first sight appear, in thinking in one language and composing in another. But when the transfusion of thought takes place, not from languages of a different family, as from German into Latin or French, but from one to another dialect of the same language, as from Milanese or Piedmontese to Tuscan, the process is far easier and simpler. The most that can be conceded to Perticari is that the Italian language, as written by its classical authors, has borrowed its forms in great measure from the Roman, Neapolitan, and Sicilian, as well as from the Tuscan dialect; that it is in fact a refinement of the dialects of central and southern Italy and of Sicily. But even this concession is liable to great objections, as any person may see who will compare the forms of the Sicilian and Roman dialects with the language of Tasso, for example, or Ariosto, who were not Tuscans. To argue, as Perticari does, that the written Italian was not borrowed from the Tuscan, because the Tuscan has many peculiar terms which are not intelligible out of Tuscany, betrays a complete misapprehension of the true question at issue: the Tuscan no doubt has peculiar *words* and *phrases*, but has it any peculiar *forms*, and have other dialects any forms which occur in the common Italian and do not occur in the Tuscan?

Note (B.)

Meidinger, in the Introduction to his *Dictionary of the Teuto-Gothic Languages*, (Frankfort, 1833,) has the following remarks on the Romance languages.

'The Italian language has for its base the *romana rustica* or *vulgaris* (plebeia) of the ancient Romans, which at a later period, after the dominion of the Franks, received the name of *lingua franca*. It is the mother of all the Romance languages. Among the Romans it formed the popular language properly so called, and the written Latin, as it is at present used, was confined to the upper classes, (*lingua nobilis* or *urbana* or *classica*.)' Introd. p. xlxix. In a note he adds: 'Originally the *romana rustica* was a mixture of the Pelasgo-Gothic, the Gallo-Celtic, and the Romano-Latin, as may be inferred from the different races which inhabited Italy.' Speaking of the French, he says, that 'the Gaelic or Celtic, mixed with the *Romana rustica*, formed the Romance language.' He afterwards adds: 'In the thirteenth century there were two principal dialects of the Romance language. These were the Romance language properly so called, or Provençal-Romance, or *langue d'oc*, spoken in the countries to the south of the Loire and in Catalonia, and 2, the *langue d'oil*,' p. 1. Of the language of Spain, he says, that 'the modern Spanish, like the French, has for its basis the *Romana rustica*, which has also undergone numerous changes, and is mixed with Arabic and Gothic words.' p. lii.

In this passage there is scarcely a single proposition to which I am able to assent. In the first place, there appears to be no evidence whatever for the opinion that the *Romana rustica* or *vulgaris* was a language distinct in its forms or roots from the Latin, and spoken by the lower classes or the peasants of Italy: still less is there any proof that this language was the base of the Italian. The statement that the *lingua Romana rustica* after the dominion of the Franks, received the name of *lingua franca* is equally unfounded: for the *lingua franca* was the corrupt and truncated language spoken by the various inhabitants of the Romance nations who met in the Levant and in the ports of Greece and northern Africa, and was called *lingua franca*, as being spoken by the *Franks*, the general name given by the Mussulmans to Europeans. So far from being identical with the language which formed the base of the Italian, it is itself a mutilated and imperfect form of the Italian, mixed with the Spanish, Provençal, and perhaps other languages. (See above, p. 22, note [1].) Having assumed the existence of this inferior dialect of the Latin, the *rustic* or *vulgar*, as opposed to the *classical* language, or that *of the city;* he proceeds to account for its origin by the races which inhabited Italy, viz. the Pelasgo-Gothic, the Gallo-Celtic, and the Romano-Latin. What the Pelasgo-Gothic race may be, or how it differs from the Romano-Latin; or how the language of the Romans, so far as it agrees with the Hellenic, differed from that of the Pelasgian part of the 'Pelasgo-Gothic' tribe; I confess myself wholly unable to comprehend. Nor is it very obvious why the Gallo-Celtic race should have produced so powerful an influence on the *lingua rustica* of Italy, and have produced no influence on its *lingua urbana:* or how, if the *lingua Romana rustica* was full of Celtic words, the languages supposed to be derived from it (as the Ital. and Span.) should be nearly destitute of them. It may be here observed, that if, in ancient Italy, the inhabitants of Rome and of the other large towns had spoken a language different from that of the inhabitants of the country, the latter would not have been called the 'lingua *Romana* rustica:' as at that time the appellation of Romans was not extended to the inhabitants of the entire peninsula. It was only at a much later period when the name of *Romani* was given to all the provincials, to all the subjects of the Roman empire, that the name of *rustic Roman* language could by possibility have arisen. (See above, p. 29.)

With regard to the origin of the Romance languages of France, Mr. Meidinger says that they were formed by the mixture of the *Romana rustica* and the Celtic; which is much the same as if any one were to say that the English was formed by the mixture of the Anglo-Saxon and the Celtic: for in both cases the true origin of each language would be omitted, and a false origin would be asserted. The Latin language of France was transformed into the Romance by the operation of the Teutonic, as the Anglo-Saxon language of Britain was transformed into English by the operation of the Norman French: nor had the Celtic, the native language both of Gaul and Britain, exercised any influence on either language before the invasion of Gaul and Britain by the Teutons and the Normans. There is not (as far as I am aware) any instance of a Celtic having been amalgamated with either a Teutonic, a Latin, or a Romance language: a remarkable circumstance, when the diffusion of the Celts over the whole of western Europe is considered.

As to Mr. Meidinger's account of the Spanish, it is not easy to understand why he should have mentioned the influence of the Gothic invaders on the *Romana rustica* of Spain, while he makes no mention of any influence exercised by the Teutonic invaders of France on the *Romana rustica* of that country. Moreover the influence of the Arabic on the Romance of Spain was by no means equal to that of the Gothic, and ought not to be placed on the same level with it.

I have selected the above passage in Mr. Meidinger's introduction to his Teuto-Gothic Dictionary, as it occurs in a book of reference, compiled with great industry, and considerable ability, which may be supposed to express the opinions on the origin of the Romance languages generally current even among persons who have a more than superficial acquaintance with the subject: and I have examined it in order to justify myself for contributing my mite to the destruction of accredited and received errors, although they might seem to have been already overthrown by former writers, such as Schlegel and Diez, and in part by M. Raynouard himself. [This theory is still maintained by Burguy, *Gramm. de la Langue d'Oïl*, vol. i. p. 7—10. He lays it down that 'les langues romanes sont un développement organique du viel idiôme latin vulgaire.' 1862. Diez likewise attributes this origin to the Romance languages, *Rom. Gr.* vol. i. p. 6.]

NOTE (C.)

'*Ausonian* in Priscus *Excerpt. Legat.* p. 59, B, seems to mean *volgare* as opposed to the Latin,' says Niebuhr, *Hist. of Rome,* vol. i. note 46. The passage of Priscus is as follows: Διατρίβαντι δέ μοι καὶ περιπάτους ποιουμένῳ πρὸ τοῦ περιβόλου τῶν οἰκημάτων, προσελθών τις, ὃν βάρβαρον ἐκ τῆς Σκυθικῆς ᾠήθην εἶναι στολῆς, 'Ἑλληνικῇ ἀσπάζεταί με φωνῇ 'χαῖρε' προσειπών, ὥστε με θαυμάζειν, ὅτι γε δὴ ἑλληνίζει Σκύθης ἀνήρ. ξύγκλυδες γὰρ ὄντες πρὸς τῇ σφετέρᾳ βαρβάρῳ γλώσσῃ ζηλοῦσιν ἢ τὴν Οὔννων ἢ τὴν Γότθων, ἢ καὶ τὴν Αὐσονίων, ὅσοις αὐτῶν πρὸς 'Ρωμαίους ἐπιμιξία· καὶ οὐ ῥᾳδίως τις σφῶν ἑλληνίζει τῇ φωνῇ, πλὴν ὧν ἀπήγαγον αἰχμαλώτων ἀπὸ τῆς Θρᾳκίας καὶ Ἰλλυρίδος παραλίου. p. 190, ed. Bonn. It does not appear to me that this passage affords any reason for supposing that there was in the time of Priscus, any language spoken by the Romans different from the classical Latin. Priscus had accompanied Maximus on an embassy to Attila, (448 A.D.) and being in the interior of Scythia he was surprised by hearing a person address him in *Greek:* 'for, says he, besides their own language the Scythians in general speak either that of the Huns, or of the Goths, or sometimes that of the *Ausonians,* in cases where they have had intercourse with the *Romans;* but it rarely happens that any of them speak Greek, except those who have been brought captive from the Thracian and Illyrian coast.' It appears to me quite evident that Priscus here used *Ausonians* for *Romans*, in order to avoid the repetition of the word Ῥωμαῖος, and that the two terms are precisely synonymous: his meaning being that the Scythians, from their intercourse with the Romans, occasionally learnt to use the *Latin* language. Even if there had been a difference of dialects in the spoken language of Italy, it is very unlikely that Priscus, who was a Greek by education and habits, should have noticed such a distinction.

Note (D.)

On the non-Latin part of the Romance Languages.

It has been stated in the text that the object of the above essay is to elucidate the *form* and *structure* of the Romance languages, without reference to the *origin* of the words themselves, and therefore no mention was made of those foreign terms which were introduced into these languages at, or soon after, the Teutonic conquest of Western Europe. This is properly a question of etymological research: nor could it be satisfactorily determined without making a dictionary of all the Romance languages with their several dialects, in which the corresponding words should be arranged together, and their etymology explained.

It has, however, occurred to me that a few facts illustrative of the foreign or non-Latin part of the Romance languages might be conveniently given in this place; and with that view I shall first subjoin some of the chief derivatives of German words in the Italian, Spanish, and French languages, merely as instances of the manner in which foreign terms were adopted in those tongues, and not as making any claims to completeness. Most of them are selected from Menage's *Origini Italiane*, and the Glossary attached to Muratori's thirty-third Dissertation on the *Italian Antiquities of the Middle Ages*: from the list of French and Italian words derived from the ancient northern languages in Hickes' *Thesaurus Ling. Vet. Septent.* vol. i. p. 91—100, and from the index of French words at the end of Wachter's *Glossarium Germanicum*. Other remarks on the same subject will also be found in the treatise of G. J. Vossius, *De Vitiis Sermonis et Glossematis Latino-barbaris*, printed in his works, vol. ii. Amsterdam, 1695, folio. [The following list has been compared with the vocabularies of Diez and Burguy. The number of words might be much augmented. 1862.]

Words in Italian, Spanish, and French derived from the Teutonic:

Agraffe Fr. from *krappen*, to *hook*, to *grapple*.

Alabarda It. *halabarda* Sp. *hallebarde* Fr. from *helmbarte*.

Albergo It. *albergue* Sp. *auberge* Fr. from *herberge*.

Alesna Sp. *alesne* or *alêne* Fr. *lesina* It. from *alansa*. (Grimm, *D. Gr.* vol. ii. p. 346.) *Lesina* in Italian is for *alesina*, like *pecchia* for *apecchia*, above p. 137. [See Burguy in *alesne*.]

Aldea Sp. is probably Gothic, according to Grimm, *Deutsche Rechtsallerthümer*, p. 309. [Diez approves of an Arabic origin.]

Alto It. and Sp. *halte* Fr. from *halten*.

Ambasciatore It. *embaxador* Sp. *ambassadeur* Fr. from *ambacht, ministerium* or *minister*.

Amuser Fr. from *musse*. [Compare Diez in *muso*.]

Anca It. and Sp. *hanche* Fr. from *anke*.

Andare It. *andar* Sp. *andar* and *anar* Prov. (Raynouard, *Gr. Comp.* p. 300,) *aner* and *aller* Fr. from *anden* or *wanden*, the same as the English *to wend*, of which the preterite is still in use. (Wachter in *anden* and *wallen*, p. 1814.) The initial *w* has been preserved in the Italian *galleria* and the Fr. *galerie*. [Compare Diez in *andare*.]

Araldo It. *heraldo* Sp. *héraud* Fr. from *herold*.

Aringa It. *arenga* Sp. *hareng* Fr. from *häring*.

Aringo It. *arenga* Sp. *harangue* Fr. from *ringen*. [Diez derives it from *ring, a circle*.]

Arnese It. *arneses* Sp. *harnois* Fr. from *harnisch:* see Grimm quoted above, p. 141.

Aspo It. from *hasp-el*.

Astio It. *hastio* Sp. *hair* Fr. from *hass, hassen*. See Muratori in *astio:* Orell, *Altfranzösische Grammatik*, p. 154.

Attaccare It. *attacher* Fr. from *tekan* Goth. [See Diez in *tacco*.]

Avviso, avvisare It. *aviso* Sp. *avis, aviser* Fr. from *weisen*. [Diez, in *viso*, derives these words from *visum*.]

Azza It. *haz* Sp. *hâche* Fr. from *hacke*.

Bacino It. and Sp. *bac, bachot, bassin* (i.e. *bacin*) Fr. from *becken*. See Adelung in v.

APPENDIX. 261

Baldo It. *baud* Fr. from *bald*. See Menage, *Dict. Fr.* in *baud*. [Diez in *baldo*, Raynouard, *Lex. Rom.* vol. i. p. 32.]

Balla It. *bala* Sp. *balle* Fr. are probably from the German *ball*, though nearly the same word is in Latin, (*bulla*, see *Philological Museum*, vol. i. p. 411.) [See Diez in *balla*.]

Ballare It. *baylar* Sp., *to dance*, are probably from *ballen*, in the sense of *turning*, like *walzen*.

Baluardo It. *baluarte* Sp. *boulevard* Fr. from *bollwerk*. [See Diez in *boulevard*.]

Bambino It. The Greek had βάβιον; but *bambo* (whence *bamb-ino*, above p. 132,) was probably derived from a Teutonic form *bab*, (*bube* High German, *babe* English,) and the *m* was inserted before *b*, as in *amb* Prov. from *ab*, and other words mentioned above, p. 198. [Diez in *bambo*, derives the word from the Greek βαμβαλὸς, a stammerer, whence *bambalio* in Cicero.]

Banco It. and Sp. *banc* Fr. from *bank*.

Banda It. and Sp. *bande* Fr. from *band*. Also *benda* and *bendare* It. from *binde* and *binden*.

Bandire It. *bannir* Fr. from *bannen*.

Bando It. and Sp. *ban* Fr. from *bann*.

Bara It. *bière* Fr. from *bären*.

Barone It. *baron* Sp. and Fr. from *baro* or *varo*. [See Diez in *barone*, Burguy in *baron*.]

Barca It. *barco* Sp. *barque* Fr. from *barke*.

Basso It. *baxo* Sp. *bas* Fr. whence *bastardo* It. and Sp. *bâtard* Fr. (above, p. 142,) from *bas*, *below*. See Wachter, p. 126. [Diez in *basso*, Burguy in *bas*.]

Batello It. (*batto* in *Giov. Villani*) *bateau* Fr. from *bat*, or *bot*. Above, p. 139.

Beau-frère, beaupère, etc. Fr. The first word is probably a mistranslation. See Wachter in *Schönbruder*.

Berger Fr. from *bergen*. See Muratori in *parco*.

Biada It. *bled* Fr. from *blatt*. [Diez in *biado*, Burguy in *bled*.]

Bianco It. *blanco* Sp. *blanc* Fr. from *blank*.

Bicchiere It. *picher* Fr. from *becher*: compare βίκος.

Biglietto It. *billete* Sp. *billet* Fr. from *bille*. See above, p. 143.

Biondo It. *blondo* Sp. *blond* Fr. from *blonde*.

Birra It. *bière* Fr. from *bier*. [Diez in *birra*.]

Bloquer Fr. from *lukan* Goth. *belocan* A. Sax. *to shut*. Wachter in *lucken*.

Bordello It. *burdel* Sp. *bordel* Fr. from *bord*. See above, p. 138. [Diez in *bordu*, Burguy in *borde*.]

Borgo It. *burgo* Sp. *bourg* Fr. from *burg*.

Bosco It. *bosque* Sp. *bois* Fr. from *busch*. [Diez in *bosco*.]

Botte It. from *botte, butt*. [Diez in v.]

Bouc Fr. from *bock*. [Burguy in *boch*.]

Bout Fr. from *but: abutan*, or *butan*, Ang. Sax.

Brando It. *brand* Fr. from *brand*.

Bravo It. and Sp. *brave* Fr. from *brav*. [See Diez in *bravo*.]

Breccia It. *brecha* Sp. *brèche* Fr. from *brechen*.

Bridu It. *bride* Fr. from *brid*, whence *brit-til* old H. German, *blid-le* English. The Ital. changed *d* into *l* (see above, p. 76, note [1],) and made *briglia*.

Bruno It. and Sp. *brun* Fr. from *braun*. [Burguy in *brun*.]

Busto It. and Sp. *buste* Fr. from *brust*, according to Hickes. [The derivation from *brust* is rejected by Diez in *busto*.]

Butiro, butero It. *beurre* Fr. from *butter*. The Sp. has not this word.

Buttare It. *botar* Sp. *bouter, pousser* Fr. from *bossen, to push*. Wachter in *bossen*. [See Diez in *bottare*.]

Canif Fr. from *kneif, knife* Eng. [Burguy in *cnivet*.]

Canto It. and Sp. from *kant*. Perhaps *coin* Fr. may have the same origin. [Diez in *canto*.]

Cacciare It. *cazar* Sp. *chasser* Fr. from *hetzen, to hunt*, (i. e. *chetzen*, according to the Frankish pronunciation.) Wachter. [See Diez in *cacciare*.]

Cappa It. *capa* Sp. *chape* Fr. with their numerous derivatives, from *kappe*. [See Diez in *cappa*.]

Carro It. and Sp. *char* Fr. from *karr*. See Wachter in v. Above, p. 62, note *.

Chiasso It. from *gasse*.

Choisir Fr. from *chiusan* or *kiusan*, old H. German, (now *kiesen*.) See Schlegel, *Observ.* p. 110. [Diez in *choisir*.]

Cloche Fr. from *glocke*. [Burguy in v.]

Coc Fr. from *coc*. See Wachter in *küchlein*. [Burguy in *coc*.]

Daga It. and Sp. from *degen*. [Diez in v.]

Danzare It. *danzar* Sp. *danser* Fr. from *tanzen*.

Dardo It. and Sp. *dard* Fr. from *dard*.

Dogue Fr. from *docke* Germ. *dog* Eng.

Douve Fr. from *daube*, whence *adouver* or *adouber* and *radouber*, (Wachter,) *addobbare* It. [See Diez in *doga*, who derives the word from δοχή, Burguy in *dove*.]

Drudo It. *drut* Pr. *dru* Fr. from *draut* or *drut*: see v. Hagen, Glossary to the *Nibel. Lied* in *trut*, Wachter in *draut*. [Diez in *drudo*, Burguy in *drut*.]

Elmo It. *helmo* Sp. *héaume* Fr. from *helm*.

Elsa It. from *halten.*
Fallare It. *fallar* Sp. *faillir* Fr. from *fehlen.* *Fello, fellone* It. *follon* Sp. *felon* Fr. also come from the same root.
Falda It. and Sp. from *falte, fold* Eng. [*Faldistorio* It. and Sp. *fauteuil* Fr. from *faltstuhl.*]
Feltro It. *fieltro* Sp. *feutre* Fr. from *filz, felt.*
Fiasco It. *frasco* Sp. *flasque, flacon* Fr. from *flask.* [See Diez in *fiasco.*]
Fino It. and Sp. *fin* Fr. from *fein.*
Fodero It. *forro* Sp. *fourrier* Fr. from *führen.*
Folla It. *foule* Fr. from *fülle.*
Folle It. *fol* Fr. from *faul, fool* Eng. [Diez in *folle.*]
Foresta It. *floresta* Sp. *forêt* (*forest*) Fr. from *forst.* [See Diez in *foresta,* Burguy in *forest.*]
Franco It. and Sp. *franc* Fr. from *frank.*
Fresco It. and Sp. *frais* Fr. from *frisch.* Above, p. 131.
Freccia It. *flecha* Sp. *flèche* Fr. from *flitsch* or *flitz.* [See Diez in *freccia.*]
Frisson and *affreux* Fr. from *freis-lich.*
Gamuza Sp. *camozza* It. *chamois* Fr. from *gemse.*
Garzone It. *garçon* Fr. See above, p. 133, note [e]. [Diez in *garzone,* Burguy in *gars.*]
Gaspiller i.e. *ge-spillen, to spill.* See Wachter in *verspillen. Spillan* Ang. Sax.
Gerbe Fr. from *garbe.*
Ghirlanda It. *guirnalda* Sp. *guirlande* Fr. probably from *gairdan* Goth. (*gürten* H. Germ. *gird* Eng.) On the change of *d* into a liquid, see above, p. 76, note [1]. So 'Οδυσσεὺς and *Ulysses.* [Diez in *ghirlanda.*]
Giallo It. *jaulne* Fr. from *gelb.*

Giardino It. *jardin* Sp. and Fr. from *garten*. See above, p. 132.

Girfalco It. *girifalte* Sp. *gerfaut* Fr. from *geier*. [The word *falco* is Latin. The first syllable of *girfalco* is derived by Diez in v. from *gyrare*.]

Glaive Fr. from *glef, hasta*. Wachter. [See Diez and Burguy in v.]

Gramo It. *gram* old Fr. from *gram*.

Gridare It. *gritar* Sp. *crier* Fr. from *gridan* Goth.

Grifo It. *griffe* Fr. from *greifen*. [Diez in *griffe*.]

Grosso It. *grueso* Sp. *gros* Fr. from *gross*.

Guadagnare It. *ganar* Sp. *gagner* Fr. from *winnen*. [Diez in *guadagnare*, Burguy in *gaagnier*.]

Guajo It. from *weh*.

Guancia It. from *wange*.

Guanto It. *guante* Sp. *gant* Fr. from *wante*. [Diez in *guanto*.]

Guardare It. *guardar* Sp. *garder* Fr. from *wahren*.

Guarentire It. *garantir* Fr. from *weren*. See Grimm, *Deutsche Rechtsalterthümer*, p. 603. *Guarire* It. and *guérir* Fr. appear to have the same origin.

Guarnire, guarnigione It. *guarnacer, guarnicion* Sp. *garnir, garnison* Fr. from *warnen, munire*: 'postea sensus ab apparatu militari ad quemcumque apparatum translatus est.' Wachter. [See Diez in *guarnire*.]

Guatare It. *guet, gueter* Fr. from *wachen, wacht*.

Guerra It. and Sp. *guerre* Fr. from *werra*. Grimm, *D. R.* p. 603. Schlegel, *Observ. sur la Langue Prov.*, p. 97. [Diez in *guerra*, Burguy in *guerre*.]

Guiderdone It. *guerdon* Fr. from *widerthun*.

Guisa It. and Sp. *guise* Fr. from *weise*.

From the foregoing examples it will be perceived that

the Romance form of the Teutonic *w* is *gu*, and sometimes *g* in French.

Harpe Fr. *arpa* It. and Sp. from *harpfe*, harp. [See Diez in *arpa*, Burguy in *harpe*.]

Havre Fr. from *hafen*, formed (as Hickes remarks) like *Londres* from *London*. See above, p. 81, note [1].

Indarno It. Grimm, *D. Gramm*. vol. iii. p. 107, note, and p. 163, explains this word from the Sclavonic *darom*, *darmo*, *darno*, gratis from *dar*.

Landa It. *landes* Fr. from *land*.

Lanzichenecco It. *lansquenet* Fr. from *lanzknecht*.

Lasciare It. *dexar* Sp. (above, p. 76, note [1],) *laisser* Fr. from *lassen*.

Leccare It. *lecher* Fr. from *lecken*. [Diez in *leccare*.]

Lindo It. and Sp. from *ge-linde*, *lindern*. [Diez in *lindo* derives the word from *limpidus*.]

Lotto It. *lot* Fr. from *loos : hlauts* Goth.

Marca It. and Sp. *marche* Fr. from *marke*.

Masto It. *mastil* Sp. *mât* Fr. from *mast*.

Matar Sp. *ammazzare* It. *massacrer* Fr. from *metzen*, whence *maçon* Fr. Wachter. [Diez in v. derives *mazza* It. from the Latin *matea*, of which a lengthened form *mateola* is used by Cato.

Matto It. from *matt*, *mad* Eng.

Meurtre Fr. from *maurthr* Goth. See Schlegel, *Observ.* p. 99. [Diez in *meurtre*.]

Mignon, *mignard* Fr. either from *minne* love, or *min* small. [Diez in *mignon*.]

Milza It. *melsa* Sp. from *miltz*. [Diez in *milza*.]

Mischiare It. *mezclar* Sp. *mesler (mêler)* Fr. from *mischen*. [Diez in *mischiare* derives the word from *miscere*.]

Mouton Fr. Wachter derives this word from *mutzen*, truncare: but *montone* It. creates a difficulty, which signifies a ram. See Muratori in v. [Diez in *montone* and Burguy in *molton* trace the word to the Latin *mutilus*. Compare Ducange in *multo*. Blanc, *Voc. Dant.* in *montone* derives it from *montare*.]

Mutiner Fr. *ammunitarsi* It. from *motjan* Goth. to meet. See Muratori in *ammutinarsi*. [Diez in *meute* and Burguy in *movoir* derive *meute* from *movere*, and suppose *mutin* to be formed from *meute*.]

Nord, sud, est, ouest Fr. from the German. The German names for the points of the compass appear to have been introduced into the Spanish from the French, which has also been the case more recently with the Italian.

Palco It. and Sp. from *balck*. [Diez in *balco*.]

Pancia It. *panza* Sp. *panse* Fr. from *bansen*, paunch Eng. [Diez in *pancia* derives these words from the Latin *pantex*.]

Panziera It. from *panzer*.

Partigiana It. *partesana* Sp. *pertuisane* Fr. has probably a Teutonic origin. See Muratori in *partigiana*. [Compare Diez in *partigiana*.]

Perla It. and Sp. *perle* Fr. from *perle*, [a word of obscure origin, see Diez in *perla*.]

Pezzo, pezza, It. *pieza* Sp. *pièce* Fr. from *fetz* (i. e. *pfetz*.) See Wachter in v.

Piazza It. *plaza* Sp. *place* Fr. from *platz*. [Diez in *piazza* derives the word from the Latin *platea*.]

Piccare It. *picar* Sp. *piquer* Fr. from *picken*.

Piffero It. *pifaro* Sp. *fifre* Fr. from *pfeiffer*.

Poltrone It. *poltron* Sp. and Fr. *poltrire* It. from

polster. See Muratori in *poltrone* and Wachter in *polster.* [Diez in *poltro.*]

Prigione It. *prision* Sp. *prison* Fr. from *prisund* Goth. [Diez in *prigione* derives the word from *prehensio* or *prensio.*]

Randa It. from *rand.*

Raspare It. *raspar*, Sp. *râper* Fr. from *raspen.*

Ratto It. *raton*, Sp. *rat, raton* Fr. from *ratte*. [Diez in *ratto* remarks that this animal was unknown to the Romans.]

Recare It. from *reichen.*

Ricco It. *rico* Sp. *riche* Fr. from *reich.*

Riga It. *raya* Sp. from *reihe.*

Rima It. and Sp. from *reim.*

Rocca It. *rueca* Sp. *roque* Fr. *colus*, from *rocke.*

Ronz-ino It. *rocin* Sp. *rouss-in* Fr. from *ross.* See above, p. 132.

Rostir Fr. *arrostire* It. (Muratori in v.) from *rost.* [Diez in *rostire.*]

Rubare It. *rubar*, Sp. *rober*, *dérober*, Fr. from *rauben.* [Compare Diez in *roba.*]

Sciabla, It. *sabre* Fr. from *säbel.* [Compare Diez in *sciabla.*]

Sala It. and Sp. *salle* Fr. from *sal.*

Scalco It. from *schalck;* whence *mariscalco* and *siniscalco.*

Schermo, schermire It. *esgrimir* Sp. *escrimer* Fr. from *schirm, schirmen.*

Scherzo It. from *scherz.*

Schiatta It. from *schlacht* (now *ge-schlecht.*)

Schiera It. *eschiere* old Fr. from *schaar.* [Burguy in *eschele.*]

Schietto It. from *schlecht.*

Schifo It. *esquife* Sp. *esquif* Fr. from *schiff*. See above, p. 107.
Schinca It. from *schenk-el*, *shin* Eng.
Schivare It. *esquivar* Sp. *esquiver* Fr. from *scheuen*.
Schiuma It. *écume* Fr. from *schaum*.
Schizzo It. *esquisse* Fr. a drawing hastily *thrown down*, from *schiessen*. See Tooke, *Div. of Purley*, vol. ii. p. 144. [Diez in *schizzo* derives the word from the Latin *schedium*.]
Scotto It. *escote* Sp. *écot* Fr. from *schooss*.
Senno It. from *sinn*. *Bi-sogno* It. and *soin* and *be-soin* Fr. are derived from the ancient Teutonic word which is written *sonnis* and *sunnis* in the Salic law. See Muratori in *bisogno*.
Smacco It. from *schmach*.
Smaltire It. from *schmelzen*. [The derivation from *maltha* seems preferable. See Diez in *smalto*.]
Snello It. from *schnell*.
Spanna It. from *spann*. [Diez in *spanna*.]
Sparviere It. *épervier* Fr. from *sperber*.
Sperone It. *espuela* Sp. *éperon* Fr. from *sporn*.
Spiare It. *espiar* Sp. *épier* Fr. from *spähen*.
Spruzzare It. from *sprützen*. [See Diez in *sprazzare*, p. 438.]
Stampare It. *estampar* Sp. *étampe* Fr. from *stampfen*.
Steccare It. *estacar* Sp. from *stechen*.
Stelo It. from *stiel*.
Stivale It. from *stiefel*.
Stocco It. *estoque* Sp. from *stock*. [Diez in *stocco*.]
Stormo It. from *sturm*.
Strale It. from *strahl*.
Stucco It. *estuque* Sp. from *stück*, 'because' it is made of pieces of marble.' Menage in v. [Diez in *stucco*.]

Stufa It. *estufa* Sp. *étuve* Fr. from *stube*.
Tasca It. from *tasche*. [Diez in v.]
Toccare It. *tocar* Sp. *toucher* Fr. from *tekan* Goth. *to take*. [Diez in *toccare*.]
Tomare It. *tomber* Fr. from *dümen, daumeln* Germ. *tumb-le* Engl. [See Diez in *tombolare*.]
Tonel Sp. *tonneau* Fr. from *tonne*. [Diez in *tona*.]
Torba It. *turba* Sp. *tourbe* Fr. from *torf, turf* Eng.
Tregua It. and Sp. *trève* Fr. (to which may be added *intrigue* Fr.) from *treuga*, equivalent to *treue*.
Trincare It. *trinquer* Fr. from *trinken*.
Tuer Fr. from *tödten*. Wachter. [Diez and Burguy derive this word from the Latin *tutari*.]
Tuffare It. *étouffer* Fr. from *taufen*. [Diez in *tufo* derives the word from the Greek τύφος.]
Uosa It. *heuse* and *houseaux* Fr. from *hosen*. Menage in v. [Compare Diez in *uosa*.]
Urtare It. *heurter* Fr. from *horten*, to hurt.
Usbergo It. *haubere, haubergeon* Fr. from *halsberge*.
Zanna It. from *zahn*. [Diez in *zanna*, p. 448, gives the preference to the Latin *sanna*.]
Zuppa It. *sopa* Sp. *souppe* Fr. from *suppe, sop*. [See Diez in *sopa*.]

With regard to the classes of words introduced from the Teutonic into the Romance languages, Wachsmuth remarks that they are for the most part the names of outward objects, as food and implements, or they relate to customs and institutions, especially the use of arms and the feudal system. (*Athenæum*, vol. i. p. 298.) Many words relating to warlike subjects will have been observed in the list of words just given: the introduction of which, as well as of political terms, is quite consistent with the existence of a dominant military class of foreigners[1].

In many cases, however, it is not obvious why a Teutonic word should have been naturalized: as in the following instances, where the original Latin term has been retained by some of the Romance languages, and a new German term been substituted by others.

Latin.	Ital.	Span.	French.
æramen	rame	cobre (*kupfer*)[2]	airain
attonitus	attonito	atonito	estonné (*to stun*)
cerevisium	birra (*hier*)	cerveza	bière
pastor	pastore	pastor	berger[3]
saburra	savorra	lastre (from *last*)	lest
sedes	sede	sede	siège (from *sitz*[4])
socer	suocero	suegro	beaupère[5]
spuma	spuma and schiuma (from *schaum*)	espuma	escume
suber	suvero	corcho (from *kork*)	liége

[1] The following Latin terms occurring in the Greek of the New Testament, furnish a curious parallel of the introduction of foreign names for military and political subjects by a dominant nation: κολωνία, Acts xvi. 12; σπεκουλάτωρ, Mark vi. 27.; κεντυρίων, Mark xv. 39; πραιτώριον, Matt. xxvii. 27; κουστωδία, Matt. xxvii. 65; μίλιον, Matt. v. 41; δηνάριον, Luke vii. 41; ἀσσάριον, Matt. x. 29; κοδράντης, Matt. v. 26; κῆνσος, Matt. xvii. 25. [On the introduction of military terms from the German into the Romance languages, see Diez, *Rom. Gramm.* vol. i. p. 66.]

[2] *Cuprum* (for *æs Cyprium*) was a Latin word, Spartian, *Carac.* 9. See Ducange in v.

[3] See above, p. 202. The French has *pasteur*, but only in a metaphorical sense.

[4] That *siège* is not derived from *sedes* is proved by the gender.

[5] See above, p. 202.

It will be perceived that some of the words above enumerated as derived from the Teutonic are among the commonest and most familiar in the Romance languages, as *albergo, andare, bambino, basso, biancho, bicchiere, birra, biglietto, borgo, bosco, bravo*, etc. Ital.; *albergue, baxo, blanco, billete, burgo, bosque, bravo*, etc. Span.; *auberge, airain, balle, bas, berger, blanc, bière, billet, bourg, bois, brave*, Fr. In this respect there is a remarkable difference between the foreign words introduced by conquest into the English and into the Romance languages. In English the more familiar, idiomatic, and simple the style, the more exclusively Saxon it is, and the fewer are the foreign or French terms: whereas in the Romance languages the converse is generally the case. In Italian, for example, the more elevated the style, the more purely Latin is its character: in Tasso many successive stanzas often occur in which every word is of Latin origin; but if we take a composition in the familiar spoken language, as a comedy or a satire, it will be found scarcely possible to find a long passage entirely free from Teutonic derivatives. Dante is a much more idiomatic writer than Tasso, and uses a much less stilted style: but his language abounds far more in words not of Latin origin.

Some words have passed into the Romance languages, either mediately or immediately, from the Greek: as *spada* It. *espada* Sp. *espée* Fr. from σπάθη; *parola* It. *palabra* Sp. *parole* Fr. from παραβολή. (Schlegel, *Observ.*, p. 109.) To these Wachsmuth adds *frissonner* Fr. from φρίσσω, *lisse* Fr. from λίσσος, *golfo* It. from κόλπος, *gaio* It. from γαίω, (*Athenäum*, vol. i. p. 299.) With regard to *frisson*, the Teutonic derivation mentioned above, p. 264, is more probable than a Greek one; κόλπος may have been easily introduced by the intercourse with the Greek mariners of the Mediterranean: as to the other two words it seems unlikely, notwithstanding the agreement of sound and meaning, that the etymology suggested should be true.

[Diez derives *liscio* It. and Sp. and *lisse* Fr. from the German *leise* (in *liscio*); he derives *gajo* It. *gai* Fr. from the German *jähe* (in *gajo*). In his *Romance Grammar*, vol. i. p. 57—60, he gives a list of Greek words which have passed into Romance languages: compare p. 92. Many of these however made the transition through the medium of the Latin. Thus *zio* It. *tio* Sp. came ultimately from θεῖος; but the word *thius* signified uncle in Low Latin: see Ducange in v. *Agonia* It. and Sp. *agonie* Fr. were derived from ἀγωνία, and *agognare* It. from ἀγωνιᾶν; *accidia* It. was derived from ἀκηδία; *borsa* It. *bolsa* Sp. *bourse* Fr. from βύρσα; *ermo* It. from ἔρημος; *emicrania* It. *migrano* Sp. *migraine* Fr. from ἡμικρανία; *salma* It. and Sp. *somme* Fr. from σάγμα; but *agonia, accidia, byrsa, eremus, hemicrania,* and *sagma* were also used as Latin words: see Ducange *Gloss.* in *agonia, acedia, bursa, eremus, hemigranea, sagma.* In *baleno* It. from βέλεμνον; *colla* It. *cola* Sp. *colle* Fr. from κόλλα; *fanale* It. from φανός (Diez in *falò*); *mustaccio* It. from μύσταξ; *paggio* It. *page* Fr. from παιδίον, *pitocco* It. from πτωχός, and *stuolo* It. from στόλος, the passage from one language to the other may have been direct. Several words connected with navigation and trade passed directly from the Greek into Romance languages, a circumstance naturally growing out of the maritime communication between the shores of the Mediterranean: see Diez, *Etym. Wört.* in *barca. Fanale* and *golfo* are words of this class: *noc-*

T

chiere It. and *nocher* old Fr. (Burguy in *neif*) is derived from ναύκληρος, Latinized by Plautus as *nauclerus*. *Calare* It. as 'calare le vele,' *calar* Sp. *caler* Fr. derived from χαλᾶν, is a nautical phrase. *Calare* is used by Vitruvius. Also *cala* It. and Span. *cale* Fr. a landing place. Some names of weights, as *salma* from σάγμα, *mine* or *émine* Fr. *hemina* Low Lat. from ἡμίνα (Burguy in *mine*, Ducange *Gloss. Lat.* in *hemina*, *Gloss. Gr.* in ἡμίνα) belong to the same class. *Carato*, a carat, is derived by Blanc, *Vocabolario Dantesco* in v. from κεράτιον, the fruit of the carob-tree. In like manner, the Greek word μνᾶ was of Babylonian or Phœnician origin, Boeckh, *Metrologie*, p. 34.

The word *racaille* Fr. which has been traced to ῥάκος, and *tapino* It. which has been derived from ταπεινός, have probably other origins, (see Diez in *raca*, p. 711, in *tapir*, p. 731, also Burguy in *tapir*.) *Bramare* It. *bramer* Fr. which Diez in his grammar derives from βρέμειν, and *entamer* It., which he there derives from ἐντέμνειν, are in his *Etymological Dictionary* correctly explained by other etymologies.

Numerous words passed from Latin, the language of the conquerors, into Greek, the language of the conquered, in later times. See the *Glossaries of Low Greek* by Ducange and Meursius, and the curious treatise of Wannowski, *Antiquitates Romanæ a Græcis Fontibus explicatæ*, Regim. Pruss. 1846.

An etymological vocabulary of French words, whose origins are explained in the two glossaries of Ducange, is appended to his *Glossarium Mediæ et Infimæ Græcitatis*, vol. ii. p. 251—316.

A list of French words derived from the Greek is given by Voltaire, *Dictionnaire Philosophique*, art. *Grec*.]

APPENDIX. 275

On the introduction of Arabic words into the languages of the Spanish peninsula, my entire ignorance of Arabic prevents me from offering any remarks of my own: I am, however, enabled, through the kindness of Dr. Rosen, to annex the following notes, communicated to me by that able oriental scholar.

ARABIC WORDS IN SPANISH AND PORTUGUESE.

The Arabic words in the Spanish and Portuguese languages have already engaged the attention of several scholars, chiefly natives of the peninsula. The works of some of them I have had an opportunity of consulting in the library of the British Museum; and the extracts which I have made from them, and which are now before me, form the basis of the following remarks.

In the *Origines dela Lengua Española, compuestos por varios autores*, etc. edited by Don Gregorio Mayúns i Siscár, (Madrid, 1737, 2 vols. 12mo.) some observations are made on the Arabic words in the Spanish language, (vol. i. p. 235—264,) but apparently with too little knowledge of Arabic to be of much utility.

Of more value are the etymological remarks occasionally given in the *Diccionario Español Latino Arabigo*, by Francisco Cañes, (Madrid, 1787, 3 vols. folio.) This work is intended for a purely practical purpose as a Spanish and *modern* Arabic dictionary; and the author seems to be familiar only with the Arabic *now spoken* in Mauritania, etc.; otherwise he might have given a far greater number of Arabic synonymes, and would probably have assigned more satisfactory derivations for many Spanish words from the ancient and literary Arabic.

In the *Tesoro dela Lengua Castellana Española*, by D. Sebastian de Cobarruvias, (Madrid, 1611, fol.) etymologies from the Arabic are frequently reported on the authority of others, but the author seems in many instances to admit them with reluctance, as he endeavours to account differently for the origin of the words thus explained.

In Portuguese there exists a separate treatise on the subject of our enquiry, Joaõ de Sousa, *Vestigios de la Lingua Arabica em Portugal*, (Lisbon, 1789, 4to.) In his preface the author makes an assertion which I subjoin in his own words, as it is much at variance with what you seem to anticipate as to the quantum of Arabic in European languages[1]: '*e tambem ficámos conservando tantas palavras Arabicas, que dellas bem se póde compor hum arrazoado lexicon, como já notou* José Scaligero *Escript.* 228 *ad* Isaac Fontan. '*Tot puræ Arabicæ voces in Hispan. reperiuntur ut ex illis justum lexicon confici possit.*'— Sousa makes mention of several writers that preceded him in his enquiry: Duarte Nunes de Leaõ, who in 1606 published a work, *Origem da Lingua Portugueza*, (reprinted in 1781,) containing a list of two hundred and seven Arabic words in the Portuguese language; Manoel de Faria e Sousa, author of the *Europa Portugueza;* and Dom Raphael Bluteau, who in 1712 edited a *Diccionario da Lingua Portugueza*.

I hardly know whether the remark just extracted from Sousa's preface is justified by the body of his work,

---

[1] The author had ventured to express to Dr. Rosen an opinion that the number of Arabic words in Spanish and Portuguese is not considerable.

which consists of an alphabetic list of Portuguese words explained from the Arabic, and filling one hundred and sixty pages of small quarto. Many of his etymologies are stated at great and unnecessary length. Some of the words explained do not, I apprehend, owe their existence in the Portuguese language to the Arabian dominion, but to the subsequent intercourse of the Portuguese with the East. With regard to other expressions, it would seem that they have become obsolete, and can no longer be considered as forming part of the living and popular language of the Portuguese nation, as Sousa finds it necessary to adduce passages from Portuguese authors in which they occur.

Besides Sousa's work I know only of one other treatise exclusively devoted to the subject of our present enquiry: it is written in English, and bears the title *Remains of Arabic in the Spanish and Portuguese Languages*, by S. Weston, (London, 1810, 8vo.) It contains two copious lists of Spanish and Portuguese words derived from the Arabic and other oriental languages, but it should be used with great caution, as the Arabic words are not always correctly reported, and many of the etymologies given are evidently farfetched and fanciful: the word *Alhambra*, for instance, the name of the celebrated castle of Granada, is by Mr. Weston derived from *hem bera*, which words he says signify '*sans souci*,' whereas, according to the etymology commonly received, it is the regular feminine form of the Arabic adjective *ahmar*, 'red,' with the article prefixed, *al-hamrâ*, i.e. '*the red (castle)*,' in allusion to the colour of the materials of which it was built. Again, the Spanish word *Alqueria*, also written *Alcarria*, 'a farm,' is by Mr. Weston traced back to the

Persian *khargâh*, 'a pavilion or tent, a moveable Turcoman hut:' but it seems much simpler to consider it as identical with the Arabic *karyah* or *karyat*, 'a village,' with the article *al* prefixed to it.

Sousa premises a few general remarks on the change which certain letters have undergone in the passing over of Arabic words into the Portuguese. One of them, of which the glossary affords the most ample confirmation, is on the transition of the Arabic *H* into *F* in Portuguese. The following are examples collected from the glossary.

Alfeloa (mélasse en caramel) from *hahoah*, sweetness, any thing sweet.

Azafeme from the Arabic *zahmah:* 'Aperto de gente em lugar pequeno o estreito; tambem se toma por pressa, fervor, cuidado, diligencia, etc. Deriva-se do verbo *zahama*, apertar, coarctar, restringir.'

Almofalla, an encampment, from the Arabic *mahallah*, a halting place or encampment of a caravan.

Refens, from the Arabic *rahen*, a pledge.

Amofinar, from the Arabic verb *mahana*, to afflict, to vex.

There are also a few instances in which the Arabic *kh* (or *ch* as pronounced by the Germans and the Scotch) is thus changed into *f* in Portuguese: e.g.

Alfange, from the Arabic *khanjar*, a poniard.

Alface, from the Arabic *khass*, pot-herbs.

The same transition from *H* and *Kh* into *F* may also be observed in Spanish: e.g.

Alfageme (according to Cobarruvias, a barber) from *hajim*, a surgeon, a barber.

Alfombra, the measles, from *homrah*, redness, erysipelas.
Alforja, from *khurj*, a portmanteau.
Alfayata, from *khayyât*, a tailor.

It is remarkable that Latin words have in Spanish undergone the opposite change, substituting *H* for *F*, as in *hijo, filius: hacer, facere,* etc. I am not aware of any instance of a similar transition of an Arabic *F* into a Spanish or Portuguese *H*.

I subjoin a few more words from Sousa's list, but slightly changing the spelling of the Arabic words, so as to suit it to the English pronunciation of the consonants: the vowels being always taken in their German or Italian value.

Açougue, (in Spanish *azoque,*) Arabic *sûk,* (with the article, *as-sûk,*) a market, a market-place.
Adail, Arabic *dalil,* (with the article, *ad-dalil,*) a guide.
Adarme, Arab. *dirhem, (ad-dirhem,)* a particular coin.
Adibo, Arab. *dib* or *zib, (ad-dib, az-zib,)* a wolf.
Albafor, Arab. *bakhûr, (al-backhûr,)* incense.
Almofariz, Arab. *mihrâs, (al-mihrâs,)* a grinding-stone.
Azeite, Arab. *zait, (az-zait,)* an olive.

The great proportion of words that begin with *A* in Sousa's and Weston's lists is striking. The Arabic article, as usually pronounced, begins with that vowel, and it would appear that words restricted in their meaning to one special and definite object by the prefixed article, and thus losing, as it were, according to the conception of hearers unacquainted with Arabic grammar, their general or appellative nature, and becoming a sort of *proper name* of the things designated by them, found a way most easily into the vocabulary of a foreign language.—The *L* of the Arabic article is always assimilated to the initial consonant of the word to which it is prefixed, if that consonant is either a sibilant or a dental letter, or *R*, or *N*. Sousa draws attention to this euphonic rule, as it explains a number of words in his glossary.

The remark as to the preponderance of words beginning with *A* and *Al* applies equally to the Arabic terms found in Spanish. I submit a few Spanish words with their explanations from the Arabic.

Algebra, algebrista, from the Arab. verb *jabara,* to restore any thing broken.

Acemita, from the Arab. *samid, (as-samid,)* white bread.

Açofar, (according to Cobarruuias, *æs fusile,*) from the Arabic *sofr, (as-sofr,)* copper.

Albarda, Arab. *barda'ah, (al-barda'ah,)* a saddle.

Albeytar, Arab. *baitâr, (al-baitâr,)* a farrier, a horseleech.

Alboque, Arab. *bûk, (al-bûk,)* a trumpet, a clarion, a pipe.

Alcala, Arab. *kal'ah, (al-kal'ah,)* a castle, a fort.

Alcantara, Arab. *kantarah, (al-kantarah,)* a bridge.

Albufera and *albuhera,* probably the Arabic *bohairah, (al-bohairah,)* a small lake.

Almaizar, Arab. *mizar, (al-mizar,)* a girdle.

Alberca, Arab. *birkah, (al-birkah,)* a tank, a pond, a reservoir.

Alcohol, Arab. *kohl, (al-kohl,)* antimony used as a collyrium to paint the eyelids; hence *alcoholado,* said of animals that have around the eyelids a darker colour than over the remaining part of their body.

Alhamel, Arab. (*hámil, al-hámil,*) a carrier.

Alcayde, Arab. *kádi*, (*al-kádi,*) a judge, a magistrate.

Alcrebite, Arab. *kibrit*, (*al-kibit,*) sulphur.

Arraez, Arab. *raïs* (*ar-raïs,*) a master or lord.

Atalaya, (an observatory, a barbican,) Arab. *ittilâ*, (from the verb *tala'a,*) the ascending to a high place for the purpose of taking a survey.

Bellota, Arab. *ballût*, oak, acorn.

Cafila, Arab. *káfilah*, a caravan.

Cid, Arab. *sayyed*, (commonly pronounced *sîd,*) master, lord.

Fulano, Arab. *fulân*, such an one, *un tel.*

Guada, Arab. *wâdi*, a river: in many proper names, e.g. *Guadalquivir*, i.e. *Wâdi-al-kabîr*, 'the Great River.'

Horro, Arab. *hurr*, free.

Jarro, Arab. *jarrah*, a water-pot.

Naranja, Arab. *nâranj*, an orange.

Taça, tasi, Arab. *tâs*, a cup.

Tahona, Arab. *tahhânat*, a mill turned by either camels or asses.

Matraca, (a rattle,) Arab. *mitrakat*, a smith's hammer, a wooden rod for beating cotton or wool.

Mascara, (a cover to disguise the face,) Arab. *maskharat*, a buffoon, a jester; sport, pleasantry.

Xeque, Arab. *sheikh*, an old man, a chief.

Xarate, Arab. *sharâb*, any beverage.

Rambla, Arab. *raml*, sand, a tract of sandy country.

F. ROSEN.

[For examples of Romance words derived from the

Arabic or from some other oriental tongue, compare Diez, *Etymological Dictionary*, in *alcohol, alcova, almirante, arsenale, assassino, baracane, baracca, barbacane, caracca, catrame, carmesino, feluca, fondaco, gesmino, magazzino, mugavero, ricamare, ataballo, tamburo, zecca*, (p. 448.) On Arabic words in Spanish, see Diez, *Rom. Gramm.* vol. i. p. 97.

For some Arabic words in the Sicilian dialect, see Abela, *Malta Illustrata*, vol. i. p. 682, Ed. 1772.

For an etymological vocabulary of French words derived from oriental languages, see Pihan, *Glossaire des Mots Français tirés de l'Arabe, du Persan, et du Turc*, 1 vol. 8vo. Paris, 1847.]

NOTE (E.)

The following extract from the Evidence of Dr. Chalmers, before the Committee of the House of Commons on the State of the Poor in Ireland, also throws light on the gradual extinction of the Gaelic language in Scotland.

'Does the use of Gaelic at the present day operate to impart instruction better among the Highlanders?— It has given them an additional taste and demand for knowledge in general; so that in virtue of that change they are more acquainted with English books and English literature than they were.

'Are you not of opinion that the operations of the Gaelic Society have turned rapidly, though indirectly, to the extinction of the Gaelic language?—I am not aware that they have had that effect.

'Have not they operated considerably to give an increased knowledge of the English language?—They have, certainly.

'Do you consider it probable that the English and Gaelic language will continue to go on *pari passu* for any considerable time in the country?—The retrogression on the part of the Gaelic language is very slow: the line of demarcation between the Gaelic and the English being still, I believe, very much what is was fifty years ago. We can ascertain that from a circumstance that is noticeable enough; in the Guelic parishes, the minister is bound to preach in Gaelic once every Sunday. There has certainly been a slow progress in a northern direction towards preaching exclusively in English, but the progress is exceedingly slow. In a large period of time, however, the tendency is to the subsiding, and at length to the ultimate disappearance of the Gaelic language.

'Do you not think that the course which has been taken in the management of Highland property has tended materially to diminish the number of those that speak the Gaelic language?—I should think so.

'Has it ever occurred to you that the extension of paper currency has had the effect of extending the knowledge of the English language?—I am not aware of it.'—*Qu.* 3361, 3665—9.

INDEX.

ACCUSATIVE used for the nominative case in the Latin of the middle ages, 59; tendency to substitute it for the nominative, 88, 152 note ¹.

Adjectives, Provençal, their declension, 79, 80.

Adverbs, Romance, in *mente*, 209, 210.

———————— derived from the Latin, 212:

from *aliorsum*, 212
—— *aliquoties*, ib.
—— *foras*, ib.
—— *hodie, heri*, ib.
—— *jam*, 213
—— *ibi*, ib.
—— *inde*, 214
—— *insimul*, ib.
—— *intus, deintus*, 215
—— *jusum, susum*, ib.
—— *magis*, ib.
—— *mane*, 216

from *medium*, 216
—— *minus, pejus, plus*, 217
—— *quando*, ib.
—— *quare*, ib.
—— *retro*, ib.
—— *satis*, ib.
—— *semper*, 218
—— *subinde*, ib.
—— *tunc*, ib.
—— *ubi*, 219
—— *unde*, ib.
—— *unquam, nunquam*, ib.

Adverbs, Romance, modern, not derived from Latin adverbs:

amon, aval, 219
ades, adesse, des, 220
entorn, environ, ib.
lev, 221
malgrat, ib.
mantenen, ib.

hora, 222
pron, ib.
tost, ib. 223
trop, ib.
veti, ib.

Aimoin, *De Gestis Francorum*, 175 note ².
Alboacem, charter of, its genuineness examined, 106 note ¹.

Analytic forms of grammar, 25.
Arabic words in Spanish and Portuguese, 126, 156, 275.
Articles, their origin, 54; Romance definite article, 56.
At, its changes in French, 135, note ².
Auxiliary verbs, in Provençal, 167; in the other Romance languages, 169.

B, inserted between *m* and a consonant, 71 note ¹.

C, its changes in the Romance languages, 100.
Cases, their confusion in Latin after the German invasion, 57.
Celtic languages, their extinction in Western Europe, 20, note ¹, 45; were not mixed with other languages, 250.
Comparison, degrees of, in Provençal, 142; in the other Romance languages, 148.
Conditional tense in the Romance languages, 170.
Conjunctions, Romance, from Latin:

    aut, 224   *et*, ib.   *nec*, 227.

DANTE, his usage of proper names, 103; Provençal passage of, cited, 114, note ²; his use of *sipa*, 234.
Dialetto, 10 note ¹.
Diez, 20.
Diminutives, 132.
Drusi, 99.

E, before *s*, followed by a consonant, 107.

FRENCH, its ancient form 31; its nominative and accusative, 60; its genders, 114; its degrees of comparison, 148; its pronouns, 153; its numerals, 163; its auxiliary verbs, 169; its regular verbs, 177; its prepositions, 197; its adverbs, 214; its conjunctions and particles, 224; it has departed further from the Latin than the other Romance languages, 247.
Future tense in the Romance languages, 173.

GENDERS, how far changed in the Romance languages, 112.
German, its influence on the Latin, 21, 54, 57, 90, 97, 113, 142, 146, 166, 179, 190, 194, 220, 223, 224, 232, 235.
——— words in the Romance languages, 258.

Gibbon, 24 note [1], 100 note [2].
Greek, its relation to the Romance languages, 148.
Grimm, (Jacob,) 112 note [1], 114 note [2], 133 note [1], 143 note [2], 225 note [3].

IMPERFECT tense in French, 177.
Infinitive mood, in the Romance languages, 179.
Italian, theory as to its origin from a plebeian dialect of the Latin examined, 10—18, 225, 257; its dialects, 44, 251; divided into those with and without vowel terminations, 93; its genders, 113, 114; its degrees of comparison, 148; its pronouns, 152; its numerals, 103; its auxiliary verbs, 160; its regular verbs, 171; its prepositions, 107; its adverbs, 209; its conjunctions and particles, 224; its close adherence to the Latin, 240.

LANDOR, (W. S.) on *cattivo*, 141 note [2].
Language of the Troubadours, difficulty in finding an unobjectionable name for it, 51.
Langue d'oc, its dialects, 42.
——— d'oïl, its dialects, ib.
Lanzi, 11.
Lassen, 10 note [1].
Latin, its relation to the Greek, 9; its extension over Western Europe, 18; changes undergone by it in consequence of the Teutonic invasion, 24; its close agreement with the Italian, 240; had not a *patois* or a dialect spoken by the lower classes, 11, 257.
Lingua Franca, 22 note [1], 254.
——— Romana rustica, 30, 253.
——— vulgaris, 30, 257.

M, elision of final, in Latin, 66.
Maffei, 11.
Meidinger, 107 note [1], 253.
Muratori, 11, 59 note [4], 60 note [1], 214 note [2].

NEGATION, means of strengthening, 237.
Negro corruption of the English, 22 note [1], 91 note [1].

Niebuhr, 136 note *, 257.
Notaries, Latin of the, 60 note¹.
Nouns, Romance, their formation from the Latin, 61; whether from the accusative or the ablative, 68; formed from Latin neuter nouns, 73.
—— Italian and Spanish, formed from the Latin accusative, 75; Provençal and French formed from the Latin nominative, 76.
Numerals, Romance, 102.

O, in Italian, its origin, 62 note¹.
Oi, in French, its origin, 106 note¹.

P, Latin, changed into b and v in Romance languages, 109.
Particles, negative and affirmative, in Romance languages:

gaire, guari, guere, 224
mica, 226
non, 227
passus, 229

persona, 229
punctum, 230
res, 231
sic, 233

Participles, Provençal, their declension, 70, 80; their formation in Provençal, 183; in the other Romance languages, 185.
Patois, 16 note¹.
Perticari, 8, 11, 47, 125 note*, 129 note¹, 231 note¹, 243 note*, 251.
Prepositions, Romance derivatives of Latin:

ab, a, 197
ad, 199
ante, ib.
apud, 200
circa, ib.
contra, 201
cum, ib.
de, 202
extra, ib.
in, ib.
infra, ib.
inter or intra, 203
juxta, 204

per, 204
post, ib.
prope, 205
secundum, 206
sine, ib.
subtus, 208
super, 207
supra, ib.
trans, 208
versus, ib.
ultra, ib.
usque, 209

Present tense in French, 177.
Preterite tense in French, 178.
Priscus, 257.
Pronouns, possessive, in Provençal, 78; French, 82.
————— personal, in Provençal, 150; in the other Romance languages, 151.
————— demonstrative, in Prov., 155; in the other Romance languages, 156.
————— indefinite, 158.
————— relative, in Prov., 157; in the other Romance languages, 158.
Proper names, declension of in French, 91.
Provençal, 53; its genders, 114; its degrees of comparison, 147; its pronouns, 150; its numerals, 162; its auxiliary verbs, 166; its regular verbs, 100; its prepositions, 107; its adverbs, 209; its conjunctions and particles, 224; its relation to the other Romance languages, 247.

REGULAR verbs, in Provençal, 100; in the other Romance languages, 171.
Romance languages, M. Raynouard's theory as to their origin, 4; generally adopted by subsequent writers, 6; proper meaning of the word, 52.
Romans, 29.

SARDINIA, its dialects, 49 note 1.
Schlegel, (A. W. von,) 7, 27, 225.
Se, used with an active verb in a passive sense, 179.
Southey, 106 note 1.
Spanish, its dialects, 43; its genders, 113; its degrees of comparison, 148; its pronouns, 152; its numerals, 163; its auxiliary verbs, 169; its regular verbs, 171; its prepositions, 197; its adverbs, 209; its particles and conjunctions, 224; its relation to the Latin, 247.
Synthetic forms of Grammar, 25.

TERMINATIONS, Latin, and the corresponding Romance forms, 121.

U

In *ago*, 121
— *antia, entia*, 122
— *arius, aris*, 123
— *aster*, 126
— *atium*, 127
— *ia, itia*, 129
— *inus*, 132
— *ista*, ib.

In *o, onis*, 132
— *or*, 134
— *tas, tus*, 135
— *ulus, ellus, illus*, 136
— *ura*, 140
— *ensis*, ib.
— *ivus*, 141
— *osus*, ib.

Terminations, Romance, not derived from the Latin:
  ard, 142
  etto, ito, ete, et ; otto, ote, ot, 143
  asco, esco, isco, esc, esque, ib.

U, Latin, its modifications in Romance languages, 67, note ¹.

U, final, in Italian, 67.

Verbs, their syntax in the Romance languages, 191.
Vowels, final, in Italian, 91, 94, 102, 172.

ADDENDA.

Page 69.

Latin.	Italian.
aloer	cece

Page 73.

Latin.	Italian.	Spanish.
phantasma	fantasima	
schisma	scisma	cisma

www.ingramcontent.com/pod-product-compliance
Lightning Source LLC
Chambersburg PA
CBHW022118230426
43672CB00008B/1424